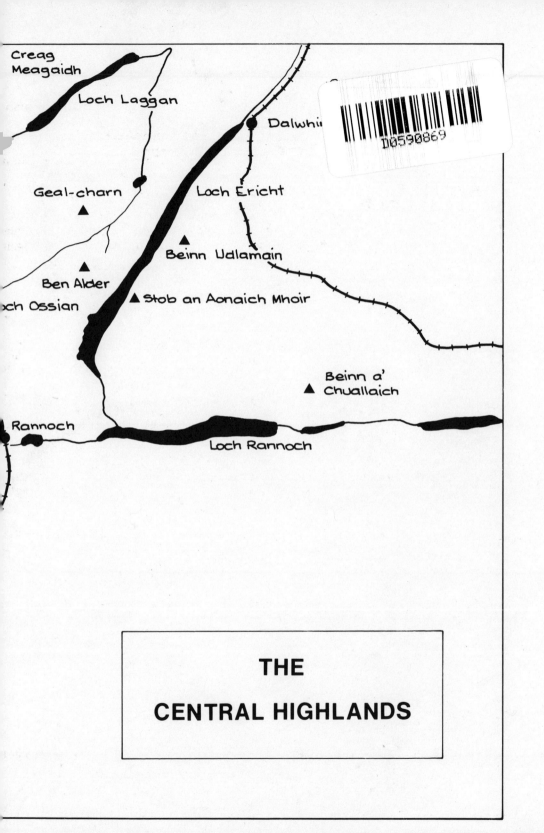

THE

CENTRAL HIGHLANDS

Scottish Mountaineering Club
District Guidebooks

THE CENTRAL HIGHLANDS

Series Editor: D J BENNET

Published by
The Scottish Mountaineering Trust

This guidebook is compiled from the most recent information and experience provided by members of the Scottish Mountaineering Club and other contributors. The book is published by the Scottish Mountaineering Trust, which is a charitable trust.

Revenue from the sale of books published by the Trust is used for the continuation of its publishing programme and for charitable purposes associated with Scottish mountains and mountaineering.

THE
CENTRAL HIGHLANDS

Peter Hodgkiss

Scottish Mountaineering Club District Guidebook

PUBLISHED BY THE SCOTTISH MOUNTAINEERING TRUST:1994
© THE SCOTTISH MOUNTAINEERING CLUB

First Edition   1934
Second Edition   1952
Third Edition   1968
Reprinted   1972
Fourth Edition   1984
Reprinted   1989
Fifth Edition   1994

British Library Cataloguing in Publication Data
Central Highlands. - 5 Rev. ed
I. Hodgkiss, Peter
796.522094115

ISBN 0-907521-44-4

Front cover: Bidean nam Bian and Stob Coire nan Lochan *P. Hodgkiss*
Back cover: View south from Sgurr a'Mhaim to the Glen Coe mountains
      D.J.Bennet

Book design by Donald Bennet
Maps drawn by Jim Renny and Noel Williams
Production by Scottish Mountaineering Trust (Publications) Limited
Typeset by Westec, North Connel
Colour separations and graphic work by Par Graphics, Kirkcaldy
Printed by Pillans and Wilson, Edinburgh
Bound by Hunter and Foulis, Edinburgh
Distributed by Cordee, 3a DeMontfort Street, Leicester, LE1 7HD

CONTENTS

Introduction   1

1. Cruachan   19

2. The Glen Strae Hills   29

3. Ben Starav Group   34

4. The Black Mount   46

5. Appin   58

6. Glen Coe   74

7. North Glen Coe and Rannoch Moor   91

8. The Mamores   102

9. Ben Nevis and Carn Mor Dearg   116

10. The Aonachs and the Grey Corries   135

11. Ben Alder to Rannoch   148

12. Loch Ossian to Loch Laggan   158

13. Drumochter   168

14. The Loch Laggan Hills: Creag Meagaidh and Glen Roy   175

15. Monadh Liath and the Corrieyairack   184

Appendix I   Gaelic Place Names   196
Appendix II   Bibliography   202
Appendix III List of Climbers' Huts   204

Index   206

LIST OF ILLUSTRATIONS

The Black Mount from Rannoch Moor *J.Renny*   Title page
Stob Ban in the Mamores *A.O'Brien*   x
The Eastern Traverse on Tower Ridge, Ben Nevis *J.Renny*   4
Looking south-west from Bidean nam Bian towards Ben Cruachan *M.Baker*   8
Purple Saxifrage *P.Hodgkiss*   12
The truncated spurs of the Three Sisters of Glen Coe *G.S.Johnstone*   17
Ben Cruachan from Ben Sgulaird across Loch Etive *D.Bennet*   20
Ben Cruachan from the Stob Dearg col *D.Bennet*   21
The summit of Ben Cruachan from the east *D.Bennet*   24
Beinn a'Bhuiridh and the Cruachan Reservoir *P.Hodgkiss*   26
The northern ridges and corries of Ben Cruachan *J.Renny*   27
Beinn a'Chochuill and Beinn Eunaich across Loch Awe *J.Renny*   30
Looking up Glen Strae to Beinn Mhic-Mhonaidh *J.Renny*   31
Looking up Loch Etive to Ben Starav and Beinn Trilleachan *P.Hodgkiss*   35
The north ridge of Ben Starav *P.Hodgkiss*   38
Glas Bheinn Mhor from the north ridge of Ben Starav *P.Hodgkiss*   39
Looking west from Mam Carraigh to Ben Starav, Glas Bheinn Mhor,
            Stob Coir'an Albannaich and Meall nan Eun *P.Hodgkiss*   40
Beinn nan Aighenan and cloud-topped Ben Starav from Victoria Bridge *P.Hodgkiss*   42
The shattered granite crags below Stob Coire Dheirg *G.S.Johnstone*   43
The serried ranks of the Black Mount from Bidean nam Bian *D.Broadhead*   47
The east face of Stob Ghabhar *D.Bennet*   49
Clach Leathad and Meall a'Bhuiridh *J.Renny*   51
Sron na Creise from Kingshouse *D.Bennet*   53
Clach Leathad from Beinn Maol Chaluim across Glen Etive *P.Hodgkiss*   54
Skiing down the east ridge of Meall a'Bhuiridh *D.Bennet*   57
Beinn Sgulaird from Beinn Fhionnlaidh *D.N.Williams*   60
Looking west from Ben Starav over Beinn Trilleachan to Beinn Sgulaird *G.S.Johnstone*   61
Ben Starav from Beinn Sgulaird *J.Renny*   64
Sgor na h-Ulaidh from Gleann Leac na Muidhe *P.Hodgkiss*   65
Fraochaidh and Beinn a'Bheithir from the east *D.Bennet*   68
Sgorr Dhearg from Sgorr Dhonuill *D.Bennet*   70
On the Trilleachan Slabs, looking towards Ben Cruachan *D.Ritchie*   73
Stob Dearg *D.Bennet*   76
Rannoch Wall from Curved Ridge *A.O'Brien*   77
Looking west from Buachaille Etive Mor to
            Buachaille Etive Beag and Bidean nam Bian *D.N.Williams*   81
The summit of Bidean nam Bian *D.N.Williams*   84
Aonach Dubh and Stob Coire nan Lochan *P.Hodgkiss*   85
Stob Coire nan Lochan *P.Hodgkiss*   88
Spacewalk, a modern extreme on the North-east Nose of Aonach Dubh *D.Ritchie*   89
The Aonach Eagach above Loch Achtriochtan in Glen Coe *G.S.Johnstone*   92
Looking east along the Aonach Eagach to Meall Dearg and Am Bodach *P.Hodgkiss*   93
The narrow section of the Aonach Eagach between Meall Dearg and Stob Coire Leith *J.Renny*   96
Sgorr na Ciche from Kinlochleven *J.Renny*   97
Rannoch Moor, looking towards the Black Mount *J.Renny*   100
Binnein Beag from Binnein Mor; the Grey Corries beyond *P.Hodgkiss*   105
Binnein Mor from Stob Coire a'Chairn *D.Bennet*   108
An Gearanach above Steall waterfall *D.N.Williams*   109
Sgurr a'Mhaim, An Garbhanach and An Gearanach from Binnein Mor *B.Jenkins*   110
Looking up the north ridge of Stob Coire a'Mhail *D.J.Bennet*   111
Sgurr a'Mhaim from the col between Stob Ban and Sgor an Iubhair *G.S.Johnstone*   112

The north-east face of Stob Ban *G.S.Johnstone*   113
Stob Choire a'Mhail from Sgurr a'Mhaim *D.J.Bennet*   114
Carn Mor Dearg and Ben Nevis from Corpach *A.O'Brien*   117
The Ben Nevis Observatory in winter *SMC Collection*   118
The north face of Ben Nevis *D.Bennet*   120
The summit of Ben Nevis at the top of Tower Ridge *D.N.Williams*   121
The North-east Buttress *G.S.Johnstone*   122
Carn Dearg Buttress and Castle Ridge *D.N.Williams*   124
At the top of the Comb, the Great Tower behind *D.Ritchie*   125
Carn Dearg Meadhonach from the east *D.N.Williams*   129
Early morning at the CIC Hut *B.Jenkins*   130
Evening descent from the summit to the Carn Mor Dearg Arete *W.Mockridge*   131
Reaching the summit of Ben Nevis at the top of Observatory Ridge *D.Bennet*   132
Aonach Beag from Ben Nevis *D.N.Williams*   137
Stob Choire Claurigh *R.Wood*   140
Stob Coire na Ceannain *J.Renny*   141
Stob Ban from the Lairig Leacach bothy *D.Bennet*   143
On the cliffs of Stob Coire an Laoigh *R.Wood*   145
The ascent of Beinn na Socaich, looking towards Aonach Beag *D.Bennet*   146
Loch Ossian youth hostel and the Bealach Dubh *N.Ritchie*   149
Ben Alder and Sgor Iutharn *D.N.Williams*   152
The northern and eastern corries of Ben Alder *D.Bennet*   156
Stob Coire Sgriodain from Chno Dearg *J.Renny*   160
Geal-Charn from Carn Dearg *G.S.Johnstone*   164
Binnein Shuas from Lochan na h-Earba *J.Renny*   164
Ardverikie Wall *D.Bennet*   167
Looking across Loch Ericht from Geal-charn to Ben Alder *D.Broadhead*   169
Stob an Aonaich Mhoir from Benalder Cottage across Loch Ericht *P.Hodgkiss*   172
A'Mharconaich from Sgairneach Mhor *D.Bennet*   173
Creag Meagaidh from Coire Ardair *D.Bennet*   176
Meall Coire Choille-rais *D.N.Williams*   177
Beinn a'Chaorainn from Luiblea *J.Renny*   180
The Parallel Roads of Glen Roy *G.S.Johnstone*   180
The Post Face of Creag Meagaidh *D.Ritchie*   181
The east side of the Corrieyairack Pass near Melgarve *G.S.Johnstone*   186
The Allt a'Chaorainn below A'Chailleach *R.Wood*   187
Looking west from Geal-charn Beag *D.Broadhead*   190
Carn an Fhreiceadain from A'Chailleach *R.Wood*   191
The ascent to Carn Dearg at the head of Gleann Ballach *D.Bennet*   194

PREFACE

It is wholly appropriate that this guide should begin with a brief account of a traverse from Dalwhinnie to Inveroran that almost bisected the Central Highlands.

William Naismith and Gilbert Thomson, two stalwarts of early Scottish mountaineering, had been dissatisfied with the time taken and their state of near exhaustion after a traverse from Clachaig to the Kingshouse over Bidean nam Bian, Buachaille Etive Beag and Buachaille Etive Mor. Concluding that lack of calories had been the major debilitating factor, they undertook to reach the 1892 Easter meet of the SMC at Inveroran, starting at Dalwhinnie and carrying sufficient food to enable them to arrive fresh. Starting from Glasgow on the overnight train, they left Dalwhinnie at 3.30 am on April 14th, crossed Ben Alder by ascent of the Short Leachas and descent of its south ridge, forded the River Gaur at Dunan, and then marched near the present line of the West Highland Railway to finish by fording the River Orchy at its outlet from Loch Tulla.

They arrived at Inveroran by 8.00 pm having walked 41 miles, yet still with food left, fresh enough to enjoy dinner, and to be out on the hills the following day when Naismith led an ascent of the Upper Couloir on Stob Ghabhar.

There have been many changes since Naismith and Thomson strode from Atholl to the Black Mount - crofts are now open bothies; and afforestation, the railway and hydroelectricity have all left their mark - but anyone wishing to emulate their feat is still free to do so. Those relishing that freedom would do well to be vigilant and active in protection of that value.

I wish to thank all those photographers who have contributed toward illustrating this guide. Also I thank Jim Renny whose clear maps are both a pleasure to look at and a great help in planning trips to the hills. Most of all I acknowledge my debt to Donald Bennet who has been a most careful and thorough editor. Any errors remaining are, nevertheless, my responsibility.

Peter Hodgkiss

THE CLIMBER AND THE MOUNTAIN ENVIRONMENT

With increasing numbers of walkers and climbers going to the Scottish hills, it is important that all of us who do so should recognise our responsibilities to those who live and work among the hills and glens, to our fellow climbers and to the mountain environment in which we find our pleasure and recreation.

The Scottish Mountaineering Club and Trust, who jointly produce this and other guidebooks, wish to impress on all who avail themselves of the information in these books that it is essential at all times to consider the sporting and proprietory rights of landowners and farmers. The description of a climbing, walking or skiing route in any of these books does not imply that a right of way exists, and it is the responsibility of all climbers to ascertain the position before setting out. In cases of doubt it is best to enquire locally.

During stalking and shooting seasons in particular, much harm can be done in deer forests and on grouse moors by people walking through them. Normally the deer stalking season is from 1st July to 20th October, when stag shooting ends. Hinds may continue to be culled until 15th February. The grouse shooting season is from 12th August until 10th December. These are not merely sporting activities, but are essential for the economy of many Highland estates. During these seasons, therefore, especial care should be taken to consult the local landowner, factor or keeper before taking to the hills.

Climbers and hillwalkers are recommended to consult the book HEADING FOR THE SCOTTISH HILLS, published by the Scottish Mountaineering Trust on behalf of the Mountaineering Council of Scotland and the Scottish Landowners Federation, which gives the names and addresses of factors and keepers who may be contacted for information regarding access to the hills.

It is important to avoid disturbance to sheep, particularly during the lambing season between March and May. Dogs should not be taken onto the hills at this time, and should always be kept under control.

Always try to follow a path or track through cultivated land and forests, and avoid causing damage to fences, dykes and gates by climbing over them carelessly. Do not leave litter anywhere, but take it down from the hill in your rucksack.

The number of walkers and climbers on the hills is leading to increased, and in some cases very unsightly erosion of footpaths and hillsides. Some of the revenue from the sale of this and other SMC guidebooks is used by the Trust to assist financially the work being carried out to repair and maintain hill paths in Scotland. However, it is important for all of us to recognise our responsibility to minimise the erosive effect of our passage over the hills so that the enjoyment of future climbers is not spoiled by landscape damage.

As a general rule, where a path exists walkers should follow it and even where it is wet and muddy should avoid walking along its edges, the effect of which is to extend erosion sideways. Do not take short-cuts at the corners of zigzag paths. Remember that the worst effects of erosion are likely to be caused during or soon after prolonged wet weather when the ground is soft and waterlogged. A route on a stony or rocky hillside is likely to cause less erosion than on a grassy one at such times.

Although the use of bicycles can often be very helpful for reaching remote crags and hills, the erosion damage that can be caused by them when used 'off road' on soft footpaths and open hillsides is such that their use on such terrain must cause concern. It is the editorial policy of the Scottish Mountaineering Club that the use of bicycles in hill country may be recommended on hard roads such as forest roads or private roads following rights of way, but it is not recommended on footpaths or open hillsides where the environmental damage that they cause may be considerable. Readers are asked to bear these points in mind, particularly when the ground is wet and soft after rain.

The proliferation of cairns on hills detracts from the feeling of wildness, and may be confusing rather than helpful as regards route-finding. The indiscriminate building of cairns on the hills is therefore discouraged.

Climbers are reminded that they should not drive along private estate roads without permission, and when parking their cars should avoid blocking access to private roads and land, and should avoid causing any hazard to other road users.

Finally, the Scottish Mountaineering Club and the Scottish Mountaineering Trust can accept no liability for damage to property nor for personal injury resulting from the use of any route described in their publications.

The Mountaineering Council of Scotland is the representative body for climbers and walkers in Scotland. One of its primary concerns is the continued free access to the hills and crags that we now enjoy.

Information about bird restrictions, stalking and general access issues can be obtained from the National Officer of the MCofS. Should any climber or walker encounter problems regarding access they should contact the National Officer of the MCofS, whose current address is published in CLIMBER AND HILLWALKER magazine.

Stob Ban in the Mamores

Introduction

AREA

The area of the Central Highlands is clearly demarcated within the lines made to the west by Loch Linnhe and the Great Glen, and to the east by the A9 road. To the south a more broken line follows Loch Etive into the Pass of Brander and beyond it swings north up Glen Orchy and along the West Highland Railway to Rannoch Station, where it turns east along the B846 to reach the A9.

Within the area there are 74 hills of over 914.4m (3000ft) complying with Sir Hugh Munro's list. In addition there is a similar number of tops subsidiary to the main hills and over 40 separate hills between 762m (2500ft) and 914m.

TRANSPORT

For those who do not wish to travel by car, and also as an extension to private transport, the Central Highlands are served by three railway lines. The most important of these is the West Highland Railway which runs throughout the year, Sundays included, between Glasgow and Fort William and provides access to one of the most remote areas in Scotland. Starting on the early morning train from Glasgow or later at Bridge of Orchy, one can enjoy a day's hillwalking on the hills about Loch Ossian and a fast-moving party can make the round trip from Corrour Halt to Ben Alder in between the morning and evening trains. Distances between the stations on this line seem almost designed for hill traverses and allow one to leave the morning train at say Corrour and to walk across the hills to either Rannoch or Tulloch for the evening train.

From that part of the line between Crannach Wood and the Blackwater, the view across Rannoch Moor on a clear winter's day is breathtaking. Particularly if there is no snow on the moor, its vast brown expanse with a back-cloth of white jagged peaks gives a marvellous sense of distance and magnitude to the distant hills of the Black Mount and Glen Coe.

Of lesser importance to the Central Highlands are the lines to Oban and to Inverness. The latter provides access at Dalwhinnie to the Ben Alder Group and to the Drumochter Hills, and, at Newtonmore to the Monadh Liath; while the former can be used to approach the Cruachan range from Dalmally or Loch Etive from Taynuilt.

Though not fitted for travel to and from the hills in a day from the main Scottish conurbations, bus services on all the main roads in and around the periphery of the Central Highlands add greatly to the flexibility of travel and enable the carless hill-goer to reach some very remote corners. One can for example penetrate the north-eastern fringes of the Monadh Liath by the postbus — a 4-seater Land-rover — from Tomatin to Coignafearn; or, use the local service plying between Fort William and Glen Nevis (July and August only) to save one's feet from the tarmac at the end of a traverse from Corrour Halt.

Another way of extending freedom of movement in one part of the area is to make use of the steamer that plies up and down Loch Etive between Easter and the end of September. This service runs from Auchnacloich, which is a few kilometres west of Taynuilt, and there are two sailings each day of the week, Sundays included, at approximately 10.15am and 2.00pm. Normally passengers make the round-trip but prior arrangement may be made for a party to be put off at Barrs or Ardmaddy. Phone Taynuilt 430 (STD Code 08662).

An essential reference work is the publication of the Highlands and Islands Development Board entitled *Getting Around the Highlands and Islands* which is, as it claims, a comprehensive guide and shows the intriguing possibilities for long hill-traverses aided by a conjunction of train and bus (with or without a car). Postbus routes and times are also available in a separate guide — the *Scottish Postbus Guide*, from Royal Mail PR, 102 West Port, Edinburgh EH3 9HS.

ACCESS

Outwith the stalking season (mid-August to mid-October) there should be no problem with access, but during this period the estates do rely on lets of stalking to produce much of their income and unrestricted access would not be compatible with successful stalking. That said, a courteous approach to the estate in question from small parties of hill-goers, either by phone on the evening prior to the planned hill walk or in person before setting out on the hill, will rarely meet with a blanket refusal. Such parties will more than probably be asked to avoid certain stretches of hill or particular glens and corries, but again the probability is that constructive sug-gestions as to alternative expeditions will be offered. However, it is difficult for estates to accommodate large parties on the hills at this time and it would be diplomatic for clubs to organise their meets during this period to areas not carrying deer, or to others owned by the National Trust for Scotland.

The representative body for estate owners, the Scottish Landowners' Federation, has cooperated with the Mountaineering Council of Scotland in compiling a most informative guidebook to estates, the mountains they contain and the telephone numbers of stalkers and other contacts. This essential reference book is *Heading for the Scottish Hills* published by the Scottish Mountaineering Trust (1993).

With regard to the bothies owned by the estates and left open for use by hill-goers, access to small parties outside the stalking season presents no problem, but any party in excess of two planning use of a bothy for more than two nights should seek permission from the estate factor or stalker.

ACCOMMODATION

Anyone wishing to spend time in the more remote parts of the Central Highlands
will need either to carry a tent or to make overnight use of the bothies left open by
the various estates. In most cases the Mountain Bothies Association help to maintain
these bothies, and this organisation has done much to engender good relationships
between landowners and hill-goers. Otherwise the area is well served by hotels,
guest houses, bed and breakfast houses and youth hostels. Details of official camp
and caravan sites, youth hostels, mountaineering club huts and other accommodation are given in the relevant chapters. There follows a short list of useful addresses
and publications.

> 1. Mountain Bothies Association — General Secretary
>   Jim Ross
>   2 Dungallan Terrace
>   Oban PA34 4PB
>
> 2. Scottish Youth Hostels Association
>   7 Glebe Crescent
>   Stirling FK8 2JA
>
> 3. *Getting Around the Highlands and Islands*
>   from Highlands and Islands Development Board
>   27 Bank Street
>   Inverness IV1 1QR
>
> 4. *Where to Stay in Scotland*
>   Self-Catering Accommodation in Scotland
>   Scottish Tourist Board
>   23 Ravelston Terrace
>   Edinburgh, EH4 3EU

MAPS

The current source of information concerning heights, distances and Gaelic spelling
used in this guide is the OS 1:50 000 Landranger Series; only occasionally has
recourse been made to the OS 1:25 000 Pathfinder Series for spot heights and greater
physical detail. Five of the 1:50 000 Landranger Series — Nos. 34, 41, 42, 50 and 52
— cover almost the whole of the Central Highlands, with only the coastal strip of
Benderloch and Appin, and the northernmost triangle between the Great Glen and
the A9 road, missing.

While admiring the clarity of the 1:50 000 Landranger Series and the thorough-
ness with which their content has been metricated, the OS One Inch to One Mile
Tourist Map *Ben Nevis & Glen Coe* has the advantage of covering the heart of the
Central Highlands and includes Ben Nevis, Ben Alder, Glen Coe and Stob Ghabhar.
That said, the Ordnance Survey's latest 1:50 000 maps have the decided advantage
of later revision — variously between 1974 and 1984; they contain paths additional

The Eastern Traverse on Tower Ridge, the classic route on Ben Nevis

to the previous One Inch to One Mile series, and other new information such as the extended boundaries of afforestation. With regard to this latter subject, the 1:25 000 maps have particular value, showing access tracks, paths and cuttings through afforestation that are not included in the 1:50 000 maps. Additionally the 1:25 000 Pathfinder Series have generally a later revision date than the 1:50 000 maps and include greater detail about features such as waterfalls, and the siting of named crags.

For convenience on the hill, the 1:50 000 maps are unmatchable and can only be improved by marking in such detail from the 1:25 000 as is considered relevant to individual needs. It is assumed that readers of this guide will be using the latest Landranger maps with a revision date of 1984.

ROCK, SNOW AND ICE CLIMBING

Those who come to the Central Highlands intent on more than general mountaineering will want the specialist publications of the Scottish Mountaineering Trust. Their three climbing guides to *Glen Coe*, *Ben Nevis* and *Highland Outcrops* are comprehensive guides to all the major mountain crags in the district. This book will not include descriptions other than the occasional classic route in the well-known climbing areas.

The *Scottish Mountaineering Club Journal*, published annually, is a useful source of additional information about mountaineering in the area covered by this guide and particularly about new routes and first ascents, significant changes in mountain shelters, bridges, paths and general access, as well as alterations to designated mountain heights and the status of Munros.

SKI-ING

The piste slopes on Meall a'Bhuiridh are sufficiently mechanised to allow a day of frequent runs, but have yet retained an air of informality and low density that is perhaps a reflection of the fickle weather in the west. Access is from the A82 road opposite the Kingshouse Hotel and there is a large carpark beneath the lift system.

Further north there is a new facility on the northern slopes of Aonach Mor, access to which is gained from the A82 road 5½ kilometres north-east of Fort William. From the carpark there a gondola takes skiers up to 650m.

Mountain skiers will find a great variety of usually long expeditions where the use of two cars, one at each end of a traverse — as with the crossing of Meall a'Bhuiridh and Stob Ghabhar — is of great advantage. Good use can be made of the West Highland Line for traverses such as that from Corrour over Beinn na Lap and Chno Dearg to Tulloch. Creag Meagaidh remains unsullied by mechanisation and, with its great bulk and numerous corries, offers more mountain ski-ing than most other hills in the Central Highlands. Other notable catchment areas are described in their relevant chapters.

MOUNTAIN SAFETY

The area described in this guide is mountainous and in winter there are very few genuinely easy descents from the summits. Even paths that are pleasant summer highways, such as the one leading up into Coire Gabhail (Lost Valley), can become icy traverses over steep drops needing an ice-axe and crampons, and confidence in their use. Efforts have been made to describe a straightforward descent route from all the tops, but it has to be assumed that users of this guide will have sufficient navigational and mountaineering skills to cope with adverse conditions, particularly in winter. This season often lasts from November to May.

Summer hill-walking in less mountainous areas is not an adequate preparation for winter expeditions on the Glen Coe peaks or the Mamores. Those without experienced friends to guide their progress should adopt a very cautious approach in winter, tackling only the easiest peaks such as Stob a'Choire Odhair, where one can learn something about the use of an ice-axe and crampons. Prior reading of one of the many manuals on mountaineering technique is essential.

One of the greatest perils, even to well-equipped and experienced mountaineers, is a high wind. Navigating against a strong wind, probably to avoid steep and dangerous ground, requires a strength of mind and body difficult to appreciate without experience. It can be impossible to face into snow or spindrift blown horizontally.

Avalanches are another danger more common than a casual acquaintance with Scottish winters would indicate. Scottish radio forecasts give daily assessment in winter of avalanche risk and these are very useful. However background reading of one of the books recommended in Appendix II and regular observation over a number of winters are necessary before an informed opinion can be formed of the danger on any particular slope. Knowledge of recent snowfall and of radio avalanche forecasting will make for better informed decisions.

Avalanches and Rock-fall

The growing number of people going out on the Scottish hills in winter has brought a greater appreciation of the frequency and scale of avalanches. There is no doubt that avalanches of most types occur frequently in Scotland and the sceptics, who in the past would not acknowledge the serious danger of Scottish avalanches, have retreated in the last decade before the weight of evidence. Anyone intending even simple winter hill walks in the Central Highlands would do well to read one of the standard texts on this subject (see below) and to absorb knowledge of the more predictable avalanche conditions. Then close attention to weather forecasts and to weather changes during the course of a hill day is equally important. For those intending to climb one of the snow and ice routes, and particularly one of the gullies, a thermometer is a worthwhile adjunct to winter climbing equipment. From knowledge gained by reading about avalanches and from observation, avoidance of the more obvious hazards, such as a cornice in thaw conditions, is a straightforward matter. It is in avoidance of the less predictable that the trick (and a certain amount of luck) lies, and in this context it is well to remember that the seeming extreme examples of slab avalanches occurring at angles of 22 degrees and of parties being engulfed on much-frequented paths, have both caused fatalities in the last few winters (both in the Allt a'Mhuilinn glen of Ben Nevis).

A last sobering thought on this subject is that there is a consensus among those who have studied and written about the phenomenon that a certain percentage of avalanches (some put it at 30%) are not predictable in the state of present knowledge.

Avalanche Enigma	C.Fraser. Murray
Avalanche Handbook	R.I.Perla & M.Martinelli Jr.
	US Dept. of Agriculture
SMCJ — XXXII, 172	Two articles by R.G.W.Ward
XXXI, 170	Statistical article by Blyth Wright
XXXI, 168	Snaba's by Roger O'Donovan
Mountain Leadership	E.Langmuir. Scottish Sports Council
A Chance in a Million	Barton & Wright. Scottish Mountaineering Trust

Rock-fall

Though not in the same order of occurrence as avalanches, rock-fall as an objective danger during scrambling should be guarded against. Increased numbers of climbers have again brought to light a hitherto unrecognised problem, both as human initiating agents on the ridge above one and in terms of increased observation. On some of the easier rock-climbs on Ben Nevis (Observatory Ridge) and on Buachaille Etive Mor (North Buttress) several incidents have been reported in recent years.

Weather

The Central Highlands has a higher rainfall than most areas in the British Isles, with only a belt of land west of the Great Glen recording greater precipitation. That said, the climatic variation over a distance from west to east of merely 50 kilometres is wide, as is shown by the following mean figures drawn from a publication by the Meteorological Office in Edinburgh.

1941-70 RAINFALL
Glen Etive and Glen Coe — more than 3200mm pa.
Eastern Rannoch — less than 1600mm pa

or SNOW LYING AT 9.00 am
Glen Coe 50% coverage — valley observation 20 days
Ben Alder 50% coverage — valley observation 60 days

and TEMPERATURE — JANUARY MINIMUM
Glen Coe at 1000m — minus 4 degrees C
Ben Alder at 1000m — minus 6 degrees C

Looking south-west from Bidean nam Bian towards Ben Cruachan over a cloud-sea covering Loch Etive

Much of the weather is of Atlantic origin with the mild, moisture-bearing south-westerlies seeming more predominant than is the case: almost as much wind comes from the south-east quadrant and consistent south-easterlies, when not carrying rain, produce strong haze which make it difficult to see the outline of hills only a few kilometres away, even when there is blue sky above. North-westerlies are also frequent and normally bring a lowering of temperature, blustery showers and, in between, periods of excellent visibility. The stable conditions of an anti-cyclone are often of short duration and those that last for longer periods, usually in association with blocking zones of high pressure over Scandinavia, are recalled in revered tones at climbing club dinners. Another anti-cyclonic condition even more infrequent is that where the usual altitudinal gradient becomes inverted and cold air sinks into the glens to form a cloud-sea, leaving the tops clear. To be on a mountain ridge on such a day is a heady experience, especially if the Moor of Rannoch is close enough for the blanket of cloud to suggest the one-time glacial ice-dome.

Those limited to weekend climbing have little choice in the matter of weather, which is therefore of some fascination, and careful consideration of the alternatives can be repaying. One example would be when south-westerlies prevail and a day of infrequent showers could be spent on the Drumochter hills while Cruachan is blattered with those 'frequent showers' of the meteorological forecast that are, on the hill, indistinguishable from continuous rain.

A too obsessional consideration of weather can be discouraging, but regular study of radio forecasts and of weather reports from coastal stations, allied to personal observation, is worthwhile. From such attention over the past twenty years, two patterns have been regular — a period of low temperature often accompanied by snowfall in November, and a subsequent thaw in the path of south-westerlies in time for the holiday break at the end of December !

A good reference work is Gordon Manley's *Climate and the British Scene* (Fontana New Naturalist) and for its fascinating insight into the life of the meteorologists in the Ben Nevis Observatory around the turn of the century as much for its weather data, William T. Kilgour's *Twenty Years on Ben Nevis* (The Ernest Press). Though out of print, the public library service should find a copy for the determined enquirer.

HISTORY, HUMAN

Man's presence on and among the hills of the Central Highlands is well documented only in recent historical times. Gaelic, the sole language of the Central Highlands until the 18th century, had no written history. Indeed its first book, known as *Carswell's Liturgy*, did not appear until 1567 and though its oral tradition is accepted as an art form, it is not viewed as historically reliable. The higher reaches of the glens have been used for centuries by pastoralists and evidence of their summer residence can be seen in the 'rickle heap stane' remaining from shielings and in Gaelic names such as 'airidh' (shieling) or 'blar' (a cleared space), both often found in names for places deep in the recesses of the hills. Evidence of man as a hunter on the hills is also found in Gaelic, there being innumerable references to 'eilde' (hind), 'gaibhre' (goat), 'daimh' (stag) and other prey in names of hill-form. However the great Caledonian forest of red pine would have been an enormous hindrance to either activity until it was cleared by felling and burning, a process that did not commence until the 1st century AD. Those activities that have been well described are related to warfare, commerce, road and rail building.

From these a personal selection that seems particularly relevant to man's movement on and through the hills starts, and with pride of place, with the awe-inspiring night crossing in winter of the hills between the Great Glen and Glen Spean by Montrose and his small army of 1500 men. Early on the morning of 31st January 1645, Montrose started his band of Atholl, Appin and Glen Coe clansmen together with Irish mercenaries and Camerons on a flank march intending surprise as a weapon to defeat opposing forces more than four times the number of his own, that were gathered north and south of him in the Great Glen. They struck south up Glen Tarff and over a bealach of 620m to descend glens Turret and Roy, not reaching Glen Spean until the morning of 1st February. There were then a further 13 miles, skirting the hills on the south of the glen, to reach the base of Meall an t-Suidhe, where the clansmen soaked their plaids in order that they should be more windproof for their night's rest in the snow. This epic march is well described by John Buchan in his biography of Montrose (op).

Another group of men who tackled the rigours of long journeys on foot were the drovers who brought their beasts for sale at the trysts of Falkirk and Crieff. By 1840 great quantities of black cattle — about 150 000 — were being delivered annually to Falkirk Tryst alone. From Mull they used the Pass of Brander and Glen Lochy to Tyndrum; from the north-western glens they came over the passes of Corrieyairack and Drumochter to Dalnacardoch; and from Skye they cut directly across the grain of the Central Highlands, either using the lines of weakness provided by Glen Spean and the Lairig Leacach and then skirting Leum Uilleim and the lochans that were used as the site of the present Blackwater, to cross to the Kingshouse by the bealach east of Beinn a' Chrulaiste, or, going over the Lairig Mor from Fort William to Kinlochleven and then the Devil's Staircase to Altnafeadh. Both latter routes converged on Inveroran, which has become, through literature, the acme of droving stances. Dorothy Wordsworth would 'have given £20 to have been able to take a lively picture of it' — the concourse in the kitchen at Inveroran — and goes on to draw as lively a picture in words as anyone could wish (*A Tour in Scotland:* 1803; James Thin Edinburgh, 1974).

Another intriguing insight into droving customs is given in the descriptions by 19th century travellers of drovers' dogs returning north alone to be fed at each stance by prior arrangement while the master took the easier route by sea from Glasgow to Oban or Fort William. The magnum opus on the subject of droving is A.R.B. Haldane's *The Drove Roads of Scotland* (Edinburgh University Press, 1968). Following the drovers, the road-makers avoided some of their high passes and generally took more circuitous routes. Here again A. R. B. Haldane has written a fine book, *New Ways through the Glens* (Nelson, 1962), that is almost as much a tribute to three honest public servants — Messrs Telford, Rickman and Hope — as a masterly evocation of 19th century road-building.

However the only significant new road in the Central Highlands in which the three had a part was that from Fort William to Kingussie, to be used about the turn of the century by Edinburgh-based climbers such as Raeburn, Tough and Brown who took the overnight train to Dalwhinnie and cycled to Aberarder or Fort William for a day out on Creag Meagaidh or Ben Nevis. The main route through the Central Highlands from Tyndrum to Inverness originated much earlier, with George Wade in the 18th century responsible for that part between Fort William and Inverness, as he was also for the road over the Corrieyairack. Considering the lack of resources other than men and hand implements, the speed with which some of these military roads were completed is remarkable. That from Dalwhinnie to Fort Augustus over the Corrieyairack took 500 men only the summer of 1731 for its 31 miles and several bridges. It took rather more men to construct the section between Loch Tulla and Kingshouse, there being a total of 1100 men camped on either side of the Black Mount in the summer of 1752 (when Wade had left Scotland and Caulfield was responsible for military road-building). Later travellers crossing the Black Mount remarked on finding rocks engraved with regimental names.

More recently about the turn of the century, the railway, and especially the West Highland Line from Glasgow to Fort William, had some influence on the development of mountaineering in the Central Highlands. Although stalwarts such as W.W.Naismith and W.Inglis Clark had made the approach to Ben Nevis by the steamer service plying between the Clyde and Fort William, it was not until the opening of the West Highland Line in 1894 that climbers made regular visits and it is notable that before the railway reached Fort William there were only two mountaineering routes on the mountain (Tower Ridge — descent 3rd September 1892 and North-East Buttress — ascent 6th September 1892; both by the brothers Hopkinson). By the end of the century, eighteen more routes had been made on the mountain.

The building of the West Highland Line bred its own legends, the foremost of which was the attempted crossing in winter of the Moor of Rannoch from Loch Treig head to Inveroran by seven men, only one of whom had crossed the Moor before. Of the rest one was the 60-year-old factor to the Marquis of Breadalbane. Their intention was to examine the proposed route, but not only did they intend to complete over 30 miles of the roughest going in the short span of January daylight, but had included in their itinerary a noon rendezvous at the River Gaur for a site inspection with the landowner. Not surprisingly they failed to reach Inveroran and spent most of the night in varying states of collapse on the Moor. Help eventually arrived from Gorton but one Macalpine, described in accounts of the time as 'stout, full-blooded, and loquacious', actually got the length of Barravourich, a mere 6 miles from his destination.

Before the line could be laid, stretches of moor between Rannoch Station and the rising ground 5 miles to the south, plus further stretches to the north, required substantial drainage after which a great trench was filled with ash and glacial till on a bottoming of brushwood and heather. A temporary light railway was used to transport the spoil across the moor, and when one of the small engines in use was derailed at the wettest part of the moor, it sank 12ft in the course of the night. Thousands of navvies were involved in building the line; a large number from Ireland and Highlandmen from all parts including a contingent from the Western Highlands where a recognised destitution brought them the benefit of a one-way fare from the contractor. Fixed camps were built at intervals for the occasional recuperation of the navvies, who normally slept in hutting or 'turf-dwellings' along the line. At one such — Achallader Camp — the Marquis of Breadalbane presided over the Black Mount Literary Association set up to 'excite a spirit of inquiry combined with healthy amusement among men employed upon the West Highland Railway during the winter season'. Programmes comprising pianoforte selections, light vocals and a service of fruit, and rules barring entry of 'intoxicated or swearing men' can have done little to capture such audiences.

And so the droving routes fell into disuse as Highland-bred cattle were transported by train across the Moor of Rannoch by much the same route as that surveyed in 1811 when looking for an improved route to the cattle trysts of Central Scotland.

Purple Saxifrage

FLORA

The Central Highlands contain mainly acid soils most of which are poorly drained so that blanket bog is common. In few places does the birch bring its golden glow to autumn and even rarer are the remaining stands of oak in occasional southern exposures. In most seasons the Scottish hills present a subdued display of russets, olive greens, bleached oranges and purples, giving startling exception to the brilliant orange berries of the mountain ash and to the underfoot luminescence of the wine-red and orange in sphagnum moss. Only in early summer can one follow Principal Shairp's instruction to

> 'Stoop and see a lowlier kind,
> Creeping milkwort, pink, white, blue,

and find the bright tints of wild orchid and sea-pink, or see a southern hillside fresh with green new shoots of bracken. The climber ascends through indistinct stages of vegetation. Not often in the Central Highlands does one avoid the lower, boggy ground where the aroma of bog myrtle and the tattered fleece of cotton grass vie with sphagnum moss and purple moor grass.

Above 300m, plants of the bog give way to grass heaths such as mat grass, deer grass and stiff sedge with heather more predominant on the eastern hills. Once on the tops, the striking feature is the dwarf-like nature of all growth. Indeed, those hill-goers not specifically interested in flora will only notice the miniature forms when perhaps recumbent on the tops in sunny weather. Then one may examine the tiny antlers of stag's horn moss or on rarer occasions, usually in gravelly clearings, the china-pink flowers of moss campion clustered several dozen in a green cushion of perhaps 20cm diameter. This beautiful flower survives in the arctic conditions above 900m by driving down a tap-root often greater in length than the diameter of its cushion. On the eastern tops of the district, blaeberry and crowberry are more common and mix with the tawny Nardus grasslands. The autumn blaeberry presents another delight for the hill-goer, the succulence of its berries as much appreciated by birds as can be seen from the purple stain of their droppings on the rocks at this time of year. These berries seem to grow as large and sweet on northern slopes as on more sunny exposures.

In only a few places in the Central Highlands can the hill-goer enjoy the variety that indigenous trees bring to landscape. By the 16th century, when Elizabeth I took fright at the inroads being made into the deciduous woodlands of England and passed legislation that forced the charcoal burners to pursue their pillage into Scotland, the vast Caledonian forest of Scots pine had already been laid waste by various human agencies. The Norse raiders almost by custom, as much as for any purpose of flushing out defenders, burnt vast tracts of timber and also culled material for boat-building. Their depredations stretched well inland from the western seaboard and were continued by the warfaring Scottish clans. Then the smelting industry and next the land clearance for the coming of the sheep completed the destruction. Here and there remnants can be seen — oakwoods in Glen Creran, Scots pine beside Loch Tulla and birch above Loch Etive — but man can now move freely about the hills.

FAUNA

Few city-dwellers are accustomed to watching a hillside for the tell-tale movement of a fox, otherwise indistinguishable in his perfect camouflage, but the ever-present red deer are readily seen from most hills in the Central Highlands. In the Black Mount and Corrour estates vast herds congregate in the corries and, when disturbed, their wonderfully light, flowing movements can enliven many a dreich day. A peculiarly autumn noise is the roaring of the stag in rut — at a distance often terminating in a gloomy, coughing, groan — while the hind has a short, clear bark used rarely to warn a grazing herd of an intruder. Other signs of deer are the wallows that stags and hinds use for the removal of parasites: a pit of wettish peat with a substantial piece of pine in its midst is the place favoured by the stag, who will churn the peat with his fore-feet and use the old trunk as a rubbing post. As with other wild animals, deer have an extraordinary awareness of weather change. Deer watchers have frequently noted an otherwise inexplicable large-scale movement of deer to low ground two to three days before the onset of heavy snowfall.

With the exception of the blue (alpine) and brown hares, few other quadrupeds will be seen by the casual observer. Very occasionally, walking upwind and hidden by an intervening ridge, one might surprise a fox; otherwise only his winter tracks, often on a high ridge, will be seen. Even rarer sightings at low level will be had of stoat, weasel, pine marten, wild-cat and red squirrel, while there is little enough forest in the Central Highlands for the roe deer to be much seen. Unlike the case with land beasts, many species of birds will be seen in the course of a hill-walk. Even in winter, grouse, ptarmigan and snow buntings will enliven most days, the first rising lower on the hill, almost from underfoot with its alarm call of 'awah, awah, awah', and flocks of the latter on the tops wheeling and banking to show their white undersides. Then in spring and early summer on high and open ground, the mournful whistle of the golden plover will sometimes be heard.

But it is surely the ptarmigan that is the bird of the tops. A native of Scotland, spending its whole year above 650m, and relying so much on its camouflage that one frequently approaches within spitting distance before it breaks from cover and runs, as often as not until choosing a take-off point allowing a gliding descent. In winter both cock and hen are white all over apart from their black tails and a black eye patch on the cock. When they have scooped out a lee hollow in the snow, either to shelter from high winds or to uncover the plants on which they feed, they become undetectable. In summer, when their plumage changes to a mottle of grey and brown, they blend just as well against lichen-covered boulders. Their young also have great confidence in the camouflage of their plumage and will remain perfectly still while a camera is moved to within a metre, though the hen will be several yards away desperately dragging a wing. Ptarmigan shooting has been one of the hill sports, and whatever one's attitudes to such pastimes, grudging admiration must surely be accorded to the writer of an article years ago who claimed that for the birds to have a sporting chance, they should be stalked until close enough to shoot with a hand-gun (a pistol). He was also of the opinion that a pair of stout, nailed shoes were essential for this activity.

Few of the raptorial birds will be seen. The buzzard's mewing call will be heard more often than the bird is seen and casual sightings of eagles are fairly rare. This splendid bird is highly intolerant of human activity near to its nesting site and as over 4 months are involved between the laying of eggs and the eaglets becoming fledged, the potential for disturbance is large. Of the migratory birds, greylag geese provide a splendid sight, and sound, during their April flight north, in echelon with the lead position changing frequently in strong headwinds and the whirr of their pinions audible from as much as 100m below. In the wooded glens and on the lochsides a much greater variety of bird-life can be readily seen — particularly this is the case in the Etive basin. Lapwing, curlew, sandpiper and oystercatcher among the waders are common as are many of the passerines including the yellowhammer, grey wagtail and wheatear. Those having the leisure to wander up the eastern shore of Loch Etive and stop to eat beside a burn will be unlucky not to catch sight of a dipper. (On the same shore, with a detour to the headland north of Inverliver Bay, grey seal can often be seen basking on the islets not 100 metres out into the loch.)

Last under this heading, a little must be said about those small creatures which, on a still humid day in July and August, can try the humour of the most ardent hill-goer. Worst by far is the midge and it will be found at its most maddening density in poorly drained glens such as Glen Etive. Indeed it is claimed that they were far less numerous before the glens were cleared of crofters who, with their need to drain the land for cultivation, removed much of the insect's habitat. There is certainly little mention of the midge — meanbh-chuileag (little fly) — in Gaelic lore, although Prince Charles Edward Stuart seems to have found them trying during his flight across the Central and Western Highlands. Various proprietary creams and lotions are sold as repellants in all Highland chemists. Many have an active constituent of di-methyl-phthalate and these can usually be applied to the skin. For increased protection some authorities recommend application of a repellent to clothing and these may contain chemicals unsuitable for use on the skin. One repellant that the author has found effective, though this is a relative term in the context, has the trade name of Autan, and many people claim noticeable relief from the burning of Moskill in a tent. The midge is preyed upon by dragonflies, frogs, palmated newts and, in the midge's pupal stage, by trout — there would seem strong argument for regarding all these predators as protected species!

Other pests lesser in numbers but more unpleasant in their individual effect are blood-sucking clegs, the bite from which causes painful swellings, and sheep-ticks, another bloodsucker that burrows into the skin of humans and sheep alike. Against midges and clegs, a hat with a drooping brim provides some relief. Those wishing to mount a campaign against these pests could start by reading *Insecticide Resistance and Vector Control:* 17th Report of the Expert Committee on Insecticides. Technical Report, World Health Organisation, No. 433, 1970.

For those hill-goers who wish to acquire a little knowledge about what they see on the hills, perhaps the widest overview is provided by F. Fraser Darling and J. Morton Boyd's *The Highlands and Islands*, (Collins New Naturalist, 1969) which itself contains a comprehensive bibliography. To those wanting to know more about red deer is recommended F. Fraser Darling's fascinating study *A Herd of Red Deer*, first published in 1937 and with several other printings over the years (OUP, 1969).

LANDFORM

The Central Highlands are the remains of a great range that reared up 400 million years ago, was first planed down to a plateau and then dissected to give the landform that we see today. They are composed of ancient metamorphic rocks known as Dalradian schists that stretch in a great belt with a SW to NE bias and are only broken to any large extent by the intrusive granites of Cruachan, Etive and Rannoch, though extrusions of volcanic rocks at Glen Coe and Ben Nevis are of great interest for rock-climbing and have had impact on the local landform. To the west and, to a lesser extent, to the south, the area is moated by valleys eroded along natural faults — the Great Glen and the Pass of Brander — while to the east the boundary follows

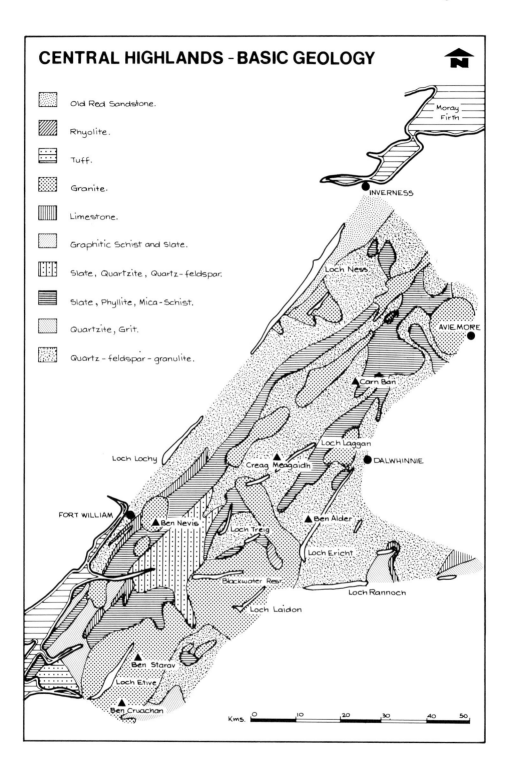

CENTRAL HIGHLANDS - BASIC GEOLOGY

Old Red Sandstone.

Rhyolite.

Tuff.

Granite.

Limestone.

Graphitic Schist and Slate.

Slate, Quartzite, Quartz-feldspar.

Slate, Phyllite, Mica-Schist.

Quartzite, Grit.

Quartz-feldspar-granulite.

Moray Firth

INVERNESS

Loch Ness

AVIEMORE

Carn Ban

Loch Laggan

Loch Lochy

Creag Meagaidh

DALWHINNIE

FORT WILLIAM

Ben Nevis

Loch Treig

Ben Alder

Loch Ericht

Blackwater Resr.

Loch Rannoch

Loch Laidon

Ben Starav

Loch Etive

Ben Cruachan

Kms. 0 10 20 30 40 50

The truncated spurs of the Three Sisters of Glen Coe

the Dalradian trend of Glen Orchy and then, more prosaically, the West Highland Line to Rannoch Station, the B846 road to Killiecrankie and the A9 to Inverness. Though contained within a tall oblong leaning to the north-east of only 150 kilometres height, this area shows a wonderful variety of hills from the jagged outline of Cruachan's granite in the south-west to the rolling plateau of the Monadh Liath's mica-schist in the north-east. In between, weather-resistant quartzite gives the distinctive sharp ridges of the Mamores and Grey Corries; the Etive granites show in cream-coloured slabs of great extent and roughness on both sides of the loch; and at the centre cauldron-extrusions of lava have left compact rocks and the dramatic structure of the Glen Coe hills and of the northern cirque of Ben Nevis. Through it all run the ice-gouged faults with that SW to NE trend so apparent in lochs Etive and Ericht. Evidence of that effortless and most recent leveller, glaciation, is prominent on all sides, from the U-shaped valleys with truncated spurs and hanging corries, such as Glen Coe itself, to the lesser but still evocative evidence in the furrows left as glaciation planed down the rock on the summit of Aonach Beag.

It is thought that the last remnant of the great Laggan-Spey glacier died about 9000 years ago in the recess of Coire Leis. After a winter of heavy snowfall when on a day in May one may peer down 20m into the bergschrund beneath Observatory Ridge, it needs little imagination to picture glaciation recurring with a slight deterioration in climate. Those wishing a more than passing acquaintance with the landform of the area would find the definitive text in A.Geikie's *The Scenery of Scotland* (op) with another, more accessible text in J.B.Whittow's *Geology and Scenery in Scotland* (Penguin, 1979). For those with some knowledge of geology, G.S. Johnstone's *British Regional Geology-Scotland: The Grampian Highlands* (HMSO, 1966), contains much interest and a comprehensive bibliography.

ABBREVIATIONS, DIRECTIONS AND TERMINOLOGY

Only those abbreviations in general usage are used in this guide. The directions left and right refer always to the direction faced by the climber, whether in ascent or descent. Gaelic words adopted by the English language, such as cairn and bothy, are used in their English spellings unless they form part of a name, e.g. the corries of the Black Mount but Coire Chat.

SMCJ: Scottish Mountaineering Club Journal
  OS: Ordnance Survey
  op: out of print
   m: metres (but metres for horizontal distance)
   ft: feet

CHAPTER 1

Cruachan

Ben Cruachan	1126m	069 304
Stob Diamh	998m	095 308
Beinn a' Bhuiridh	897m	094 283

ACCESS
From the A85 Crianlarich — Oban road. There are a few spaces for car parking near the Cruachan Power Station Visitors' Centre. Further east on the B8077 road parking space is limited near the junction with the A85.

TRANSPORT
Train from Glasgow — Oban actually stops at the Falls of Cruachan station; also at Dalmally and Taynuilt. Daily service all year.
Bus service Glasgow — Oban and Stirling — Oban both stopping at Taynuilt and Dalmally. Daily service May — October.
Postbus between Bridge of Orchy and Dalmally (Mon — Sat).
Local bus service Oban — Taynuilt.

ACCOMMODATION
There are hotels and guest houses at Dalmally, Lochawe and Taynuilt. At Crunachy, Bridge of Awe there is a guest house with a caravan and camp site.

MAPS
OS 1:50 000 Landranger Sheet 50

From whatever direction one approaches this splendid group, some feature of its detached and mountainous nature impresses one immediately. As a whole its extent is best seen from the south, where from some point on the eastern side of Loch Awe the full length of its ridge can be appreciated. However, it is from the north that the jagged nature of its three western tops becomes clear and indeed the view of the tops in winter from Loch Dochard, on the path between Loch Tulla and Loch Etive, is positively Alpine.

The Cruachan massif is bounded on three sides by the deep trenches of Loch Etive, the Pass of Brander and Glen Strae, while to the north the through valley of Glen Noe almost completes its isolation. A narrow ridge runs east-west for 4 kilometres dropping below 900m to 860m at one point only, and it has four distinct peaks within its length, while its easternmost peak throws out ridges to the north-east and to the south, giving two more tops above 900m. This latter cirque, well seen from the main road east of Dalmally, is known as the Dalmally Horseshoe. Almost

Ben Cruachan from Beinn Sgulaird across Loch Etive

to its full height the southern slopes of this range are well grassed on the granular dioritic rock of which they are partly composed. However, the ridge itself and most of the spines it throws out to the north have an extensive exposure of granite. The acid soil supports little variety of flora, but the lower southern and western slopes carry fine woods of hazel, birch, alder, ash and small oak and the easternmost tops of the Dalmally Horseshoe produce a succulent crop of blaeberries each autumn.

Much was written about Ben Cruachan and its environs by the early travellers, though the Pass of Brander made as much impression on them as the Ben itself. In 1791 Thomas Newte rather tremulously and exaggeratedly wrote of the road through the pass as being 1000ft up Ben Cruachan and having no parapet. That part of the old road he was describing climbed from the church west of Lochawe village to a maximum height of 519ft and is now under the tarmac of the road up to the Cruachan dam. Dorothy Wordsworth's sharply observed account of the journey between the heights south of Dalmally and Taynuilt is still relevant today, as with the exception of the railway and the lower-level road at the east end of the pass, the general appearance of the ground can have changed little.

It needs little more than a glance at the OS 1:50 000 map (Sheet 50) to show the attractiveness of a traverse of the main ridge, and possibly the most attractive of the possibilities is to start up the long eastern ridge of Beinn a' Bhuiridh from the western junction of the A85 with the Stronmilchan road (B8077). After the next ascent north

Ben Cruachan from the Stob Dearg col

from Beinn a'Bhuiridh onto the tops of the Dalmally Horseshoe, there is a switch-back running west of an increasingly rugged nature terminating at Stob Dearg, Cruachan's Taynuilt Peak. If there is time left and the sky is clear, it is well worth the extra effort of descending the steep, coggly slopes west-north-west from Stob Dearg in order to be at the top of Meall nan Each for the sunset, which particularly late and early in the year can throw a path of crimson from behind the hills of Mull down the seaward length of Loch Etive. Such a traverse of course assumes either two cars in a party and a sure meeting at some point on the ridge for an exchange of keys, or prior research into the use of the bus and train services between Glasgow and Oban.

Another way of traversing the tops involving return to the departure point is that starting from the old Falls of Cruachan railway station up the path on the west side of the burn. When the dam wall comes in sight a westerly line leads onto the broad, southern ridge of Meall Cuanail and from its top there is a mere 60m of descent before the climb up Ben Cruachan itself. An easier, though considerably longer, way of reaching the dam is to walk or cycle up the surfaced road starting from the A85 at 115 266. Private cars are not allowed to use this road.

Those who traverse north-north-west from the bealach just north of Meall Cuanail in order to reach Stob Dearg without climbing Cruachan twice, should be wary, particularly in winter, of the extensive belt of compact red granite slabs that lie in the way. These are best skirted by taking a low traverse line until almost below the bealach between Stob Dearg and Cruachan. In winter the space of a full day should be allowed for the traverse. A party starting from the Falls of Cruachan will probably take 8 hours, exclusive of stops, and fresh snow could add substantially to this allowance.

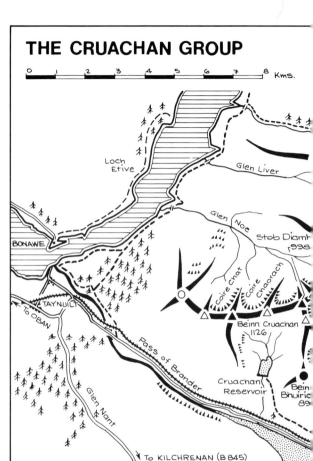

THE HILLS

Stob Dearg *(red peak)* (1104m)
This Gaelic name for Cruachan's Taynuilt peak highlights the colour change in the granite from the grey cliffs on Drochaid Ghlas to the pink blocks that litter the west side of the Stob. If approach is being made directly to this peak, then straight-forward though laborious routes can be taken from the Pass of Brander either beside the Allt Brander or the Allt Gruiniche. A little above the railway line on either of these approaches, remnants of 'Anderson's Piano Wires' may yet be found. These were installed as an alarm system before the turn of the century, when a derailment impressed upon the railway owners the danger of falling boulders. A fence of 5659 yards length, composed of 9ft posts carrying ten strands of steel wire, was erected through the Pass of Brander. Any boulder inflicting sufficient shock to the wires of this fence, triggered the signals and warned drivers of impending danger. The name itself originated from that of the engineer in charge of the line toward the end of the last century.

Ben Cruachan *(stacky hill)* (1126m)
All the natural routes to the summit of the main peak in the group are fittingly steep and up well-defined ridges. The easiest approach is to the south ridge from the bealach north of Meall Cuanail, which can be reached by the route previously described under traverses. (Also on this side of the peak an unpleasant path ascends steeply over crumbling ground from east of and below the bealach north of Meall Cuanail. It reaches the main ridge somewhat to the east of the summit.) Both west and east ridges involve a little scrambling, the latter having a tricky step requiring care in winter.

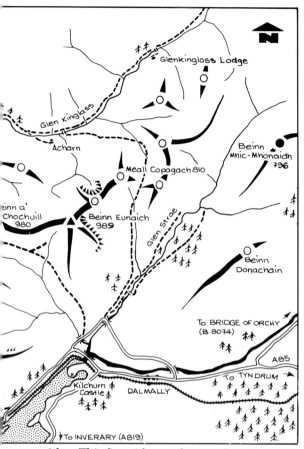

However, pride of place goes to the north ridge, whose aerial highway amply repays the effort of the long approach. Two ways of reaching the north ridge and the north side of the range in general are described; both involve a walk of 9 or 10 kilometres. The first is from Bridge of Awe on the Taynuilt side of the group and uses the old military road for 2 kilometres before taking the private road to Glennoe Farm. Cars can not be taken on this road, which is in any event very rough, but a bicycle would save time. On a fine day the views from the road through the trees across Loch Etive are particularly fine.

Once the farmhouse has been skirted, the path continues up Glen Noe on the north side of the burn, which should be held for 4 kilometres and up to the 250m level in order to enjoy best the views of the northern cliffs on Stob Dearg and Cruachan and in order to pick the best line to the foot of the north ridge. This fine ridge curls round to the north-east at its foot where it is well-defined. After an initial steep climb the angle eases for 100m until the ridge steepens again to become more rocky and narrow, and to involve a little scrambling. It finishes at a shoulder just north-east of the summit. In good winter conditions an ice-axe and crampons will be needed.

The second approach is shorter, but does involve 250m of descent and reascent. It uses the dirt road built during the construction of the Cruachan Dam that commences on the B8077 on the north-east side of the Allt Mhoille and reaches a point 100m below the Lairig Noe. This approach over the Lairig Noe offers obvious possibilities of mountaineering circuits on the northern ridges. It is also a convenient means of approaching and observing the gullies on the north face of Sron an Isean's east-south-east ridge.

Meall Cuanail (918m)
This southern spur of Cruachan itself is a modest lump in very grand surroundings and is usually ascended on the way to the main peak by the route from the Falls of Cruachan.

The Summit of Ben Cruachan from the east

Drochaid Ghlas *(grey bridge)* (1009m)

This fine peak set in the middle of the main ridge, and often a mere incident in the course of a traverse, deserves more attention. The most repaying approach is over the Lairig Noe, from where a descending westerly traverse of 100m and 1½ kilometres leads to a spur thrown down north-east from the peak's north ridge. This ridge is a narrow and exhilarating route to the summit over the occasional difficulty and a final arete between the peak's two tops. In winter it would be classed as Grade I. Its east face is composed of very steep granite riven by vertical cracks and chimneys, while a deep gully rises to the neck between the two tops. Rock climbs have been made here, but the rock is badly shattered and routes are short.

When traversing this peak in poor visibility from either west or east, the natural and almost imperceptible trend is to the north and then onto the summit which is set back north of the main ridge. The continuation of the main ridge in either direction is not well-defined and a compass course will save time.

Stob Diamh *(peak of the stag)* (998m)

This peak with its two satellites, Stob Garbh (980m) and Sron an Isean (966m), forms an east-facing horseshoe well seen from the road east of Dalmally and better still from the Stronmilchan road (B8077). Either of the east-south-east ridges on Sron an Isean and Stob Garbh can be approached from the old railway track mentioned below in the description of Beinn a' Bhuiridh. Bridges cross the Allt Coire Ghlais and the Allt Coire Chreachainn; for the first there is one close above the junction, and for the latter more than one below the junction.

Once one of the outer tops has been climbed there is only an extra 150m of ascent and an extra kilometre involved in the circuit of all three. Both outer peaks offer some winter climbing on their eastern and northern slopes. Stob Garbh in particular throws out a north-eastern ridge from directly beneath its summit that forms a most attractive route in winter and, if the easiest line to the north of the lowest rocks is followed, is no harder than Grade I. When making a circuit of the peaks from south to north, care is needed in poor visibility at Stob Diamh since the natural trend of the ridge is due north, eventually leading to a steep and rocky descent to Glen Noe. The true east-north-east continuation is also a steep descent for a short distance.

Beinn a'Bhuiridh *(hill of roaring {of stags})* (896 m)

From the east this peak has a distinctive and graceful pyramidal shape. Its Gaelic name perhaps arose from the reverberant properties of the enclosed corrie that lies to the north of the long east ridge, though no deer will be seen there today. This latter ridge is the pleasantest approach and the initial 300m of steep ground can be avoided by following the old railway track to the abandoned lead mine for 1 kilometre before starting uphill to the left. The track is easily found leading north from the B8077 approximately ½ kilometre from its west junction with the A85. Splendid views are to be had from this ridge, out over Loch Awe and down to Kilchurn Castle. When continuing north in winter down to the Larig Torran, the descent is often icy and

Beinn a'Bhuiridh and the Cruachan Reservoir

steep enough to require care. In poor visibility the ideal descent north is not easily found since the summit area is extensive and undulating with many rocky knolls, one of which at the western end is the summit. The Gaelic name larig (*a pass*) for the saddle north of the peak suggests that it was used as such for the black cattle grazing on the ground now occupied by the Cruachan Reservoir. It was reputed to have been used by William Wallace to outflank the men of Lorne, otherwise immovable from the narrows of the Pass of Brander.

A northerly escarpment runs along the east ridge and numerous short climbs can be enjoyed here in winter. An interesting approach to these short chimneys and gullies takes a traverse from the Larig Torran along turf ledges which eventually run out on steep ground at one of the shallow gullies which can carry thick ice.

If this hill is included at the end of a traverse of the main ridge and descent must be made to a car left at Falls of Cruachan, the best descent is due west to the dam from where the path down the west side of the burn can be picked up. Descent due south to Loch Awe involves laborious scrambling lower down on steep, tree-clad slopes, though one may well have one's evening toil enlivened by the hooting of tawny owls.

The northern ridges and corries of Ben Cruachan

CLIMBING

There is winter climbing on the east face of Stob Dearg of a length and quality not found elsewhere in the range. This face has traditionally been described as the north-east face, but there is little or no 'northing' to its general inclination and those climbing there in clear weather will find the face most attractively lit by the glancing rays of the sun even at midday. The routes can be reached either from the south with descent from the bealach between Stob Dearg and Cruachan itself, or by the longer, but pleasanter approach from the north through Glen Noe.

The east face makes a triangle between the south-south-east and north ridges, with its base descending toward the latter. It is composed of granite slabs steepening toward the north ridge and fissured by two short open gullies on its southern fringe and by two open couloirs of greater length at its centre. The first recorded ascent takes the more northerly and longer of the short gullies (Grade I), while the second with its variation start (both Grade III) takes a line from the lowest point and close to the centre of the triangle's base. A little further right there is a harder winter route (Grade IV). These climbs are described in *A Climbers' Guide to Arran, Arrochar & the Southern Highlands* by K.V. Crocket & A.Walker, published by The Scottish Mountaineering Trust (1989).

The north ridge of Stob Dearg, though not as long as its companion ridge to Ben Cruachan, is rather more difficult and makes a fine winter route with some awkward rock steps not easily turned. In poor visibility finding its foot requires careful navigation as the topography in the higher reaches of Coire Chat is confusing. All four of the northern corries have short winter climbs on their headwalls. Coire Chat has a buttress rising just east of the bealach between Stob Dearg and Cruachan that is cut by two chimneys, the westerly one being of easy angle and the easterly one vertical. Coire Caorach has some gully lines on the north-westerly aspect of Drochaid Ghlas, as has the nameless corrie to the east at the north-east angle between Drochaid Ghlas and the main ridge. The hanging corrie — Coire Lochain — presents steep ground, often icy, to the summit of Stob Diamh.

Somewhat east of the north-east ridge of Stob Garbh, there is an outcrop of granite in the form of a tall slab and a buttress that would give some hard rock-climbing. Sron an Isean's east-south-east ridge has a north face seamed with gullies and one of these, which ascends to a point on the ridge 1 kilometre from the summit, often carries steep, though short ice-pitches in its lower half. In such conditions it would be Grade II.

Meall nan Each's east face is steep enough to provide good climbing in a hard winter and, at its northern edge there is a fine crag of steep clean granite.

References

SMCJ, II, p85. For a thrilling account by W.Douglas of the first ascent of Stob Dearg's north ridge under unusually icy conditions (1882).

A Progress in Mountaineering, J.H.B.Bell, p8. For another account of a winter ascent of Stob Dearg's north ridge (1936).

SMCJ, XI, p236. *Loch Awe in the time of Bruce and Wallace.* An interesting introduction to the history of the warfare waged through the Pass of Brander.

SMCJ, XII, pp65, 137 and 189. These articles are of antiquarian interest about the islands of Loch Awe.

Prospects and Observations on a Tour of England and Scotland. Thomas Newte (1791).

A Tour in Scotland: 1803. Dorothy Wordsworth (James Thin, Edinburgh, 1974).

CHAPTER 2

The Glen Strae Hills

Beinn a'Chochuill	980m	110 328
Beinn Eunaich	989m	136 328
Beinn Mhic-Mhonaidh	796m	208 349

ACCESS
From the A85 and on to the B8077 3 kilometres west of Dalmally. There is limited parking on the B8077. (Do not obstruct the road to Castles Farm.)

ACCOMMODATION
As Chapter 1

TRANSPORT
As Chapter 1

MAP
OS 1:50 000 Landranger Sheet 50

This scattered group of hills is bounded to the east and south by Glen Orchy and Glen Noe and to the north by Glen Kinglass and by the path from the head of the latter glen to Victoria Bridge. A mail-bus service between Bridge of Orchy and Dalmally makes possible the long walk up Glen Strae and over the tops to Bridge of Orchy, but the extensive afforestation on the western slopes of Glen Orchy leaves only one approach from this side.

One natural traverse over the big hills presents itself, with a convenient approach *via* the hydro-road leading onto the southern slopes of Beinn a'Chochuill and the day's end on the track down the lower part of Glen Strae after a descent from Beinn Lurachan.

THE HILLS

Beinn a'Chochuill *(hill of the hood)* (980m)
While dwarfed and hidden by its splendid neighbour Ben Cruachan, this hill does have a distinctive form, being an elongated ridge running east to west. Indeed, a traverse from Loch Etive to the bealach between Beinn a'Chochuill and Beinn Eunaich involves a distance of 9 kilometres. Such a roundabout approach will rarely be undertaken, but anyone climbing from Loch Etive is recommended to include

Beinn a'Chochuill and Beinn Eunaich across Loch Awe

A' Chruach (271m) behind Glennoe farm for the magnificent view both up and down the loch.

The obvious approach is *via* the Hydro track from Castles Farm, described earlier in Chapter 1. After crossing the main burn descending from the bealach between Beinn a'Chochuill and Beinn Eunaich, the track should be left for the easy ascent of the south-easterly ridge that descends from Point 896m — an easterly fore-top and one of many on the 1 kilometre ridge to the summit. Once on the ridge the splendour of the view towards Cruachan's three westerly peaks becomes apparent and improves until it is at its best a little beyond the summit. So splendid is this view that it would almost be worthwhile to climb the north face of Beinn a'Chochuill in order to enjoy the breathtaking impact of it as one's head popped over the cornice. For this superb composition of ridge, corrie and peak to be enjoyed at its best, ascent before midday on a clear winter's day is recommended.

Though it provides no recognised winter climbs, the north face is continuously steep throughout its 3 kilometre breadth and care is needed on the ridge which often carries a large and continuous cornice. The ground to the north around the head of Glen Liver is a desolation of peat-bog, moraines and lochans, but has a real sense of remoteness and is as likely a place as any on the east side of Loch Etive from which to see eagles soaring and swooping, or even to spot fox and wild-cat with the aid of binoculars.

Looking up Glen Strae to Beinn Mhic-Mhonaidh

Beinn Eunaich *(fowling hill)* (989m)

Though joined to Beinn a'Chochuill at the Lairig Ianachain (728m), Beinn Eunaich has a somewhat different form. This is partially due to the band of porphyry that outcrops on a north-eastern shoulder of Beinn Eunaich and interrupts the granite of which the two hills are mainly composed, but also Beinn Eunaich has a more pyramidal shape, radiating three ridges and holding a fine corrie to the east. The ascent can be made straightforwardly from Castles Farm, over steep ground to the fore-peak Stob Maol and then along the broad, easy-angled south ridge, but this ridge is pleasanter in descent for the fine views it gives of Loch Awe and of the long ridges of the Dalmally Horseshoe.

A more interesting route will be found on the opposite side of the mountain. Starting up the track on the west of the River Strae and keeping left at the fork, a patch of afforestation is reached in 1 kilometre. From its northern rim a faint path follows the west bank of the main burn (unnamed on the 1:50 000 OS map) that drains the cirque formed by Beinn Eunaich, Meall Copagach and Beinn Lurachan. (This path, the depiction of which on various maps has been the subject of raillery for the past 90 years — William Douglas, SMCJ, Vol. II — is still shown confidently on the 1:50 000 OS map. It certainly comes and goes and should not be relied upon north of the bealach). In a little over 30 minutes a gully known as the Black Shoot and its containing buttress of porphyry will be seen steeply above to the left, and in a further 30 minutes the foot of a ridge running down east from the unnamed top (880m) will be reached. This, and then Beinn Eunaich's steep north-east ridge, give an approach of greater interest.

The hill is revered as the place where that most generous and far-sighted spirit Percy Unna crossed the Great Divide. Warned off the hill by his doctor because of a serious heart condition, Unna preferred to continue his hill wandering, but out of consideration for others chose to go alone. He did not return from one of his solitary walks and was found dead on the slopes below Stob Maol. A man of great wealth, Unna chose to disperse much of it toward the purchase of mountain land for the use of hill-goers and, using the National Trust for Scotland as a vehicle for anonymous donations, was instrumental in the purchase of mountainous areas such as Glen Coe and Kintail.

Meall Copagach (810m)
Beinn Lurachan (715m)
A traverse of Beinn a'Chochuill and Beinn Eunaich extends quite naturally over these two tops and Beinn Lurachan's south-west ridge is well drained and easy going for descent. Rough slabs of pink granite crop out lower down and, at its foot above a new bridge on the Glen Strae track, there is a magnificent swimming-pool. For those walking from Dalmally to Bridge of Orchy, Beinn Lurachan is a good point at which to take to the hills since Glen Strae narrows considerably beyond it and the view becomes restricted. A rather tenuous line can then be followed over Beinn Larachan (586m) and on to Beinn Suidhe (675m). This walk gives ever-changing views of the Ben Starav and Black Mount hills and of their deeply recessed glens. It ends in a fine situation as one descends Beinn Suidhe's north-east ridge toward an isolated stand of firs beside a confluence of burns.

Beinn Mhic-Mhonaidh (hill of the son of the moor) (796m)
From Glen Strae this hill looks every inch a mountain, presenting as it does a classical cone shape with steep sides. It is not easy of access, for the Strae can be difficult to ford opposite the foot of the south-west ridge. There is a bridge (166 315) in the second patch of afforestation which gives access to the old path up the glen and eventually to the shieling of Inbhir-nan-giubhas, but no one should be tempted here as the old path is now very rough going through densely packed spruce. (This corner is worth visiting though on an off-day for the delightful series of waterfalls and for the remnants of Scots pine that mingle with the new firs and appear majestic by contrast.)

When the river is full the first place at which it can be forded is where the track itself crosses over to the east bank (186 338) and even then great care will be needed. The slopes above are steep, riven with drainage channels, and higher, of scree. The alternative of trending diagonally right (south) to gain the south-west ridge is recommended. Descent from Beinn Mhic-Mhonaidh to Glen Orchy is not advised as a way must be found through the extensive afforestation. However the ascent route *via* the bridge over the Orchy at 243 321 is easily followed and would be a sensible choice after a wet period. Beyond the bridge a forestry track runs up beside the Allt Broighleachan for 2 kilometres. When the track runs out in a clearing, there are leads through the trees to the west.

To continue over Beinn Mhic-Mhonaidh and on to Bridge of Orchy involves some rough going at the head of Glen Strae and at the double-level bealach between Beinn Mhic-Mhonaidh, Beinn a'Churn (564m) and Meall an Laoigh (546m), where also the terrain can be confusing in poor visibility. Intervening ridges prevent the fine views that are enjoyed from the previously mentioned traverse, but this route is the quicker, avoiding the 9 kilometre walk from Clashgour to Bridge of Orchy and once Ben Inverveigh's long ridge has been traversed northward, an excellent track leads down directly to Bridge of Orchy from the Mam Carraigh. The temptation to descend due east from Ben Inverveigh's northernmost top should be resisted as the struggle through the forest will absorb any time saved.

For anyone staying in the vicinity of Loch Tulla, a walk up Ben Inverveigh on a clear evening will be amply repaid, as the westering sun highlights the ridges and models the corries of the Starav and Black Mount groups to great effect. The view of the north-west quadrant is fine enough from the Mam Carraigh, but as one gradually gains height on a good track, the panorama extends until it includes an arc from Beinn nan Aighenan to Clach Leathad and Beinn Toaig. From the Mam Carraigh one can also look down on the old enclosures and the more recent wood above the Allt Tolaghan, that marks the area of the croft in which the Gaelic poet, Duncan Ban Macintyre, was born. Even though his poetry is said not to translate with its full effect into English — losing the cadence of Gaelic and its changing rhythm, as of the piobaireachd, that Duncan Ban used deliberately — his poems, and one *In Praise of Beinn Dorain*, transmit a sense of elan at approaching a hill and an appreciation of landscape that will strike a chord with most hill-goers.

CLIMBING

At one time Beinn Eunaich was best known for its Black Shoot and a train of aspirants attacked it, and were usually repulsed, in the years about the end of the last century. There are no fewer than 21 references to it in the first 8 volumes of the SMC Journal and any modern climber contemplating an ascent could prepare himself by reading accounts by two of these ancients and one by a modern whose wit is well seasoned with awe: *The Black Shoot of Stob Maol*, W.R. Lester, SMCJ, II, p117; *The Black Shoot in White*, H.Raeburn, SMCJ, VI, p161; *Pink Elephants in the Black Shoot*, R.N.Campbell, SMCJ, XXX, p21. The climb is up a series of chimneys, well vegetated and seemingly always wet. It is at least Severe in standard.

CHAPTER 3

Ben Starav Group

Ben Starav	1078m	126 427
Stob Coir'an Albannaich	1044m	169 442
Beinn nan Aighenan	960m	149 405
Glas Bheinn Mhor	997m	153 429
Meall nan Eun	928m	192 449

ACCESS

The A8005 turning from the A82 to Victoria Bridge where there is parking for about twenty cars. Also from the single-track road leading off the A82 down Glen Etive. There is very limited space for car parking in Glen Etive at the point of access to the hills (137 469).

TRANSPORT

Glasgow — Fort William train stopping at Bridge of Orchy. Runs all year round and 7 days a week but with restricted service on Sunday.

Glasgow — Fort William bus service.

The boat plying between Auchnacloich, near Taynuilt, and the head of Loch Etive may put off passengers by arrangement at Ardmaddy.

ACCOMMODATION

Hotels at Bridge of Orchy, Inveroran and Kingshouse with bunkhouse only at the first. Climbers' huts at Clashgour (Glasgow University Mountaineering Club. 1½ kilometres west of Victoria Bridge, not at the farm of the same name); Inbhir-fhaolain (Grampian Club) and The Smiddy (Forventure Trust), both in Glen Etive.

There are no official campsites but wild camping is possible at the first bridge west of the Inveroran Hotel and at various sites in Glen Etive.

MAP

OS 1:50 000 Landranger Sheet 50

This group of hills is clearly bounded to the west and to the south by Loch Etive and Glen Kinglass and, a little less clearly to the north and to the east by the Allt Ceitlein and Allt Dochard, with the scatter of lochans below the latter burn completing the eastern boundary. The hills are characterised by deeply recessed glens and by large exposures of the creamy and rough Etive granite, sometimes in extensive pavements on the high ridges, sometimes in vast slabs spilling down from the bealachs and making idyllic summer highways in the beds of the major burns. All the tops are most conveniently reached from Glen Etive, but starting from Victoria Bridge does allow a more open view. Though at a great distance from the

Looking up Loch Etive to Ben Starav (right) and Beinn Trilleachan (left).

nearest road, there are some extensive catchment areas of snow for those who enjoy skiing away from the crowds.

THE HILLS

Ben Starav   (1078m)

From Glen Etive this hill stands up proudly above the head of the loch, looking its full height and of an appearance agreeing with the derivation of its name suggested by some Gaelic speakers, i.e. an abbreviation from starbhanach meaning a stout, bulky man with a small head. The most straightforward ascent is up the well-defined north ridge, reached by crossing the bridge a little north of Coileitir and then following the path to a second bridge crossing the Allt Mheuran. Both these bridges occupy fine situations; the first looking down on a pool of great depth shadowed by deciduous trees, and the second spanning a burn lined with a delightful variety of trees — Scots pine, holly, birch — and looking up to a series of short waterfalls dropping green into creamy granite basins. When crossing the bridge at Coileitir, it is an arresting thought that in the winter of 1906 it was immersed in a flash-flood — a rise of at least 7 metres.

The north ridge sweeps up with just one relatively level section at mid-height and with an escarpment on its eastern rim, directly to the summit cairn.

About 300 metres south-east of the summit there is a slight rise (1068m) where the ridge divides. The south ridge leads to Meall Cruidh (930m); the narrow shattered north-east ridge drops and rises to Stob Coire Dheirg (1028m) and then turns east down to the col leading to Glas Bheinn Mhor. On the flanks of this arete where the granite has eroded into gravel, can be found the cushions of moss campion flowering from June on.

Another approach to Ben Starav is extremely long, involving a round trip of about 42 kilometres from Victoria Bridge. However for those walking across country, or able to organise cars at Victoria Bridge and Glen Etive, this long walk from the east carries one beside the chuckle of the Abhainn Shira, broad and shallow for a burn of comparable drainage; then over a watershed almost

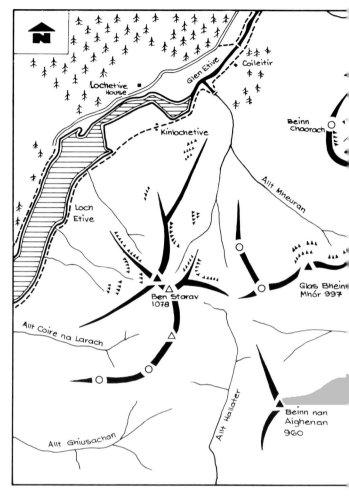

imperceptible in Highland terms, where two burns falling east from Beinn Suidhe and not 100 metres apart, diverge to flow to either side of the watershed; and last into the recesses of the great Coire na Caime where lies the source of the River Kinglass which here falls in a series of waterfalls, ravines and pools ideal for swimming and where numerous rickles of stone speak of summer shielings.

Those following this route in reverse and in poor visibility will need to exercise care with compass readings at the bealach between Ben Starav and Meall nan Tri Tighearnan (892m) to the east, also at the lower bealach at the foot of Beinn nan Aighenan's north ridge.

Stob Coir'an Albannaich *(peak of the corrie of the Scotsmen)* (1044m)
With its satellite Beinn Chaorach (850m), this hill extends 9 kilometres from south-east to north-west. To its north a narrow spur falls between gorges into Glen Ceitlein and to the south an even narrower spur drops from Sron na h-Iolaire (510m)

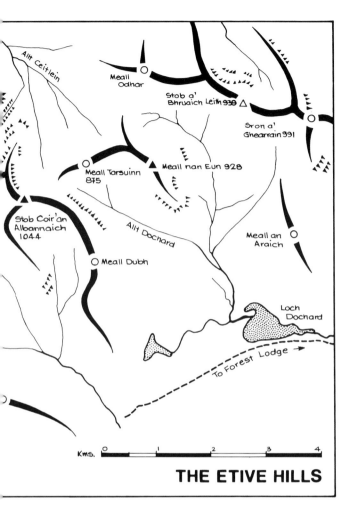

THE ETIVE HILLS

to the watershed above Loch Dochard. Both spurs make fine routes to the summit with the former adding zest to a winter ascent and the latter perhaps better appreciated without snow.

When leaving the path approximately 9 kilometres out from Victoria Bridge, the driest ground beneath Sron na h-Iolaire will be found just to the south of Lochan na h-Iuraiche; from where the ridge is soon gained. From the ridge one's eye follows the glen over lochs Dochard and Tulla in an uninterrupted view to the drainage-furrowed flanks of Beinn Achaladair, and higher there is an expanse of granite slabs on Meall Dubh at an angle and of a roughness that is a delight to walk up. The summit sports an unusually large cairn — a relic of early theodolite triangulation by the Ordnance Survey.

From Glen Etive one starts, as with all the hills in this group, at the bridge above Coileitir. The apparent bridge shown 1 kilometre to the north on OS maps previous to the Landranger series (but without the significant letters FB) is in fact a pulley bridge, i.e. a gondola suspended from wires, not intended for public use. A good track runs north from Coileitir and then east for a short distance up Glen Ceitlein, which rises little for 2 kilometres when the two gorges with their birch remnants come into view. The steep, northern spur is bedecked with blocks of granite and needs a little care in icy conditions, but the ground falls away more steeply on either side where the granite blocks seem even more crazily perched.

An easier way from Glen Etive turns south from Coileitir and up the open hillside from the junction of the River Etive and the Allt Mheuran. The angle is unrelenting for 750m but the slope is straightforward.

The north ridge of Ben Starav

Glas Bheinn Mhor from the north ridge of Ben Starav

Both the northern and main tops are fronted to the north-east by crags, that under the main summit being a sweep of very steep granite, unfortunately too short for worthwhile climbing.

If it is intended to continue from the summit to Meall Tarsuinn (875m), care should be taken in poor visibility as a dog-leg movement first east down the ridge for barely ½km to a more level section, then back west of north is needed. Care is also advised in winter as the slope is steep, rocky and often icy.

A compass bearing is again worthwhile when descending south-west in poor visibility perhaps to continue over Glas Bheinn Mhor, as the natural trend of the ground leads out onto a south-easterly spur. This south-westerly aspect of Stob Coir'an Albannaich is noted for its snow collecting properties.

Beinn Chaorach (the hill of the sheep, known locally in Glen Etive as Stob Leitir) is notable for its consistent steepness on all sides and whilst a way can be picked up or down the hillside above Glen Etive, it is barred lower down with a deer fence. Also it is steep and is pocked with granite slabs usually wet with seepage — no place to descend on a winter's evening.

Looking west from Mam Carraigh to Ben Starav, Glas Bheinn Mhor, Stob Coir' an Albannaich and Meall nan Eun

Beinn nan Aighenan *(hill of the hinds)* (960m)

One of the more remote hills in the Central Highlands, Beinn nan Aighenan is moated on all sides by the waters of the Kinglass and the Allt Hallater, above which rise steep and grassy slopes stirring admiration for the black cattle who perhaps roamed these slopes. The only break in these defences occurs in a small area to the north where a ridge drops to a bealach that itself must be reached by crossing another — that between Ben Starav and the top to its east, Meall nan Tri Tighearnan (892m). When approaching from Coileitir in Glen Etive, interest is added by climbing the long, low spur thrown out north by the latter top. It gives fine views into Ben Starav's Coire Dearg.

A second approach is that using the path from Victoria Bridge. Once over the watershed beyond Loch Dochard a descent of 100m and 1½ kilometres leads to a half-cantilever bridge at a junction of burns. Above, a very steep slope of 350m eases onto a splendid ridge undulating and twisting for 3 kilometres over exposures of rough cream-coloured granite.

The last route described is perhaps too lengthy to be used in anything but a crossing of the hills. It uses the faint path from Glen Strae over the bealach between

Meall Copagach and Beinn Lurachan (described in Chapter 2). In descent it follows the main burn down to a junction, with birch remnants about a waterfall, when a crossing should be made for a traverse to the footbridge over the River Kinglass at 153 368 with an alternative at 152 369. From there the track leads north to the Allt Hallater which descends through a wooded gorge. A good stalker's path follows the north-east side of the burn (immediately above to the north is a ravine with some short rock-pitches) and should be held until it climbs temporarily from the burn, when ascent north-east leads to a plateau at c. 700m and then to the south-south-west spur of Beinn nan Aighenan.

Despite the long and, in places, rough approach, the scenery in the lower reaches of the Allt Hallater and the remoteness of its setting make the effort well worthwhile. This approach can also be made by bicycle, starting from Bridge of Awe and continuing past Glennoe Farm. Thereafter a Land-rover track runs to Ardmaddy and then swings east up Glen Kinglass.

Though at very great distance from the nearest road, the higher reaches of the Allt Hallater gather large accumulations of snow in most winters and would provide good runs for those seeking to ski in solitude.

Beinn nan Lus (709m)
Stob an Duine Ruaidh (822m)
For those walking up the east side of Loch Etive and intending to include an ascent of Ben Starav, an approach across these two small hills will add interest. Ardmaddy and the spur behind it are an obvious starting point for the first hill, but a glance at the OS map would not prepare one for the extent of the plateau above with its scattered multitude of tiny lochans. At the foot of the hill's northerly spur is another tiny lochan, not more than 100 metres from the Allt Hallater, but draining in the opposite direction towards Loch Etive.

Few might consider descending the 100m or so from Starav's southerly ridge to sit for a while on Stob an Duine Ruaidh, but the view will compensate for the lost height, there being a lack of intervening ground to interrupt the splendour of Cruachan's northern ridges, added to which the steep slopes beneath to west and south give a sense of isolation above the Loch Etive. From the A82 road beside Loch Tulla, at a distance of about 20 kilometres, the peak is very prominent as a sharp cone to the left of Ben Starav.

Glas Bheinn Mhor *(big greenish-grey hill)* (997m)
Either of the approaches from Glen Etive or from Victoria Bridge described under Ben Starav and Beinn nan Aighenan apply equally to this hill, which presents a pleasantly symmetrical profile when seen from the road near Druimachoish in Glen Etive. Descent from the bealach east-north-east of the summit is wet going, but leads to the Robbers' Waterfall on the Allt Mheuran, which is a spectacular fall. Ascent or descent of Glas Bheinn Mhor on its northern slopes involves tiresomely steep ground well worth avoiding.

Beinn nan Aighenan and cloud-topped Ben Starav from Victoria Bridge

Meall nan Eun *(hill of the birds)* (926m)

Though accurately described by Gaels as a 'round shaped hill' (of the birds), Meall nan Eun has been unfairly dismissed as dull and uninteresting. No hill in this group is composed of such consistently steep ground, with only a north-west ridge presenting a straightforward route. Through an arc from north-north-east to south-west the flat top is surrounded by slopes that fall away uncompromisingly and the whole of the north-eastern slope is interrupted by plaques of granite set at a high angle. Ascent by dint of a little scrambling can be made at any point in this arc, but for descent open slopes will be found only in the south-western corner.

The shattered granite crags below Stob Coire Dheirg

The pleasantest approach from Victoria Bridge is to follow the stalker's path that climbs north-west from Clashgour over the bealach between Meall an Araich and Stob Ghabhar. When the path fades, a descending traverse to the Allt Dochard allows a scramble on the rough granite in the bed of the basin until the bealach is reached on the north-west of the hill. If returning to Victoria Bridge, the ground near Loch Dochard should be avoided — it is a waste of bog, tussocks and hidden pools, while skirting the loch on the west in order to reach the path involves fording deep burns.

From Glen Etive the river, when low, can be forded at a point just north of the pulley bridge at Glenceitlein and the glen then followed to the bealach on the north-west of Meall nan Eun. Alternatively, the track should be followed across the bridge at Coileitir and then up the river to Glenceitlein.

Study of the OS map (Sheet 50) shows the feasibility, even on a winter's day, of traversing all the hills in this group that front onto Glen Etive, though inclusion of Beinn nan Aighenan makes for a tall order and is in any event somewhat artificial. On a clear day without fresh snow to hinder one, this circuit from Coileitir is thoroughly recommended.

PATHS AND WALKS

Bridge of Orchy to Taynuilt. Outside that summer period from July to early September when the midge can make low-level walking a penitential exercise, this path provides fine contrast between the barren stretch of high moorland east of the Loch Dochard watershed and the lush, deciduous woodlands in the narrow Glen Kinglass. Start at Victoria Bridge where a signpost points the right of way west to Loch Etive. Follow the rough Land-rover track, keeping beside the Abhainn Shira, for about 3½ kilometres, when the track narrows to a path. After a further 500 metres a bridge leads south over the burn. The two turnings right up to Clashgour are not rights of way.

To the east of the watershed the Abhainn Shira flows broad and shallow over a bed of pink granite shingle and boulders and to the west the River Kinglass spills over great saucers of grey granite, which under strong sunlight can heat the water almost to body temperature. Bird-life abounds in lower Glen Kinglass and on Loch Etive-side, where seals can often be seen basking on the islets off the point of Inverliver Bay. The shore line at Inverliver also has interest in the spring that wells out of the shingle and is known to have been there for the last 50 years. Though the loch is salt to the taste at this point its margins freeze in hard winters, when the spring leaves a clear track in the ice as it flows into the loch.

In the lower reaches of Glen Kinglass, the remains of old furnaces and charcoal beds can be found here and there, and oak, hazel and birch still grow strongly. Though the full distance of approximately 45 kilometres makes a good step in a day, there is an excellent track. Those planning to take two days would be advised to carry a tent as the only bothy *en route* at Narrachan is often full at weekends.

Taynuilt to Kinlochetive. Another low-level walk of interest is that from Taynuilt to the head of Loch Etive and here the boat plying in summer between Auchnacloich and the head of the loch might be of use (see Introduction, p2). Start at Bridge of Awe taking the dead-end road that goes north from the A85. A tarmac surface continues for about 2 kilometres. Turn right at the first fork and at the next fork turn right onto a dirt track. Ignore the next right fork but take the second which drops to a locked single-bar gate. This situation may change as the forest is being worked and new roads cut, moreover the dense afforestation does not allow any outward view. The Land-rover track continues north for 14 kilometres.

Halfway up the loch, Ardmaddy, once renowned as the granary of Glen Etive, occupies the site of a fluvial outflow and the rich silt provides good pasture-land. Further north a low wall is all that remains of the church by the Allt Ghiusachan — evidence of the scattered community of the lochside and Glen Kinglass in previous centuries. This latter burn together with the Allt Coire na Larach and that draining the north-north-west corrie of Ben Starav are difficult to cross after heavy rain.

There is no safe crossing of the River Etive until one reaches Coileitir and the total distance from Bridge of Awe is about 30 kilometres.

CLIMBING

Ben Starav's eastern peak, Stob Coire Dheirg, is the culminating point of a fine corrie, Coire Dearg, buttressed with crazy turrets of shattered granite, but also containing some gullies which with their north-easterly aspect, and commencing at such great height, offer good winter climbing. None is more serious than Grade II and none gives more than 100m of ascent. More difficult winter routes have been made in this corrie and are described in *Glen Coe: Rock and Ice Climbs* by K.V.Crocket, R.Anderson and D.Cuthbertson, published by The Scottish Mountaineering Trust (1992). Coire Dearg is best reached from Coileitir in Glen Etive by an excellent stalker's path which follows the west side of the burn forking south-south-west at 140 451 (Allt nam Meirleach).

There are exposures of granite slabs at high angle on Ben Starav's west-facing slopes at about 400m above Kinlochetive. They are more featureless and more affected by drainage than the famous Trilleachan Slabs (as named on the 1:50 000 Landranger map, but better known as the Etive Slabs) across the loch. Though again not offering the same vertical length of route as the latter slabs, they offer a taste of exploration for those climbing comfortably at the Severe level.

On Beinn Chaorach outcroppings of granite occur over much of the summit area and granite appears again in steep ribs with a slabby apron on the slope dropping into the gorge — Coire Glas — east of the summit area. Routes have been made here and are described in *Glen Coe: Rock and Ice Climbs* (1992).

The long southern flank of Beinn nan Lus presents a bold front to Glen Kinglass. Steep crags stretching for more than 2 kilometres form a battlement above a skirt of indigenous woodland. Heavy drainage keeps the crags well lubricated, but in a dry summer they could repay exploratory climbers. The 16 kilometres distance from Bridge of Awe need not deter those with bicycles.

CHAPTER 4

The Black Mount

Stob Ghabhar	1087m	230 455
Stob a'Choire Odhair	943m	258 461
Creise	1100m	238 507
Meall a'Bhuiridh	1108m	251 503
Beinn Mhic Chasgaig	864m	221 502
Stob Dubh, Beinn Ceitlein	883m	167 488

ACCESS
The A8005 turning from the A82 to Victoria Bridge where there is parking space for about twenty cars. The A82 can also be left near Loch Ba at 308 497 and at the White Corries (ski-lift) carpark. From the western side of the range access is from the single-track road leading off the A82 down Glen Etive. There is limited space for car parking in Glen Etive. Note that access to the hills from the road in Glen Etive involves crossing the river, which can only be waded when very low. The only bridge is at Alltchaorunn (198 513), but it is often barred and difficult to cross.

TRANSPORT
As in Chapter 3

ACCOMMODATION
Hotels at Bridge of Orchy, Inveroran and at Kingshouse. The former provides bunkhouse accommodation and is open all year round.
Climbers' huts at Clashgour near Loch Tulla (Glasgow University Mountaineering Club), Blackrock Cottage near Kingshouse Hotel (Ladies Scottish Climbing Club) and Inbhir-fhaolain in Glen Etive (Grampian Club)

Wild camping is possible ½ kilometre west of Inveroran Hotel beside the A8005 road and in Glen Etive.

MAPS
OS 1:50 000 Landranger Sheets 50 & 51

The best features of this magnificent group of hills are hidden from roadside view. It is only from the old road, in the vicinity of Ba Bridge, that one can begin to appreciate the splendour of Coireach a'Ba and its sister, Coire Dhearbhadh, while from Glen Etive it is impossible to look into the twin defiles that drain Aonach Mor. More than any group of hills in the Central Highlands, other than perhaps those of the Corrour Forest, this is the province of the red deer. It is also of interest for the complexity of its geology, which though mainly of Cruachan Granite is interrupted by mica-schist, quartzite and gneiss — a junction of gneiss and Cruachan granite crossing close to the top of Stob Ghabhar.

The serried ranks of the Black Mount from Bidean nam Bian

THE HILLS

Stob Ghabhar *(goat peak)* (1087m)

For complexity of form and for the splendour of its corries and glens, this hill has few equals in the Central Highlands. It throws out a series of roughly parallel ridges to the north-west and two others to the east that enclose a fine hanging corrie: only to the south does it present relatively gentle slopes. Victoria Bridge beside Loch Tulla is the obvious starting point and also offers the shortest route to the summit. A stalker's path strikes north beside the Allt Toaig from the old schoolhouse, which is now run as a club hut by the Glasgow University Mountaineering Club. (This corrugated metal tower is reputed to sleep 12 people, a reputation which will be a source of wonder to all who walk past). The path on the east side of the burn becomes faint perhaps 1 kilometre short of the bealach between Stob Ghabhar and Stob a'Choire Odhar, but it is worth continuing to the bealach for the view on the other side of the glacier-scarred corrie with its lip dropping sharply toward the lower Coire Dhearbhadh. From the bealach a scramble over rough ground leads to the east-south-east ridge, Aonach Eagach, with the view of the cliff enclosing the Upper Couloir providing ample excuse for halts on the rough slopes. Once on the ridge there is a splendid highway to the top, narrowing in places to an arete that requires care under icy conditions.

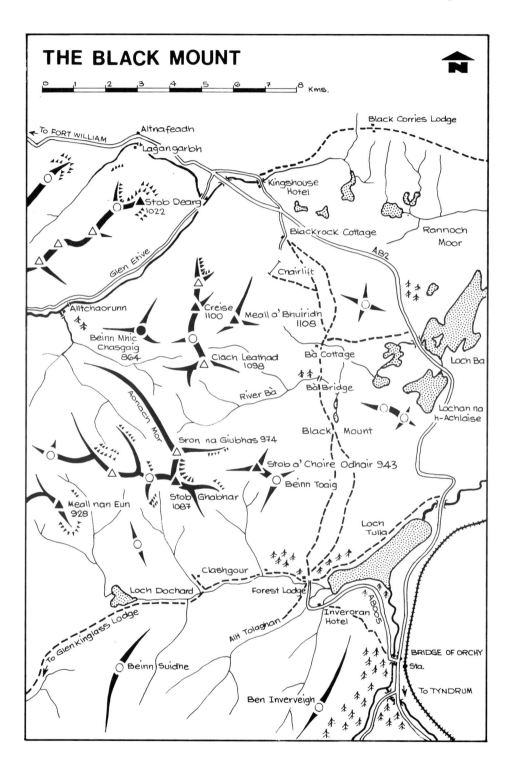

THE BLACK MOUNT

N

0 1 2 3 4 5 6 7 8 Kms.

To FORT WILLIAM
Altnafeadh
Lagangarbh
Kingshouse Hotel
Black Corries Lodge
Stob Dearg 1022
Blackrock Cottage
A82
Rannoch Moor
Glen Etive
Chairlift
Alltchaorunn
Creise 1100
Meall a' Bhuiridh 1108
Beinn Mhic Chasgaig 864
Clach Leathad 1098
Bà Cottage
Loch Ba
River Bà
Bà Bridge
Lochan na h-Achlaise
Aonach Mòr
Sron na Giubhas 974
Black Mount
Stob a' Choire Odhair 943
Beinn Toaig
Meall nan Eun 928
Stob Ghabhar 1087
Loch Tulla
Clashgour
Loch Dochard
Forest Lodge
Inveroran Hotel
A8005
To Glen Kinglass Lodge
Allt Tolaghan
BRIDGE OF ORCHY
Sta.
Beinn Suidhe
To TYNDRUM
Ben Inverveigh

The east face of Stob Ghabhar

Return from the top offers choice for all tastes. Most direct is the spur running south-south-east off the shoulder 300 metres south-east of the summit. This spur broadens out and maintains an easy angle, and should be followed down to the tree line where a Land-rover track from Clashgour leads through the afforestation. Traversing east above the tree-line in order to cross the Allt Toaig is for occasions when the burn is known to be low. In spate a crossing would be impossible.

However, more repaying by far is the circuit of the eastern hanging corrie, travelling initially north and soon crossing the junction of gneiss and granite, made obvious by the transition from short grass to a boulder-field of pink and grey granite, then trending right and east to descend over the sharp spine of Sron nan Giubhas (the nose of the firs: pronounced geevas) with the prospect of Rannoch Moor widening before one and the slopes on either side dropping steeply into glaciated corries. Returning over the bealach between Stob Ghabhar and Stob a'Choire Odhair involves a very steep descent aiming for the outflow of Coirein Lochain. This slope requires care in summer and can be decidedly tricky in winter. If a party has the intention of continuing to Ba Bridge and returning by the old road, then the north side of the River Ba should be gained directly from the foot of the Sron nan Giubhas. The river cannot be forded easily further downstream and there is a track on only the north side. A line taken directly east from Sron nan Giubhas crosses poorly drained ground that can be very wet indeed.

The two approaches from Glen Etive involve greater distances but both have interest and that over Aonach Mor has a unique scenic quality. To reach Aonach Mor's north-western toe one has first to surmount the gate of corrugated metal on the Alltchaorunn bridge where combined tactics may be needed. Once past the disused shooting lodge keep to the path, worn through to the granite, on the east side of the Allt a'Chaorainn for 1 kilometre to a junction where the burn must be crossed. This burn has cut a spectacular channel in its granite bed and falls into a series of pools culminating in very deep water beneath the bridge just above the lodge. Roughly 1 kilometre upstream from the lodge there is a square-cut cleft known locally as Fraser's Leap, from the feat performed by one of the Marquis of Breadalbane's stalkers.

There is a steep pull of perhaps 200m before the ridge begins to level out, when there is a splendid high-level walk of 5 kilometres to the summit. In thick weather the trend of the ground carries one out onto Sron nan Giubhas and a compass bearing will save time. Those with time to spare and the thirst to justify a search might turn aside and a little downhill before the final slope of Stob Ghabhar to hunt for the spring near the head of the Allt Coire a'Chaolain (at 228 459).

The second approach from Glen Etive uses the route up Glen Ceitlein described in the previous chapter under Stob Coir'an Albannaich. Once past the twin gorges with their birch remnants that lie on the northern flanks of Stob Coir'an Albannaich, a steep nose leads up in approximately 250m to Meall Odhar (876m) from where a ridge twists and undulates over Stob a'Bhruaich Leith (939m) to the top. If this route is being used for descent in poor visibility, careful navigation will be needed to avoid the natural trend of the ground carrying one north at two places. As a route to the top of Stob Ghabhar it has most to commend it as one leg of a long circuit over Stob Ghabhar and the Starav group.

Stob a'Choire Odhair *(peak of the dun-coloured corrie)*   (943m)
Beinn Toaig (827m)
From near and far, in the sector from east to north, Stob a'Choire Odhair with its satellite, Beinn Toaig, perched on an abutting shelf, shows a most distinctive shape. It blocks out Stob Ghabhar from the main road and is still prominent from the hills above Rannoch Station, while it appears as a graceful cone to those travelling the old road between the Black Mount summit and Ba Bridge. (The Gaelic pronunciation is something like corrour and from this has been derived the phoneticised English.)

A pleasant circuit of the two peaks can be made from Victoria Bridge, starting up the track beside the Allt Toaig and then up the stalker's path that carries one gently on well-engineered zigzags up most of the southern flank of Stob a'Choire Odhair. This path starts a little over 2 kilometres up the Allt Toaig at the point where a burn descends from an open gorge. Descent of Beinn Toaig's north-east ridge to the old road gives a splendid view across Rannoch Moor, being in line with the great fault occupied by lochs Laidon and Ericht.

Clach Leathad and Meall a'Bhuiridh

Clach Leathad *(stone of the slope)* (1098m)
Creise (1100m)
Meall a'Bhuiridh *(hill of the bellowing {of stags})* (1108m)

Clach Leathad (often seen abbreviated to Clachlet), the most outstanding peak in this group, makes a fine prospect when seen with its slightly higher neighbour Meall a'Bhuiridh from the A82. It looks even better from Ba Bridge, and for a circuit of the two peaks this is an ideal starting point. A little-used track between the A82 and the old road provides the quickest approach. It starts a little north of the main road bridge over the River Ba — here a link between Lochan na Stainge and Loch Ba — where parking space for cars is limited. This approach is equally convenient for an intended traverse from Meall a'Bhuiridh to Stob Ghabhar.

If only Clach Leathad is to be climbed, a pleasant circuit can be made and the splendour of Coireach a'Ba seen to advantage, by following the track on the north side of the River Ba until it runs out below a low-level promontory, Meall Tionail, jutting out east from the southern flank of Clach Leathad. Skirting this promontory to the south brings one into the heart of Coireach a'Ba with deeply recessed minor corries up to the left and slopes rising north-west to the Bealach Fuar-chathaidh. The east ridge leading down over Sron nam Forsair is an obvious descent line, but though well-defined on the 1:50 000 OS map, only experience of it on a clear day brings appreciation of its aerial nature, thrusting an elegant wedge out onto the moor.

Meall a'Bhuiridh can also be climbed from the old road. Easy slopes lead up west from a little north of the ruin of Ba Cottage. If descending the south-east ridge toward the minor top, Creag an Fhirich, which has that same sense of isolation above the moor as the other easterly ridges in the Black Mount, there is steep craggy ground that needs a right-angled turn — either south-west or north-east — to find an easy way down.

For those on their first visit to the area and possibly seeking a quick route to the tops, Meall a'Bhuiridh has a system of ski-lift and tows starting a little above the large carpark which is 1 kilometre from the A82 road. The open corrie above, Coire Pollach, has excellent snow-holding properties and became the site in 1960 of Scotland's first commercial ski-ing operation — The White Corries Ltd. The west-south-west ridge forming a connection with the rest of the Clachlet group is steeper and narrower than the 1:50 000 map indicates. In winter it is prone to be icy, and a bad place to be without crampons.

All approaches from Glen Etive to the Black Mount group contrast remarkably in their enclosed nature to that sense of space given by Rannoch Moor; and, nowhere is this more epitomised than by the glen of the Allt Coire Ghuibhasan, which has the atmosphere of a Himalayan defile, if not that scale. A good path clings to the steep slopes and is pleasantly shaded with birch and alder. From the Alltchaorunn bridge it keeps to the east side of the burn and continues on the north side of the Allt Coire Ghuibhasan until crossing at a bridge. Further on there is a fine waterfall which has cut its way around a porphyry dyke and produced an abrupt right-angle turn behind a great sheaf of rock.

Once the glen opens out, Beinn Mhic Chasgaig can be climbed *via* a gorge in its southern flank before carrying on east to Clach Leathad. This diversion is worthwhile for the splendid view of Bidean nam Bian and Buachaille Etive Mor across the deep rift of Glen Etive.

The most direct route to Clach Leathad climbs the steepening west ridge that flattens and curves northwards over a wilderness of granite boulders to a top north of the summit. This top, known as Mam Coire Easain (1068m), which name applies more properly to the slopes north-east of and beneath it, is the point where the eastern escarpment is breached by relatively easy ground for descent to gain the west ridge of Meall a'Bhuiridh. Steep granite drops east along the length of the ridge between Clach Leathad and Creise but nowhere is the height great enough for worthwhile climbing. Beyond Mam Coire Easain the ridge continues north over Creise (1100m) to a final eminence, Stob a'Ghlais Choire (996m). This top together with its northern spur, Sron na Creise, present a bold front to the north-east, seen to advantage from the lounge of the Kingshouse Hotel.

Despite its forbidding appearance, Sron na Creise can also be climbed with no more than moderate scrambling on its north ridge. West of this ridge at an altitude of c. 600m there is an exposure of steep, shattered rhyolite and were it not for the wealth of climbing across the glen, there might be more activity there. In anything

Sron na Creise from Kingshouse

other than a dry summer the River Etive can be difficult to ford. Otherwise the best approach to Sron na Creise is across the moor from the ski-lift carpark skirting the foot of Creag Dhubh.

A traverse of the Black Mount from Stob Ghabhar to Meall a'Bhuiridh offers a splendid and full day for the hillwalker, with the old road to leaven the return to Victoria Bridge on winter evenings. There is variety in the terrain, from the sylvan approach at Victoria Bridge to the long knolly ridge of Aonach Mor and the shattered granite on the sharp west ridge of Meall a'Bhuiridh. In poor visibility the Bealach Fuar-chathaidh is difficult in terms of navigation whether approached from south-west or north-east.

Stob Dubh (883m)
Beinn Ceitlein (832m)

This twin-topped hill, despite being dwarfed by its near neighbours on all sides, is easily recognised from lower Glen Etive by the gorge that cleaves the southern side of Stob Dubh and by the thumb (An Grianan) so prominent at the north-eastern extremity of Beinn Ceitlein above Alltchaorunn. It lies on the northern rim of the sea of Cruachan granite and is a complex of mica-schist, quartzite, rhyolite and dykes of porphyry almost surrounded by granite.

Clach Leathad from Beinn Maol Chaluim across Glen Etive

The only straightforward approach is from Glenceitlein and either the south-west ridge of Stob Dubh can be ascended in a long steep pull, or the gorge itself can be scrambled up with the occasional short rock pitch. (There have been severe wash-outs from this gorge in the last few years, and loose rock must be expected). Ascent can also be made from Alltchaorunn leaving the track on the west side of the Allt a'Chaorainn once well south of the remarkable pinnacle, An Grianan. This extraordinary hump can be reached easily from the neck to its west, but otherwise should be avoided as its slopes are composed of rotten granite, heavily vegetated and at high angle. Its Gaelic name is usually taken to mean a sunny place or bower, but local opinion has it that the name relates to the similarity of a thumb to the shape in which peats or hay are stacked for drying.

This chapter closes fittingly with a reference to the Marchioness of Breadalbane, whose book *The High Tops of Black Mount* shows her deep appreciation of these hills and a refreshing respect for flora and fauna, despite her huge enjoyment of deer-stalking, for it was she who first recognised the need to preserve the Scots pine about Loch Tulla and who had constructed the enclosure at Doire Darach (now under the supervision of Scottish Natural Heritage). She had also an immense respect for the stalkers and ghillies employed in the Black Mount Forest, some of whom apparently had little time for the propriety of the day, as she engagingly recounts in stories at her own expense. One such concerns Sandy McLeish of Ardmaddy who, when during one stalk was remonstrated with for speaking in Gaelic to the ghillies, sharply rejoindered to his employer — 'It is a pity you had not learned such a useful thing (Gaelic) before taking to the hill.'

PATHS AND WALKS

Loch Tulla to Glen Etive. For parties crossing the hills, or with transport to Victoria Bridge and from Glen Etive, and wanting to avoid the tops in poor weather, the following makes a fine walk through a great variety of scenery. (Parts of it are recognisable in the novel *The New Road* by Neil Munro.) Take the stalker's path from Clashgour to the bealach north of Meall an Araich, drop then to follow the Allt Dochard to the bealach north of Meall nan Eun, from where drop again before trending north to cross the last bealach between Meall Odhar and Beinn Ceitlein to follow the Allt a'Chaorainn, with a path on its west bank, down to the bridge at the shooting lodge. This stravaig has more mountain flavour to it than many a hill-walk, and here and there in the middle section one can find traces of the path evidencing century-long use of such routes through the hills. (16 kilometres).

Two connected routes give rewarding low-level walks. The first is the track that remains from the old road, which was not replaced until 1936. It starts from Victoria Bridge and finishes at Blackrock Cottage close to the A82. Throughout its length of about 15 kilometres there are fine views of the Black Mount peaks. 10 kilometres from the start it is crossed by the path from the A82 (starting 278 497) that runs into the vast Ba corrie.

CLIMBING

There is climbing of a general mountaineering nature on three sides of Stob Ghabhar. It is all satisfyingly remote with the only likelihood of meeting another party being in the Upper Couloir. In the deep-cut corrie — Coire Ghabhar — lying to the west, there is a winter route that takes the 100 m gully cleaving the headwall and finishing steeply not 50m east of a point 991m above Sron a'Ghearrain. This route often carries steep ice in its lower half and is therefore Grade II. Almost directly below the summit and facing a little north of east lies the buttress cloven by the Upper Couloir. This climb occupies a place in the early annals of winter climbing on a par with Tower Ridge and the Black Shoot of Beinn Eunaich. Successive waves of SMC parties attacked the route, as impressed by its surroundings as by the difficulties of the climbing. The first complete ascent took place in 1897 when A.E. Maylard led Professor Adamson, Mrs. Adamson and Miss Weiss. Most of these early parties made the Lower Couloir part of their approach, but this involves a leftward traverse to reach the foot of the Upper Couloir across a snow-slope very prone to avalanche. If there is deep snow in the corrie, it will be quicker to traverse the Aonach Eagach, descend the broad gully at the neck between it and Stob Ghabhar and make a rightward traverse above more open slopes. In thick weather the narrow entrance to the Upper Couloir is not easily found.

Particularly in early winter, before snow fall has banked out the lower pitch and shortened the frozen waterfall above, the route can be very difficult and fully deserving a Grade III category.

Further north still, where the rim of the ground between Sron nan Giubhas and Aonach Mor drops steeply into Coireach a'Ba, there are short but steep north-facing gullies (concentrated in Coire Dhomhnaill 232 468). These were first climbed by J.H.B.Bell and Colin Allan and can be approached most conveniently from Ba Bridge.

Apart from the general winter mountaineering on Stob Ghabhar, rock-climbs have been made on the Upper Couloir Buttress and are recorded in *A Climbers' Guide to Arran, Arrochar & the Southern Highlands* by K.V.Crocket and A.Walker, published by the Scottish Mountaineering Trust (1989). In Glen Etive there are rock climbs on the high crag on the west face of Beinn Mhic Chasgaig, and on the north-east face of An Grianan. Both are reached by the bridge at Alltchaorunn and are described in *Glencoe : Rock and Ice Climbs*, by K.V.Crocket, R.Anderson and D.Cuthbertson, published by the Scottish Mountaineering Trust (1992)

In winter the view of Sron na Creise from the Kingshouse is breathtaking as its classical shape of buttresses containing apparently vertical gullies holds a lot of snow. However, the viewpoint is misleading and all the open gullies can be climbed at Grade I standard, while the containing buttresses have also been climbed at moderate to difficult standard, though the rock is not sound. The broad V-shaped buttress in the centre of the face gives the best climb, *Inglis Clark Ridge*, Grade III.

Skiing down the east ridge of Meall a'Bhuiridh; Stob Ghabhar beyond

SKI MOUNTAINEERING

There is one magnificent ski traverse over these mountains — that between Meall a'Bhuiridh and Stob Ghabhar, which can be followed in either direction. Starting at Meall a'Bhuiridh enables the ski lifts to be used almost to the summit, and thereby makes for a painless start to the day, which ends with a long and easy run from Stob Ghabhar down towards the Allt Toaig and Clashgour. However descent of Meall a'Bhuiridh's west ridge requires great care, and the run from Clachlet down to the Bealach Fuar-chathaidh is very steep for 100m. The traverse from south to north has some advantages as once the long climb to Stob Ghabhar has been accomplished there is good downhill skiing to the Bealach Fuar-chathaidh and, at the end of the day, down the entire north-east slope of Meall a'Bhuiridh. This is a serious ski expedition, suitable for good skiers in favourable conditions.

References

The New Road, Neil Munro (op).

The High Tops of Blackmount, The Marchioness of Breadalbane (op).

Scottish Mountains on Ski, Malcolm Slesser, West Col. (1970) (op).

Always a Little Further, Alastair Borthwick. Diadem (1987). Contains a fine account of climbing the Upper Couloir in prewar times.

CHAPTER 5

Appin

Beinn Mheadhonach	714m	019 369
Beinn Molurgainn	690m	019 400
Beinn Bhreac	708m	994 403
Creach Bheinn	810m	024 422
Beinn Lora	308m	919 378
Beinn Sgulaird	937m	053 461
Beinn Trilleachan	839m	086 439
Beinn Fhionnlaidh	959m	095 498
Sgor na h-Ulaidh	994m	111 518
Meall Lighiche	772m	095 529
Fraochaidh	879m	029 517
Beinn a'Bheithir		
Sgorr Dhearg	1024m	056 558
Sgorr Dhonuill	1001m	040 555

Unlike neighbouring areas to the east and north-east, Appin and Benderloch contain few large, mountainous hills, and correspondingly fewer people will be met, particularly on the lower hills in the southern half of the district. Its major glens are heavily afforested with much recent planting, but have also a spread of healthy oak in Glen Creran and a fine birch wood on the eastern slopes of Beinn Trilleachan. To the west good tracks intersect Appin, both commencing at Ballachulish, the one veering west through Glen Duror and the other leading south over a low pass to Loch Creran; but the district of Benderloch bordered by Loch Creran, Gleann Salach and Loch Etive contains only a few minor hill-paths.

There is major rock-climbing on the great plaque of rough granite slabs on Beinn Trilleachan's east face and, on a lesser scale, some similar granite slabs high on the west flank of Beinn Sgulaird. There is also some caving in the bands of limestone that run through Glen Creran. On the northern shore of Loch Etive the quarry at Bonawe is a curiosity, its face seamed with rich colours of pink and purple, where in earlier days the quarry workers hewed granite sets for Glasgow's streets and pavements. An early and far-sighted visitor, Thomas Pennant, reported in 1769 his fear that the iron-foundry at Bunaw (sic) would soon devour the beautiful woods of the country.

```
ACCESS
From the A82 road through Glen Coe and its southern connecting road from Oban, the
A828. Also from the single-track road down Glen Etive. The narrow section of the A828
loop around Loch Creran is being improved and there is increased parking space at the
head of the loch. However the branch road up Glen Creran is still single-track.

TRANSPORT
Bus services Glasgow — Fort William and Fort William — Oban

ACCOMMODATION
There are hotels and guest houses at Glencoe, Clachaig, Ballachulish, and Duror.
Bunkhouse accommodation at Clachaig Hotel and Leacantuim (Glen Coe).
Youth hostel in Glen Coe.
Climbers' huts at Inbhir-fhaolain (Grampian Club) and The Smiddy (Forventure Trust), both
in Glen Etive.
Camp and caravan sites in Glen Coe, one at Invercoe and the other by the A82 road
1½ kilometres south-east of Glencoe village.

MAPS
OS 1:50 000 Landranger Sheets 41, 49 and 50
```

THE HILLS

Beinn Mheadhonach *(the middle hill)* (714m)
Beinn Molurgainn (690m)
Beinn Bhreac *(the speckled hill)* (708m)
For those who do not count altitude too highly in their choice of hills, this round of
rough and unfrequented country between lochs Creran and Etive involves five tops
and a longer day than the 15 kilometres distance might suggest. It gives fine views
of the sea-lochs Creran and Etive and of Lismore stretched across both their exits.
The B845 road through Gleann Salach (which is a continuation of the curving
fault-line so apparent in the Pass of Brander) provides a central starting point at its
summit and a little north of the River Esragan. This river is powerful in spate, and
even without that condition is not easily crossed dry-shod near the road. Beinn
Bhreac carries an unusually large summit cairn but nothing else is so prominent in
this round and the three bealachs between Beinn Molurgainn and Beinn
Mheadhonach are not easily found in thick weather.

Creach Bheinn *(hill of plunder)* (810m)
This twin-topped hill can be included in the round from Beinn Bhreac to Beinn
Mheadhonach or climbed singly from Druimavuic at the head of Loch Creran. Just
south of the house of that name a Land-rover track runs up to meet the Allt Buidhe.
A path comes and goes along the north bank of the burn and reaches the bealach
between Creach Bheinn and Beinn Sgulaird. Alternatively once past the trees a way
can be made to the west ridge, which in descent gives fine views out over the Firth
of Lorn. If continuing down the west ridge to find a firebreak through the trees to
Dallachulish, it is worthwhile making a short diversion south to see the gorge and
waterfall of the Eas Garbh. Also worth seeking out, under the small outcrops on the

Beinn Sgulaird from the south side of Beinn Fhionnlaidh, with a glimpse of Loch Creran and Mull beyond

western aspect, is an usually rich crop of spring flowers, with purple saxifrage and orchid prominent.

Beinn Lora (305m)

This small eminence in Benderloch lies in the westernmost corner of the Central Highlands and it can be climbed comfortably in an hour from North Ledaig, which is rather oddly south of Ledaig itself. The whole northern aspect of the hill is afforested and though a forestry track starts at Benderloch village and continues to the summit, the southern approach from North Ledaig gives more open views. There is an outlook of some splendour from thjs minor hill which has an unrestricted view across to the Sound of Mull and down the Firth of Lorn. An evening visit is particularly worthwhile for the sunset behind Mull.

Beinn Sgulaird (937m)

Standing as it does at the head of a sea-loch, Beinn Sgulaird gives a fine western panorama of scattered islands backed by almost the whole extent of Mull. To the east there is stark contrast in Beinn Trilleachan's scaly eastern aspect and an intervening moor of peat hags.

The approach described first is not the most direct but does provide access from Glen Etive. It uses an ancient path running over from the head of Loch Etive to

Looking west from Ben Starav over Beinn Trilleachan to Beinn Sgulaird

Glenure in Glen Creran that is not marked on the OS 1:50 000 map. However, a start from the southern extremity of the afforestation allows one to pick up the traces. With shallow soil cover on the underlying granite, this path can be very wet and a crossing in such conditions lends respect for the missionary preachers of the last century who used it all year round in order to read the service each second Sunday to the isolated parish in Glen Etive. Beinn Sgulaird's north-eastern outlier, Stob Gaibhre (684m), juts up unmistakably out of the moor, and beyond it the north-east ridge can be made an enjoyable scramble on sound granite.

From Glen Creran the most direct route starts at the road-end where there is car parking space at the farm of Elleric. A Land-rover track to Glenure House crosses the River Ure and continues up the south side to a bifurcation of the burn north of Stob Gaibhre. Above to the south a long steep pull leads to the neck west of Stob Gaibhre. There is fine scenery in the wooded gorge cut by the River Ure through beds of granite, limestone, and schist, and the path to the twin lochans, Airigh nan Lochan, makes a pleasanter approach than that up the steep slope to the south.

A second route from the west starts up the Land-rover track south of the house of Druimavuic and follows the west ridge thrown down from Beinn Sgulaird's south-west top (863m). There are many undulations on this ridge, but its height and the mountain's isolated position offer splendid views in compensation.

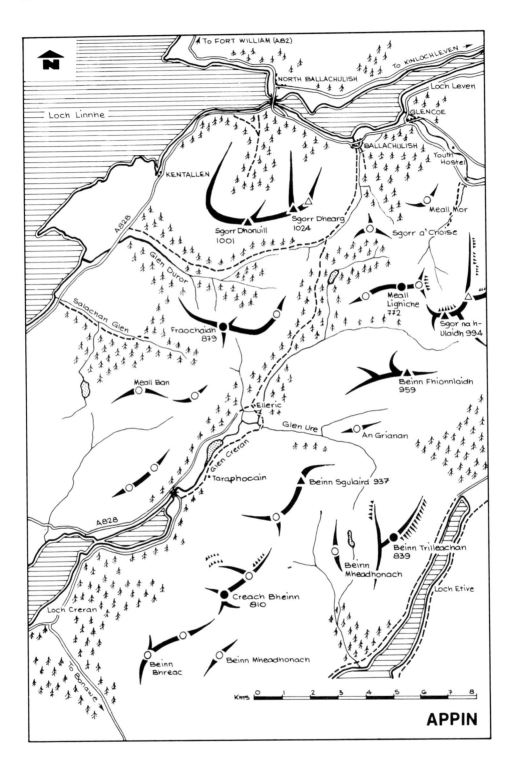

APPIN

Beinn Trilleachan *(hill of the sandpipers)* (839m)
Few Scottish hills outside Skye show such extensive exposure of rock as this hill's western aspect. Oddly the eastern slopes above Loch Etive, where occur the deservedly renowned Trilleachan Slabs (so-called on the OS map, but better known as the Etive Slabs), are steeper but more vegetated. Indeed the angle of the eastern slope is not appreciated until viewed from north or south, when also the ridge-like shape of the hill becomes apparent. The top is easily reached from the head of Loch Etive, starting up the path described under Beinn Sgulaird, but rather than ascending and returning by the north-north-east ridge, a circuit of it and the north-north-west ridge is more repaying. On Beinn Trilleachan's west face overlooking Lochan an Lair there is a sweep of granite steeper and of greater vertical length than elsewhere on the west side of the mountain. Those who tire of the weekend crowds on the Trilleachan Slabs might find worthwhile climbing there.

The ridge between Beinn Trilleachan and its northern top, Meall nan Gobhar, makes a splendid walk over tors and warts of granite, with a spectacular drop to Loch Etive on one side, but the angle is too steep for any view down towards the Etive Slabs.

Less serious entertainment can be found roughly 3 kilometres south of the Trilleachan Slabs, in the The Chasm of Beinn Trilleachan. This is the right-hand fork of a gully divided by an obvious dark tongue of rock (Teanga Dubh). There are no unavoidable difficulties but good sport can be had and the rock scenery is spectacular. The first recorded ascent was by I. Rowe and G. Tiso in 1973.

Beinn Fhionnlaidh *(Finlay's hill)* (959m)
Confusion is often expressed as to the pronunciation of this name relative to that of its neighbour Sgor na h-Ulaidh and, so near as Gaelic speech can be phoneticised, (cf *A Gaelic Guide* by I.C. and I.A.MacLeod in the The Scottish Mountaineering Trust's 1990 edition of *Munro's Tables*) the difference is something like the following: Beinn Fhionnlaidh pronounced 'yoonly' with the initial 'h' not heard and Sgor na h-Ulaidh pronounced 'hooly' (some local people have been known to confuse the issue even further by pronouncing the initial 'f' of Fhionnlaidh out of consideration for incomers).

About the peak's fine stature there is no doubt, though it is hidden from most viewpoints and appears to have been largely ignored by early mountaineers, there being only three references to it in Vols I-XXVII of the SMC Journal.

From Glen Creran a path, not marked on the OS 1:50 000 map, leads north from Glenure House, soon veering east across the southern flank of the hill. For the most straightforward ascent, the path should be left after 2 kilometres and a line east-north-east taken to gain a prominent shoulder on the west ridge. A more interesting route can be made by following the path to Lochan na h-Uraich (081 487), 1 kilometre beyond which a gully with a fine waterfall splits the southern flank. To the right of the gully a series of crags offer scrambling for 200m and lead to the final slopes south of the cairn.

Ben Starav from Beinn Sgulaird

There is a similar distance from Glen Etive with the route through the extensive afforestation clearly shown on the OS 1:50 000 map. Starting at Invercharnan, a Forestry Commission track winds south-west and then north-west through the forest for 3 kilometres until a fire-break is found where the track doubles back east. This is the only straightforward route through the forest. Beyond, a stretch of wet moor leads to steep slopes beneath an eastern satellite (821m). These slopes are easily avoided by keeping due west to the neck north of another minor top, Meall nan Gobhar. From there climb steep ground north to the 821m top and turn west descending first to a dip before the final ridge to the summit.

To the north Beinn Fhionnlaidh presents a truly mountainous appearance and in winter the open corrie beneath the summit offers general mountaineering, particularly so on the steep crags high on the eastern flank of the corrie. Further east the satellite top (821m) throws down a ridge north-north-east that is interrupted by a number of steps. These are not easy to descend in winter, with the easier turning movements to the right also on steep ground.

Sgor na h-Ulaidh   *(peak of the treasure)*   (994m)
As with Beinn Fhionnlaidh, this hill is also hidden from distant view, while even from adjacent tops its complex of ridges makes appreciation of its shape difficult. In

Sgor na h-Ulaidh from Gleann Leac na Muidhe

winter only one of the routes described below should not present difficulty — that by Meall a'Bhuiridh from Glen Etive — while, particularly in descent, all others will require care.

The hill's finest feature — Coire Dubh with its two steep gullies — is revealed only to those who approach by Gleann Leac na Muidhe. This glen commences from the A82 road in Glen Coe 2 kilometres west of Loch Achtriochtan, where a private road follows the west side of the burn for 1½ kilometres to the farm of Gleann-leac-na-muidhe itself. From the lower reaches of this track, on a clear winter's day, there is a splendid view of Aonach Eagach, its wall-like front to Glen Coe and its turreted crest showing to great effect.

Beyond the farm a path continues on the east side of the burn for a little way and just beyond the point where a large tributary joins the Allt na Muidhe from the west, there is a footbridge. The upper reaches of the glen are confined and much riven by drainage and little is gained by contouring either slope until almost beneath the north face, from where a bealach to the west is quickly gained and steep slopes climbed south to the western shoulder, Corr na Beinne.

An alternative route from Gleann Leac na Muidhe starts directly from the farm up the unrelentingly steep slopes of Aonach Dubh a'Ghlinne (the dark ridge of the glen, and well named, showing a dark front to the north with profound glens on either side) which gives a superb aerial highway to a fore-top, Stob an Fhuarain (968m; 119 523). From this ridge the view east is largely curtailed by the mass of Bidean nam Bian, but the majesty of the latter's south face, particularly when covered in snow, is consolation enough. Beyond, a drop of 100m leads to a neck beneath the final steep north-east ridge of Sgor na h-Ulaidh.

The straightforward approach from Glen Etive uses the Forestry Commission track behind Invercharnan, taking the first right turn (north) perhaps 190 metres beyond the house. When the track runs out, the quickest way through the forest is due west onto the slopes of Meall a'Bhuiridh (748m). Pleasant walking follows over schist pavements and higher over knolls until easy slopes lead down to a rocky bealach and Sgor na h-Ulaidh's south-east ridge. No difficulty need be encountered on this ridge which is a much easier option for winter descent than that to the Bealach Fhionnghaill. For those using the latter route, perhaps in a circuit including Beinn Maol Chaluim, descent of the slope from Stob an Fhuarain to the Bealach Fhionnghaill in icy conditions demands great care, for turning movements to the right are not easily found and are themselves on steep ground.

Glen Creran can also be used for approach but the track beyond Elleric, shown on the OS 1:50 000 Sheet 50, leading to Salachail runs out leaving a 2 kilometre struggle through the afforestation. Better is the track from Glenure House that runs north above and east of the River Creran. This path turns north-east and also runs out after 4 kilometres. There remains a stony hillside to be traversed to a crossing of the river beneath the steep ground falling from Corr na Beinne. In dry summer weather an alternative here is to cross the River Creran 2 kilometres beyond the end of the track to a clearing in the forest, from where the bed of the Allt Easain provides a pleasant way through the trees and on to the bealach between Sgor na h-Ulaidh and Meall Lighiche.

The northerly slope above this bealach leading to the fore-peak Corr na Beinne is steep and interspersed with slabs. During winter or in rain its descent requires great care.

Coire Dubh contains five winter climbs one of which, Red Gully, is of high quality. All are hidden from view until one is in the higher reaches of Gleann Leac na Muidhe, and then ascent to the east is needed before the left-hand aspect of the face can be studied.

Meall Lighiche *(doctor's hill)* (772m)
This minor hill is easily climbed from Gleann Leac na Muidhe, and the approach is described above under Sgor na h-Ulaidh. Follow the Land-rover track for about 2 kilometres to a confluence of burns, where the hill's north ridge looms obviously above. As is often the case with lower hills, there is splendid view; in this case of Beinn a'Bheithir and Ben Nevis. If continuing on to Sgor na h-Ulaidh *via* its western shoulder, Corr na Beinne, the latter's northern slopes are steep enough to demand care.

Fraochaidh *(heathery hill)* (879m)

The aptness of the Gaelic meaning of this name, which in Appin is pronounced free'achy, can no longer be appreciated until high up as the hill is now almost surrounded by afforestation. There are however views to be had out of proportion to Fraochaidh's relatively minor stature for it provides unrestricted views down Loch Linnhe and in winter from the lochan east of the minor top Meall Ban, Beinn a'Bheithir takes on an Alpine scale.

Approach from Ballachulish involves a long walk up Gleann an Fhiodh but gives fine views down Glen Creran and pleasant going over knolly ground on the north-eastern ridge. The left fork in the path, roughly 3½ kilometres from Ballachulish, that leads south-south-west to the pass over to Glen Creran, is faint and easily missed. Once at the pass, where a stile provides access to the path continuing down into Glen Creran, follow the forest edge south-west and up to the humpy crest of an initial top. Beyond, there are two further distinct tops before the ridge turns west for the final well-defined edge ascending steeply to the summit.

The shortest route starts from Duror using the Forestry Commission track that runs east from a little north of the Duror Inn. After 3 kilometres follow a fire-break down to the River Duror and hunt for a gated bridge (014 541). Once across the burn a Land-rover track zigzags up the hill and when this track evidently continues on a long right traverse, turn off for a struggle through the forest. Above, the afforestation gives out at c. 350m and a broad ridge leads to the top.

Salachan Glen is now too heavily afforested for approach over Meall Ban, but is mentioned for the discovery of caves there. A band of limestone runs from the south-west up Glen Stockdale and through to Glen Duror and an entrance to a cave-system has been found above the farmhouse at Bealach where, on the edge of the recent afforestation, a large burn disappears underground beside an old tree.

Beinn a'Bheithir *(hill of the thunderbolt)*

Sgorr Dhearg *(red peak)* (1024m)
Sgorr Dhonuill *(Donald's peak)* (1001m)
Dropping as it does so steeply into Loch Leven, the bulk and grandeur of this hill — pronounced vair — is not properly appreciated until one is on the north side of the loch. However, the sight from Ballachulish of Sgorr Dhearg's eastern outlier, Sgorr Bhan, under a coat of snow that highlights the horizontal strata prominent under the summit cone, gives a sense of scale and steepness not too much exaggerated.

For distant views of loch and hill, Beinn a'Bheithir's summit outlook is hard to match; there being a telescoping effect as one looks into the narrows of Loch Leven and Glen Coe that adds to the stature of the hills, while to the south-west the length of Loch Linnhe opens out to the sea beyond Mull.

The three main tops together with a remote and lower top to the north-west (Creag Ghorm, 758m), form a north-facing horseshoe with an apparently isolated

Fraochaidh (left) and Beinn a'Bheithir from the east

tower jutting out north from the main ridge east of Sgorr Dhonuill. The whole of the glen contained by this horseshoe holds afforestation of a maturity, and forestry tracks in number, to confound any stranger descending unawares. Those who plan a circuit of these tops using Gleann a'Chaolais for descent should work out their route carefully and reach the treeline in daylight. Two crucial sections of the forestry tracks are described.

For approach to both a car can be driven ½ kilometre up the glen using the metalled road signposted to Glenachulish. To reach the foot of Sgorr Dhearg's north ridge, which narrows as it gains height but maintains an easy angle, cross the main burn by a bridge and climb open slopes east-south-east to a corner in the forest edge, where a track will be found running through the forest. Follow this north-east and then east to the first burn where there is a quick passage through the forest. In descent the same burn is the best landmark.

Starting the circuit from Creag Ghorm, the track on the west side of the main burn should be followed for 1 kilometre until a small dam can be seen to the left, when the first right turn should be taken. At the third angle of the zigzags and nearing the second crossing of a burn, strike up through the trees due west. Above, open slopes are soon reached. Very recent felling in this area can only have made this approach easier.

A pleasanter way of making the traverse, though it may involve use of the Oban to Inverness bus service, is to ascend Sgorr Bhan from Ballachulish, either due west to gain its north-north-east ridge or by following the path south until the east-north-east ridge towers overhead. This latter ridge is a splendid mountain route, ever-steepening until rock steps on clean quartzite require use of the hands. In winter these rock steps ice up readily and can be trying.

Beyond Sgorr Bhan the ridge to Sgorr Dhearg forms a most graceful arc under snow, and further on the east ridge of Sgorr Dhonuill narrows and often forms an arete in winter. Under such conditions it is well worth diverging half-way up Sgorr Dhonuill to follow the even narrower arete leading north to Sgorr a'Chaolais — the tower or horn so conspicuous from the main road. Its isolated position some distance out into the corrie gives it a splendid arc of view.

From Creag Ghorm a descent can be made steeply, but forest-free, to Kentallen whose tranquil bay was observed by Dorothy Wordsworth to be sheltered from 'half the winds that travel over the lake' and where accordingly Neil Munro had Para Handy put in for shelter and refreshment. Close to the road the course of the dismantled railway line now carries enormous bramble bushes with appropriately giant berries. This idyllic backwater may be lost if plans for a super-quarry in this area are approved.

The vast southern flank of Beinn a'Bheithir will attract few, the afforestation making an unpleasant barrier and the slopes above being tiresomely steep. However, for those staying at Duror of Appin and determined to investigate this aspect of the hill, there is consolation in the scramble to be had in the gully leading up to the west of Sgorr Dhonuill's final slope. It starts at c. 550m and narrows higher where the granite rockwalls are impressive. The approach through the forest described under Fraochaidh should be followed and the same fire-break taken, this time uphill, to a clearing at the top corner of which another fire-break leads through to open slopes. At the forest edge a line due north, traversing a little left and crossing two burns, puts one in the line of the gully. On the OS 1:50 000 Sheet 41, it is the last gully shown to the west under Sgorr Dhonuill's west ridge and starts at 024 548.

Sgorr Dhearg from Sgorr Dhonuill

PATHS AND WALKS

Two routes of centuries-long usage run roughly south to north; the one on the eastern fringe beside Loch Etive and the other cutting through from Glen Creran to Ballachulish. Both make fine low-level walks.

Loch Etive. The eastern shore of Loch Etive has the greater distance and in wet weather the shallow soil on the skirts of Beinn Trilleachan becomes saturated. However there is a good track as far as Barrs and there is a grand wildness to the scenery across the loch. Remnants of oak linger south of Cadderlie near where was the school at one time, showing how the population has been reduced more than the oak woods. Roughly 1 kilometre south of Cadderlie springs bubble up haphazardly at the side of the loch, as they do on the opposite shore at Inverliver. Near Barrs, charcoal beds can be found east of the Allt Easach and, further on through the policies of the house, the old pier sits out over very deep water that is salt to the taste. South and north of Barrs and beside the burns on Beinn Trilleachan's lower slopes, regiments of conifers have been planted, merging uneasily with the parkland about Barrs and with the hazel groves on Beinn Trilleachan.

The richness of bird life makes May and June rewarding months for this walk and if one leaves the path to tread the shingle, there is some risk of stepping on a sandpiper's nest, so numerous are these delightful waders. Beyond Barrs, the view across the loch into the glens draining Ben Starav has a quality of wildness usually associated with mountainous land on a larger scale. The distance from Bonawe to the head of Loch Etive is about 22 kilometres.

Glen Creran. A right of way maintained through the new forests of conifers connects this glen with Ballachulish and provides easy access to a small, but shapely hill, Sgorr a'Choise (663 m), which commands a view out of all proportion to its lowly stature. From the road end at Elleric a great stretch of trees has been planted by the Forestry Commission and these reach up to the pass crossed by the path, curtailing much of the view. Between Elleric, at the road end in Glen Creran, and Ballachulish, there is a distance of about 14 kilometres and an ascent of c. 400m.

The lower reaches of the glen are rich in human history with one instance — the shooting of one of HM Tax Collectors some 200 years ago — immortalised by Robert Louis Stevenson in his book *Kidnapped*. This incident has its place in Scottish history for the acknowledged wrongful hanging of James Stewart of Duror after conviction for the shooting by a court working out clan bias rather than process of law. Recent researchers have suggested that, contrary to accepted belief, the tax collector — one Colin Campbell known as the Red Fox — was not shot by Jacobites out of resentment at his Government duties, but was killed by a hired assassin. This theory has it that Colin Campbell was at odds with fellow conspirators, who were highly placed in Scottish affairs of the time, over the share-out of misappropriated French gold (originally shipped to Scotland to finance the Jacobite cause).

In recent times extensive cave-systems have been discovered in the band of limestone that courses up Glen Creran from the lochside almost to the summit of Fraochaidh, though the Gaelic name Uamh Coire Sheilach — uamh being the Gaelic for a cave — given to the site suggests that A.MacKeith's first recorded descents in 1973 may have been predated by a century or two. The entrances will be found above and inside the oak wood of Coille Mheadhonach at 034 494 and 030 496, but the extent of the limestone and other parallel bands nearby suggests the likelihood of further discoveries. In detail the burn falling behind the schoolhouse should be followed to a fork and the left fork taken to its second waterfall; then 12 metres up and 15 metres left should lead to the entrance amongst birch trees. There is an initial descent by abseil of 45 metres and a total passage known to date of c. 300 metres. The second entrance will be found 400 metres further up the burn and 15 metres left at the edge of the wood.

Those wishing to potter among the old woods in the lower reaches of the glen may find interest in the disused limekiln beside the road at 004 456 — where local limestone was crushed and burned to produce fertiliser — and in the old leadmines above Invercreran.

In reverse direction a right of way runs from Ballachulish to Duror. Though the latter half of this route is easy walking on a forestry track, the outlook is very restricted by the regiment of sitka spruce.

Also at Duror, but with a fine and varied outlook, is the out-of-the-way circuit from Kentallen to Cuil Bay. From Kentallen follow the surfaced road to the Ardsheal Hotel and continue on a path through the old gardens. Ancient and splendid Scots pine and later more mixed indigenous woodland grace the first 3 kilometres of this walk. Beyond, the path deteriorates but there are splendid views across Loch Linnhe.

CLIMBING

The most important climbing in this area is on the Trilleachan Slabs where there are now over 40 routes, including three very long girdles traverses, of grades from VS to E3, and of lengths up to 400m. The climbing is almost unique in Scotland, much of it being on smooth granite slabs at an angle of about 40 degrees. Good holds are infrequent, friction climbing predominates and long pitches call for confident leading. In between the expanses of slabs there steep walls and overlaps which call for a very different style, strenuous moves contrasting with the delicate slab climbing. The Slabs are reached by a short climb from the road at the head of Loch Etive.

Creag Dhubh is a small but prominent crag at 127 470 surrounded by trees on the north-west side of Loch Etive about 2 kilometres north-east of the head of the loch. There are about ten short routes on this crag up to 35m long, and from Severe to E2 in standard.

On Beinn Sgulaird there are slabs similar to, but much smaller than, the Trilleachan Slabs. The main slabs are high up just under the summit and face south-west. A smaller crag lies a short distance further south and at a lower level below the Bealach Allt Coire Buidhe. There are about ten routes from Severe to E2 standard.

Sgor na h-Ulaidh has four gullies on its north face above the head of Gleann Leac na Muidhe; of these *Red Gully* (Grade III) is the best. There is a deep chasm on the south face of Beinn Fhionnlaidh that descends to the glen below at 091 490; it has given a good Grade IV winter climb of 350m length.

All the routes in this area are described in *Glencoe: Rock and Ice Climbs*, by K.V.Crocket, R.Anderson and D.Cuthbertson published by the Scottish Mountaineering Trust (1992).

On the Trilleachan Slabs, looking towards Ben Cruachan

CHAPTER 6

Glen Coe

Buachaille Etive Mor — Stob Dearg	1022m	223 543
Buachaille Etive Beag — Stob Dubh	958m	179 535
Bidean nam Bian	1150m	143 542
Beinn Maol Chaluim	907m	135 526

ACCESS
From the A82 road and the single-track road down Glen Etive.

TRANSPORT
Glasgow — Fort William bus service.

ACCOMMODATION
Hotels at Kingshouse, Clachaig and Glencoe.
Bunkhouse accommodation at Clachaig and Leacantium, Glencoe.
Youth hostel in Glen Coe.
Climbers' huts at Inbhir-fhaolain, Glen Etive (Grampian Club) and Lagangarbh (Scottish Mountaineering Club).
Camp and caravan sites at Invercoe and by the A82 road 1½ kilometres south-east of Glencoe village.

MAPS
OS Landranger Sheet 41.

The magnificent scenery of this glen is such that its name is renowned internationally and has achieved that indiscriminate use in advertising accorded only to the world's wonders. Discerning early travellers such as the Wordsworths, and Victorian artists such as Thomas Miles Richardson, were enraptured by its dramatic appearance and today few people will not have seen some calendar picture of it. Despite this cultural exposure, few first-time visitors will be quite prepared for the shock of the first view, whether from west or east, whether in fair weather or foul, when from the south the three huge buttresses seem almost to be pushing across the narrow bed of the glen to rest against the vast flank of the Aonach Eagach.

From a vantage point above the road at the Meeting of the Three Waters it is easy to imagine the cataclysmic forces underlying the dramatic forms before one. For the hills fronting onto the glen are part of an island of igneous rock — the remains of successive lava flows that spilled out more than 300 million years ago. Most of these have been eroded down to the underlying metamorphic rock, but an area 14 by 8 kilometres collapsed within a ring fracture and was subsequently protected from erosion so that it now stands proud. Next glaciation ground out soft rock in the bed of the glen leaving Bidean's three northern ridges, composed of more resistant rocks, with the truncated spurs that now seem to impend over the glen. One of the more resistant rocks is the rhyolite that gives such sound and impeccable material for rock-climbing on Buachaille Etive Mor's Stob Dearg and on the west face of Aonach Dubh. Today the glen is tamed by a main road, but stormy weather can still unleash forces that belittle man's efforts and after Christmas 1980 heavy rain and an overnight thaw of deep snow brought down boulders from the Aonach Eagach that blocked the road not far from the place where the village of Achtriochtan was inundated and then abandoned in the 18th century.

Since 1937 the glen and much of the high ground about it has been owned by the National Trust for Scotland — not surprisingly this area agrees closely with the boundary of the ancient ring-fracture. Prior to 1937 piecemeal purchases had brought such prizes as Bidean nam Bian under the National Trust for Scotland's wing, but in that year Dalness Forest, including Buachaille Etive Mor and Buachaille Etive Beag, came on the market and sufficient money was raised on an initiative by the Scottish Mountaineering Club to provide the National Trust for Scotland with the purchase price. Percy Unna was the driving force behind this magnificent gift to all hill-goers of the future. He had the foresight to seize the opportunity, the conviction needed to persuade others to contribute — substantial contributions from 20 English clubs and 319 other contributions from south of the border; a large sum from the Pilgrim Trust; and £1160 from his fellow SMC members — and the generosity to make the largest individual contribution from his own purse. His fund-raising circular contained a passage worth quoting in this guide — it stated, 'it was intended that the Trust (the National Trust for Scotland) should be asked to undertake that the land should be maintained in its primitive condition for all time'.

In the Central Highlands there are larger peaks more remote from main roads, but no other range is so generally mountainous, nor demands so readily in winter mountaineering techniques, skill and experience for the simplest ascents. Using the expressive terminology of Dr. Marion Newbigin, who in a most readable article about landform (SMC Journal, Vol. XIII, p. 124) maligned Scottish hills in a general comparison with other mountain ranges as 'suet dumplings scantily provided with plums'. By these standards the major peaks of Glen Coe are bare, damson stones!

From November until April, and even later in hard winters, its ridges sharpen into aretes and carry large cornices, and though the proximity of the Atlantic brings mid-winter thaws that can strip snow even from the highest points, these sudden changes in temperatures also turn easy ground into icy slopes that seem somehow to have increased in angle. Some experience in the use of crampons and an ice-axe on steep ground, and the ability to navigate in adverse conditions are essential for those planning their first winter visit.

Stob Dearg, 'Buachaille Etive's furrowed visage'

THE HILLS

Buachaille Etive Mor — Stob Dearg   *(great shepherd of Etive - red peak)*   (1022m)

One of the finest views in the Central Highlands can be had from a main road. It lies in wait for those driving north on the A82 where, after its crest, the road veers west and ahead, out of the flat expanse of Rannoch Moor, Stob Dearg springs up uncompromisingly, steep enough to show bare rock in most winter conditions and of a warm, pink hue in summer light. Well did Principal Shairp describe its front to the moor as a 'furrowed visage' for it is seamed with gullies and buttressed by a complex of pillars not easily separated by the eye unless there is early morning light.

No Scottish peak is more redolent of early rock-climbing history than Stob Dearg — Norman Collie, with Solly and Collier, made his eponymous climb up the east face in 1895, a route described by J.H.B. Bell as 'an old and superior vintage which is best tasted and savoured in very dry winter conditions'; Harold Raeburn left his mark, with the first ascent, in winter at that, of Crowberry Gully; and the ubiquitous Abraham brothers came north to pick up the plum of Crowberry Ridge. Almost all the rock on Stob Dearg's front to the moor is rhyolite, sound and clean and with small incut holds on its steeper parts. There is a comprehensive guide to Glen Coe for those wishing to rock-climb here, but this guide would be incomplete without some detail of two easy mountaineering routes and one mountaineering expedition.

Rannoch Wall seen from Curved Ridge

Curved Ridge is a moderate rock-climb that makes a logical and direct route to the summit. It winds through magnificent rock scenery and offers dress-circle seats for the rock-climbs on the Rannoch Wall. The foot of the rocks can be approached either across the flank of Stob Dearg from Lagangarbh or more directly across the River Coupal *via* the stepping stones under the carpark one kilometre west of the Glen Etive road. Both approaches converge below a conspicuous water-streaked slab, and neither avoids the steep upper path of scree. Despite the great scar of this path, the foot of the ridge is not easily found, since countless feet have diverged looking for firmer footing and to avoid steep ground. Two features help in arriving at the start of the climb. Roughly 160m above the water-streaked slab a steepening and lofty wall on the left pushes the path right-

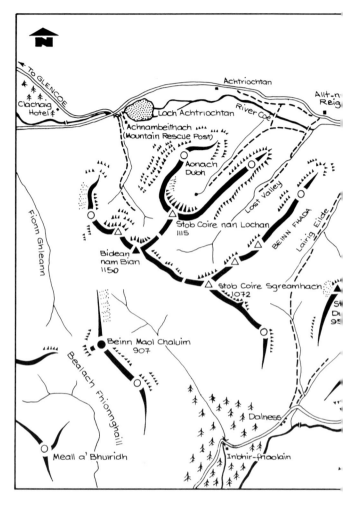

ward until it traverses horizontally into a recess with an often greasy step up to the right leading to open ground again. Above, a bay receiving drainage from gullies on either side of Crowberry Ridge should be skirted to the left, leading soon to the route. After 250m of alternate walking and steep scrambling on sound rock, the ridge flattens to merge into the hillside beneath the Crowberry Tower and scree should be followed rightward to a neck behind the Tower — in a fine situation at the top of the Direct Finish to Crowberry Gully — from where a short, steep scramble leads to the summit slopes.

Another fine mountaineering route is the North Buttress and it is reached by a rising traverse rightward from the foot of the bay beneath Crowberry Ridge. When steep rock is reached easier ground directly above leads to a broad terrace that girdles the Buttress. The best climbing will be found up an obvious system of cracks

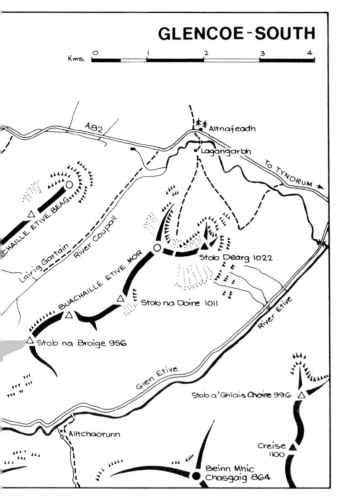

GLENCOE-SOUTH

Kms. 0   1   2   3   4

A82
Altnafeadh
Lagangarbh
To TYNDRUM
CHAILLE ETIVE BEAG
Lairig Gartain
River Coupall
BUACHAILLE ETIVE MOR
Stob Dearg 1022
Stob na Doire 1011
River Etive
Stob na Broige 956
Glen Etive
Stob a'Ghlais Choire 996
Alltchaorunn
Creise 1100
Beinn Mhic Chasgaig 864

and open chimneys at the centre of the arc made by the girdle. It is nowhere harder than Difficult. Those visiting Stob Dearg for the first time would be amply repaid by following the terrace to the west side of the buttress where there is a breathtaking view down into Great Gully and up into Raven's Gully.

Last is recommended the Chasm, which ranks as one of the finest mountaineering expeditions in the British Isles. Its rock scenery is superb, the route finding is complex and the difficulty of the climbing together with the majesty of the surroundings increase with height until the final awesome pitch of the Devil's Cauldron. In the most recent guide this exped-ition has been realistically graded Very Severe, for even after a drought the harder pitches near the top are wet. It will be found roughly 1½ kilometres down the Glen Etive road, and is the most obvious gully on this south- eastern aspect of Stob Dearg. (It is actually identified on the OS 1:25 000 map.) Climbing begins at about 400m.

Many of the early Scottish climbers were drawn to it, returning after repeated defeats and writing in awe of its obstacles. Harold Raeburn with Willie Ling in April 1906 made an ascent, using the South Wall exit from the Devil's Cauldron, which was disallowed since many of the pitches were buried under snow (these had previously been led by Raeburn in 1903), and it took 22 years before the first complete ascent was made by R.F.Stobart and Mr. and Mrs.N.E.Odell in April 1920. A winter ascent is a prize worth patient observation and is more often achievable than is generally realised, though both in difficulty and in form the individual pitches are extraordinarily variable. In March 1979 the 100ft Wall pitch — a wall of more than 100ft at an angle of about 75 degrees — was completely banked out and had become a steep but straightforward slope of hard snow, but that same day all exits from the Devil's Cauldron presented mixed climbing of the greatest difficulty. In a previous winter, of early February 1977, the position was reversed with the 100ft Wall being extremely difficult under thin ice, while the Devil's Cauldron was unrecognisable under a great snow bed. Earlier still, in late March 1974, all 16 pitches carried ice and a strong party took 10 hours to complete the route. Even in summer, conditions can be more akin to an Alpine route than a Scottish rock climb and in June 1977 a huge bed of neve obliterated the lower two of the Triple Chimneys and was only overcome by step-cutting with a peg-hammer and a spectacular leap across a bergschrund. Whatever conditions might appear to be from the Glen Etive road, those approaching the Chasm in winter should always be prepared for a route of Grade V standard.

Coire na Tulaich, almost due south of Lagangarbh Cottage, presents the most straightforward route to the summit ridge of Buachaille Etive Mor. A good path leads south from Lagangarbh and climbs the right-hand side of the corrie. After about 400m of ascent, the path deteriorates and a way must be found up scree slopes to reach the final steep narrow gully, or ledges to its left or right. From the broad bealach then reached, bouldery slopes with an occasional cairn lead to the summit.

From Glen Etive an ascent can be made to the same bealach by way of Coire Cloiche Finne, but this rough corrie is more often used as an involuntary descent in the confusing conditions that can reign in bad weather, or in winter by those deterred from descending over the cornice that often forms at the head of Coire na Tulaich. In descent this crucial bealach (870m) between the two corries will be found in poor visibility on a course from the summit cairn of 253 degrees for 250 metres and then 280 degrees for 400 metres. It should be stressed that in the wild conditions that can prevail on any winter's day, holding such a meticulous compass course is not easy and that unless the bealach is positively identified and a clear view had down the steep snow slope at the head of Coire na Tulaich, it is safer to turn down south into Coire Cloiche Finne.

Stob Dearg with its challenging front and its splendid view across the expanse of Rannoch Moor is only a part of Buachaille Etive Mor, which twists as a ridge over three other tops in a south-westerly direction, and makes a fine high-level walk. If ascent has been made via Coire na Tulaich, a traverse of the ridge and return by the deep glen to the west, Lairig Gartain, is not too long a day. Individually the tops of Stob na Doire (1011m), Stob Coire Altruim (941m) and Stob na Broige (956m) can each be ascended without difficulty from Glen Etive, although only the last-named presents a fine ridge (south-west) as an interesting climb. It also gives a particularly fine view down the glen to Loch Etive. Stob Coire Altruim has a north-east facing buttress of perhaps 100m height almost beneath its summit, cloven by a deeply recessed gully that makes a pleasant winter climb at Grade II. It was first climbed by T.Graham Brown and J.G.Parish in February 1950.

Looking west from Buachaille Etive Mor to Buachaille Etive Beag and Bidean nam Bian

Buachaille Etive Beag — Stob Dubh *(little shepherd of Etive — black peak)* (958m)
Like its larger companion across the Lairig Gartain, this hill presents a bold face to
the main road, but here the similarity ends as there is insufficient continuous rock
for worthwhile climbing on the north-eastern face of Stob nan Cabar (776m) and the
highest top, Stob Dubh, lies hidden at the south-western point of the main ridge.
Very much overshadowed by its grander neighbours, Buachaille Etive Beag is
nevertheless mountainous and from the Glen Coe road the only open, easy slopes
lie above the Lairig Eilde on the north-west side of the mountain. If turning down
into the Lairig Gartain, particularly from Stob Coire Raineach (924m), a comfortable
descent will be found from the bealach south-west of the peak. The eastern slope
between Stob Coire Raineach and Stob nan Cabar *(the top of the rafters)* is cut by a
series of gullies, well shown on the OS 1:50 000 map, all of which contain rock pitches;
the second from the north forks and the left fork contains sufficient rock-climbing
at Difficult standard to make an interesting route to the summit ridge.

On the north-eastern aspect of Stob nan Cabar an ascent can be picked through
the crags, but is not recommended for those without rock-climbing experience.

If Stob Dubh is the only peak to be climbed, then the quickest approach is from
the road bridge ½ kilometre north-west of Dalness in Glen Etive. Directly above is
the grassy south ridge, its unrelenting steepness emphasised by its constriction
between the parallel ridges of Stob Coire Sgreamhach and Stob na Broige.

Bidean nam Bian   *(peak of the mountains)* (1150m)
While Buachaille Etive Mor stands guard on the 'wrong' side of the breached
headwall of Glen Coe, Bidean nam Bian sits majestically on its throne and splays its
feet onto the very floor of the glen. From all sides its appearance is grand and
mountainous, but its complexity is such that only repeated visits bring appreciation
of its form. Its main ridge forms a north-facing arc which from its centre projects
another Y-shaped ridge. An t-Sron and Beinn Fhada are the western and eastern
outposts of the main ridge and Stob Coire nan Lochan, with its own northern ridges
of Aonach Dubh and Gearr Aonach, makes up the central prongs. A traverse in
summer from Aonach Dubh by way of Dinnertime Buttress, over all the tops to
Beinn Fhada, with a descent into the Lost Valley (Coire Gabhail) is one of the finest
outings in the British Isles and is open to hill-goers with only modest
mountaineering experience. It is of course much more demanding in winter.

Dinnertime Buttress lies on the west face of Aonach Dubh which is pleated by a
series of gullies and slim buttresses — well seen from the road near the Clachaig
Hotel — and is the left-most of the buttresses underneath the shallow bealach south
of Aonach Dubh. It is easily reached by crossing the burn below the waterfall at
about the 200m level. The only rock encountered on it is 50m of moderate scrambling
near the top and this can be avoided by traversing right into No. 2 Gully.

A simple ascent into Coire Gabhail is an enchanting experience, the approach
having the aura of that of an Alpine peak with paths clinging to steep slopes and a
jungle of boulders and trees hiding, until the last moment, the awesome view of the
cirque of jagged tops and steep walls that enclose the alluvial flats. This remarkable
feature, and much of the maze beneath it, resulted from an enormous landslide from
the eastern slope of Gearr Aonach, behind which a lake formed eventually to wash
away its retaining wall and leave exposed its flat bed of shingle. Autumn, with a
golden glow from the birches in the gorge at the head of the glen and perhaps an
early snowfall to add to the majesty of the peaks, is a good season for a visit.

For the ascent of Bidean nam Bian itself, the most straightforward approach is
from the west end of Loch Achtriochtan. A steep path climbs on the west side of the
waterfall up to the lip of the corrie and skirts the eastern slope of An t-Sron where
some mild scrambling is required. The steeper sections of this path, which were
seriously eroding the whole slope beside the waterfall, have been dramatically
repaired with stone-flagged zigzags. Where the burn divides (138 554) the path
crosses to follow the west side of the easternmost fork, though it now becomes faint.
The burn can be followed up to a tiny lochan, above which steep scree leads to the
bealach between Bidean nam Bian and Stob Coire nan Lochan. (In winter and spring
descent of this slope demands competence with crampons and an ice-axe.) Either
peak can be ascended easily from this bealach, but if descending toward it from
Bidean, great care is needed in poor visibility as the natural trend of the ridge carries
one out onto the top of Diamond Buttress. From the division of the burn mentioned
above, the south-east tributary can be followed up to the ridge west of Stob Coire
nam Beith, but in winter the headwall there may be corniced.

These bare details do no justice to the magnificence of Coire nam Beithach surrounded by steep crags which unfold slowly on the right as one ascends, until towering above are the huge buttresses of the Diamond on the left and Church Door on the right, divided by the Central Gully. Little wonder that the early mountaineers rejoiced at being able to rise from their breakfast table in the Clachaig Hotel and wander up to try new routes in this Alpine cirque. The main lodestone soon became the Church Door Buttress, probably through Norman Collie who during a fortnight in March 1894 made first ascents with Solly, Collier and Hastings of Tower Ridge, his own climb on Buachaille Etive Mor and one of the buttresses of Stob Coire nam Beith (not recorded but probably No. 4), and whose unfailing eye for a feasible mountain route would have sought out the weakness in the massive structure of the Church Door. Thereafter, between 1895 and 1898, Tough and Brown came down from Aberdeen; Hastings, Haskett-Smith and Bowen came up from the far south; and Raeburn and J.H.Bell led successive forays from Glasgow and Edinburgh. In all six attempts were made, usually in rain or snow, before Raeburn and Bell led the seventh and successful assault with R.G.Napier and H.C.Boyd. Their fascination with the buttress and with the obscure line of weakness that they followed, known now as the Flake Route, is understandable. Above the pinnacle (Collie's Pinnacle) that plugs the base of the Central Gully, there lies hidden a great split in the buttresss that allows one to 'chimney' up to a platform. Then when it appears that progress can only be made by a traverse out onto the very steep face, another hidden line of weakness slants upwards and left above The Arch formed by two enormous boulders jammed across the vertical wall. As one traverses comfortably across one can peer down vertically through a gap to the scree 60m below; above, the climbing is merely steep and difficult.

Apart from the generally hard rock-climbing on the Diamond and Church Door Buttresses, Coire nam Beithach provides great scope for general mountaineering. Four buttresses of rough, clean rhyolite all offer easy scrambling routes converging on the summit of Stob Coire nam Beith while to the right an easily identified, acute triangle of pink rock named the Pyramid offers an introduction to difficult climbing. The rock is clean, rough and sound, though near the top there is a detached flake resting on a good foundation that needs careful handling. Under snow and ice the four numbered buttresses offer a good introduction to the middle grade of winter climbing and they are split by chimneys and gullies containing harder and classic routes. The current comprehensive guide contains two very clear diagrams of the major crags — a necessity as the topography of Stob Coire nam Beith's buttresses is complex.

An-t-Sron *(the nose)* (850m)
This fore-peak, whose Chasm is so apparent from the main road (it marks the eroded line of the ancient ring-fracture), can be climbed directly from the main road and, while the initial 700m are tiresomely steep, there follows a fine ridge-walk of 2 kilometres over the tops of Stob Coire nam Beith. The ridge between Stob Coire nam Beith and Bidean nam Bian often carries in winter a delicate snow arete.

The summit of Bidean nam Bian with the Diamond and Church Door buttresses below its left-hand ridge

Another ascent of Bidean nam Bian, not an obvious approach and only recommended for winter, is by the vast south face. When stable snow conditions exist on this face its sunny exposure and complexity of ribs and couloirs give easy mountaineering in a delightful, Alpine atmosphere. It can be reached best by following the Fionn Ghleann to the bealach between Bidean and Beinn Maol Chaluim, as the southern approach up Gleann Fhaolain from Glen Etive involves a struggle through afforestation. However the burn in the Fionn Ghleann takes enormous drainage and can run its straight course with awesome force. Fortunately there is no need to ford it and its west bank can be reached around the nose of Aonach Dubh a'Ghlinne from the farm of Gleann-leac-na-muidhe.

There have appeared lighthearted accounts of descents made in error on this side of the hill, but while picking a line from below to suit one's taste on a sunny winter's morning is a straightforward affair, these slopes and those above the Fionn Ghleann are no place to descend on a winter's evening.

Stob Coire nan Lochan *(peak of the corrie of the little lochan)* (1115m)
The winter view of this peak from points above the main road and near the Meeting of the Three Waters is one of the splendours of Glen Coe. Higher up, at the lowest point between Gearr Aonach and the peak itself, there is an uninterrupted view of the vertical pillars and deeply recessed gullies on the east face of the north ridge.

Aonach Dubh and Stob Coire nan Lochan from the wooded lower part of Glen Coe near Clachaig

Perhaps the most interesting approach leads along the crest of Gearr Aonach, reached from the mouth of Coire Gabhail by The Zigzags. This path winds through the most unlikely terrain and uses a series of ledges on the steep, north-eastern nose with a little mild scrambling in between. Its base is found by following the path that forks right beyond the deer fence at the entrance to the corrie. In descent careful prospecting will be needed before the top of the path is identified. It will be found in the area between the northernmost of the steep gullies that drop to the east and the final steep nose that plummets into Glen Coe, but many false casts have left misleading traces. Under snow and with no recent tracks, those without previous knowledge could spend considerable time searching for this descent. It should be emphasised that The Zigzags is the only easy scrambling route onto and off Gearr Aonach until one reaches the shallow depression at the south-west of the ridge before the rise onto Stob Coire nan Lochan.

Two valley approaches, other than that by Coire nam Beithach, are regular routes to Stob Coire nan Lochan: that by Coire Gabhail has a path on the west side of the glen starting beyond the flats and near the point where the burn disappears underground not to reappear until beneath the debris of the great land-slip. The path continues on a gradually rising traverse across the hillside on the north-west side of the gorge of the Allt Coire Gabhail, but the ground above to the bealach between the peak and Bidean nam Bian is rough going.

The glen to the west leading to Coire nan Lochan has just as much scenic interest in the burn tumbling through the rocky gorge and higher in the spread of lochans beneath the columnar crags. A good path runs up the east side of the glen giving good views of the rock-climbing playground on the east face of Aonach Dubh and continues beyond the 600m level before fading at the rock barrier beneath the lip of the corrie. It makes the ideal approach for those planning to climb some of the classic winter routes. Easy ground can be followed from the lochans either east to gain the north-east ridge or north-west to gain the north ridge. The former ridge has steep sections of shattered rock that require care. One of the gullies, Broad Gully, seen from the corrie bed as the leftmost in the mural, makes an easy winter route to the summit and in good snow conditions a steep glissade.

Both Coire Gabhail and Coire nan Lochan are easily reached opposite their entrances by bridges crossing the River Coe.

Much has been written about Ossian's Cave, the black cleft so obvious high on the north face of Aonach Dubh. It used to contain a metal box for calling cards, but this interesting relic vanished some years ago and there remains nothing else to recommend about what is always a vegetatious and usually wet scramble with no view and with an inelegant, seated shuffle offering the only security in descent. There have been several accidents to parties descending from the Cave.

Stob Coire Sgreamhach (1072m)
Beinn Fhada *(long hill)* (952m)

These two outliers of Bidean nam Bian form the jagged outline at the head of the The Lost Valley and only from Glen Etive can easy slopes be found on the southern flank of Stob Coire Sgreamhach. When they feature as the last tops in a traverse from Stob Coire nan Lochan, they provide a sting in the tail, for there are awkward, descending steps beyond Stob Coire Sgreamhach — always best turned on the right — and the multiple tops on Beinn Fhada (truly the long hill as the Gaelic translates) seem more than their number. Purists who wish to keep high until the final nose of Beinn Fhada can scramble down the vegetatious shelf that lies east of the nose, but careful route-finding and daylight are prerequisites for a comfortable descent here.

Otherwise the only straightforward descent from Beinn Fhada is into Coire Gabhail. From the shallow bealach south of the last top of 811m, descend north-west into an open gully. There is a faint path tracing the best line down steep and loose terrain. This gully leads down onto the alluvial flats beside an enormous boulder that offers some well-polished problems.

From Glen Etive, starting up the forest edge near Dalness, a most enjoyable traverse can be made of Stob Coire Sgreamhach, Bidean nam Bian and Beinn Maol Chaluim (907m). When no snow lies the contrast between the various rock-types is remarkable with the quartzite boulder-field capping Beinn Maol Chaluim particularly noticeable. It gives some idea of the enormous forces that went to provide the underlying structure of the area to realise that an immense folding movement in the Earth's crust superimposed this quartzite on the younger Leven schist that makes up the bulk of the hill. Also, in early summer the southern spur of this peak, as it slopes down into Glen Etive, displays a rich crop of wild orchid, variegated in colour from the palest of pinks to purple.

In winter much interest can be added to this traverse by climbing the Sron na Lairig, a Grade II route that follows the ridge bounding the southern rim of Stob Coire Sgreamhach's eastern corrie. This winter climb is usually approached from the north *via* the Lairig Eilde but the southern approach by the path from Dalness leads through an impressive gorge and reserves sight of the route until the bealach at 490m. (The path continues through the Lairig Eilde to the Glen Coe road. It crosses the burn twice and the crossing nearer the main road can be a serious barrier after heavy rain.)

If icy conditions have been found in the first half of this traverse, the descent of Bidean nam Bian to the Bealach Fhaolain (not marked on the 1:50 000 map: it lies due north of Beinn Maol Chaluim) should be treated with respect. There is a dog-leg course of 1 kilometre due west then south that hinges on the steepest part of a convex slope which commences at a deceptively easy angle.

Beinn Maol Chaluim   *(Calum's bare hill)*   (907m)

Beinn Maol Chaluim is a fine mountainous peak in its own right with very steep flanks to either side of its north-south spine, and with a crag, Creag Dubh, of schist frowning down upon the Bealach Fhionnghaill. This crag of perhaps 100m height is unusually compact for schist and may well repay exploration.

For the ascent of this peak alone, a fine high-level ridge walk can be made from Glen Etive although the initial ascent from the road is very steep and afforestation restricts access to one point (149 496) just opposite Lochan Urr (from which many calendar photographs of the two Buachailles have been taken). Once up onto the spine of the hill the 1½ kilometres to the highest point provide a continuous view of some splendour.

If ascending from the north *via* the Fionn Ghleann, the only easy, though circuitous route to the summit follows a path from the Bealach Fhionnghaill skirting left around the base of the crag, and leading eventually past other smaller outcrops of porphyry.

In hard winters a deeply recessed gully on the eastern flank beneath the southern top (847m) makes an enjoyable climb at Grade II.

WALKS AND PATHS

Two through routes follow deep glens from the A82 to Glen Etive. As the two routes are about 6 kilometres (the first described) and 8 kilometres, the total distance is not too much for a day's circuit. However both paths lead through some boggy ground and the end of a long dry spell would give most enjoyment.

Stob Coire nan Lochan

The shortest route has the best path. It runs through the Lairig Eilde and starts at 188 563, where there is a signpost beside the road. It has also the more varied scenery. However after heavy rain a ford at 182 557 can be very difficult to cross.

The second starts at 213 560, follows the Lairig Gartain, reaches a greater height at almost 500m and its path runs out near the summit of the pass. Both meet in Glen Etive at a bridge (171 515) ½ kilometre north of Dalness.

CLIMBING

Significant rock and ice-climbing areas abound in these mountains. The north-eastern quadrant of Buachaille Etive Mor's Stob Dearg holds a great number and variety of routes. Starting in the east and moving west, Central Buttress offers mainly rock climbs including *Pegleg* (HVS). Rannoch Wall, easily recognised as the largest wall of pinkish rock, has classic climbs in the lower grades such as *Agag's Groove* (Very Difficult) and *Red Slab* (VS). Between Crowberry Ridge and North Buttress is the classic winter climb *Crowberry Gully* (Grade III/IV). The west face of North Buttress, Slime Wall, is an intimidating place with one of the best routes at HVS — *Bludgers Revelation* — in the UK. Tucked in beside Slime Wall and above Great Gully is the dark slit of *Raven's Gully* (HVS) rarely dry and a fine winter route. Overlooking Raven's and to the west is *Raven's Edge* (VS) with fine situations and

Spacewalk, a modern extreme on the North-east Nose of Aonach Dubh

an awesome view of Slime Wall. West of Great Gully there is a series of buttresses — Cuneiform, Great Gully, Broad, Staircase and Lagangarbh, all containing shorter rock climbs mainly in the middle grades. West of Coire na Tulaich and at a height of c. 450m lies the very steep crag of Creag a'Bhancair with many routes at the highest standard, the best-known, but not the hardest, being *Carnivore* (E2). There are also some modern bolted routes.

High in Coire Gabhail, the Lost Valley Buttresses have seen many modern hard winter routes (such as *Neanderthal* Grade VI) pioneered in the last decade.

There is good rock-climbing on the east and north-east faces of Gearr Aonach and high on the former some excellent ice routes (*Mome Rath* and *The Wabe*, both Grade V) that need a hard winter. The south-eastern aspect making for pleasant rock-climbing conditions on this east face, can in winter bring very dangerous ice and stone-fall — some huge, Damoclean icicles have been seen to fall from the upper walls when early morning frost prevailed lower down in the sunless glen. The north-east nose of Gearr Aonach has pleasant climbing in the middle grades including *The Cheek* (Severe).

The East Face of Aonach Dubh has pleasant climbing mainly in the lower grades. At a higher level than the East Face and further north, the North-East Nose has been the scene of recent development of several short extreme routes, of which *Freak-Out* (E4) and *Spacewalk* (E5) are among the best.

The west face of Aonach Dubh is a rock climbers' playground with classic hard routes (*The Big Top* E1; *Trapeze* E1; *Hee-Haw* E1) on superb rock. In hard winters there are some excellent snow and ice routes such as *No 6 Gully* (Grade IV) and *Elliot's Downfall* (Grade V).

The summit cliffs of Stob Coire nan Lochan and Bidean nam Bian offer high-quality rock climbs of all standards. In hard winters a wide range of type and difficulty in winter climbs will be found, and even in a poor season routes will still be found high on Bidean nam Bian. The comprehensive guide is *Glen Coe: Rock and Ice Climbs*, by K.V.Crocket, R.Anderson and D.Cuthbertson, published by the Scottish Mountaineering Trust (1992).

References

Always a Little Further, Alastair Borthwick (Diadem) 1987 — for a vivid account of a prewar ascent of The Chasm.

SMCJ, IX, p135. Article by J.H.Bell on the early attempts on Church Door Buttress.

SMCJ, XXII, p116. *The Geology of Glencoe*, E. B. Bailey.

Mountaineering in Scotland, and *Undiscovered Scotland*, W.H.Murray. A compendium, (Diadem 1982), containing classic accounts of first ascents in Glen Coe.

CHAPTER 7

North Glen Coe and Rannoch Moor

Aonach Eagach		
Meall Dearg	953m	161 584
Sgorr nam Fiannaidh	967m	141 583
Sgorr na Ciche	742m	125 594
Garbh Bheinn	867m	169 601
Beinn a'Chrulaiste	857m	246 567
Leum Uilleim	906m	331 641

ACCESS

From the A82 and the B863 loop road around Loch Leven.

TRANSPORT

Glasgow—Fort William train service.
Glasgow—Fort William bus service.
Fort William—Oban bus service calling at Kinlochleven.

ACCOMMODATION

Hotels at Kingshouse, Clachaig, Glencoe village, Ballachulish and Rannoch station.
Bunkhouses at Clachaig Hotel, Leacantuim (Glen Coe) and Corrour station.
Guesthouses and bed and breakfast houses at Glencoe village, Kinlochleven and Ballachulish (Glencoe Tourist Office — telephone 08552 296).
Camp and caravan sites at Invercoe, Leacantuim (Glen Coe), Caolasnacon and the Caravan Club site beside the A82 road 1½ kilometres south of Glencoe village.
Youth hostels at Glen Coe and Loch Ossian.
Climbers' huts at Lagangarbh (Scottish Mountaineering Club) and Kinlochleven (Fell & Rock Climbing Club).
Bothies at Gorton (375 481), Ciaran (289 635), Meanach (266 685) and Staoineag (295 678) These four bothies, maintained by the Mountain Bothies Association, are small cottages which only provide simple shelter.

MAPS

OS 1:50 000 Landranger Sheets 41and 42

From the constricted depths of Glen Coe the splendour of Aonach Eagach's airy crest is not well appreciated and only those who traverse its jagged pinnacles will realise how slender the ridge is. To enjoy this outing one should ideally have some rock-climbing experience and those without would probably better maintain their composure if a rope were used for short sections. In true winter conditions that part between Am Bodach (943m) and Stob Coire Leith (940m) can be very difficult indeed

The Aonach Eagach above Loch Achtriochtan in Glen Coe

and the bare standard given of Grade III is not truly indicative of the variety of problems nor of the scale. Such extreme conditions are uncommon, but any party venturing onto the ridge on one of the shorter winter days would do well to start early and to keep moving. Frequently, experienced parties have had a casual attitude on a fine winter's day repaid with a struggle to find a safe descent in darkness.

THE HILLS

Meall Dearg *(red hill)* (953m)
Sgorr nam Fiannaidh *(peak of the Fian warriors)* (967m)
Most parties carry out the traverse from east to west and this direction offers a saving of 150m on the shorter ascent to Am Bodach and, in summer, the easiest way of tackling the awkward sections. The south-south-east ridge of Am Bodach can be ascended directly by a path starting in the carpark west of the cottage of Allt-na-reigh, or a diverging path can be followed into the ravine east of the ridge for more easy ground. From the top of Am Bodach the easiest line of descent west onto the ridge is not obvious, but a cast to the right should succeed. A little north of the next top, Meall Dearg, lies a great boulder of rough and creamy granite carried there by the vast ice-sheet that once covered Rannoch Moor and all the surrounding hills — it was evidently over 700m thick. Meall Dearg is the site of another curiosity, for it was the last Munro of the first of that exclusive band to have climbed all those

Looking east along the Aonach Eagach to Meall Dearg and Am Bodach

Scottish hills designated by Sir Hugh Munro as having a separate status of more than 3000ft. The Reverend A. E. Robertson, for he it was, endeared himself to future Munroists by kissing first the cairn and then his wife.

Between Meall Dearg and Stob Coire Leith, though the ridge twists and undulates, the route is obvious and involves most pleasantly varied scrambling, the highlight of which is a particularly narrow section turreted with two crazy pinnacles; these should be clambered over directly as circumvention to the right involves loose rock and vegetation. After Stob Coire Leith the ridge broadens and near the top of Sgorr nam Fiannaidh boulders of quartzite appear underfoot. For those wishing to descend directly into Glen Coe, the steep slope due south of Sgorr nam Fiannaidh offers better going in summer than the unpleasant and dangerous path that hugs the western rim of Clachaig Gully. In places this path has been worn down to the underlying rock, it approaches very close to the lip of the gully where long strips of turf have been undermined, and in wet weather it makes a thoroughly nasty descent. A more comfortable descent will be found by following the ridge from Sgorr nam Fiannaidh west-south-west and then north-west to the col below Sgorr na Ciche, and then south-west down to the old road in Glen Coe.

There is no easy summer descent to the south between Am Bodach and Stob Coire Leith, and in winter this caution should be extended to include the corrie above Loch Achtriochtan and also that above the cottage of Allt-na-reigh, both being potential avalanche sites. If a party suspects dangerous snow conditions it is far safer to continue to the bealach between Sgorr nam Fiannaidh and Sgorr na Ciche or, at the eastern end, to face the steepness of the south-south-east ridge of Am Bodach. There are easy descents north from both Meall Dearg and Stob Coire Leith to Loch Leven, but these would be desperate measures indeed for a party returning to Glen Coe.

Sgorr na Ciche (742m)

This prominent cone, usually known as the Pap of Glencoe, offers a fine viewpoint for an evening's walk. A good path leads up the hill from a point almost 1 kilometre east of Bridge of Coe on the old road. It runs up to the bealach between the Pap and Sgorr nam Fiannaidh and can be followed up the steep, south-eastern slope to the top of the Pap. A little west of the summit smooth slabs of

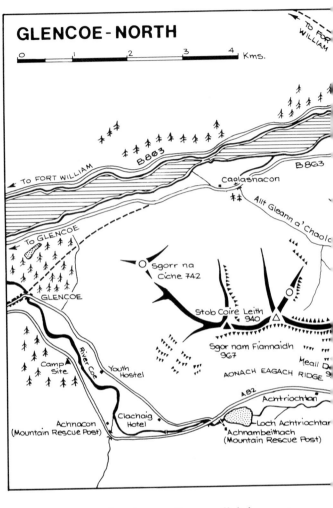

quartzite are scored with south-westerly directed striae — the parallel furrows ground out by glaciation — and further down the slope (at the 250m level; 115 586), ancient man has left his mark in a series of trenches thought to have been dug by Fingal's horde as fortification against the Norse invaders.

Stob Mhic Mhartuin (706m)
Sron Gharbh *(rough nose)* (874m)

These two hills, separated by two other unnamed tops, form the eastern continuation of the Aonach Eagach, with the ridge between Am Bodach and Sron Gharbh falling only to a bealach at 816m. They make a fitting start, or finish, to a traverse of the Aonach Eagach and in themselves offer an easy afternoon's exercise from Altnafeadh. Views from them are out of proportion to their relatively minor status and a sense of perspective is gained of the Bidean range and of its corries that is lost from the confusing proximity of the Aonach Eagach itself. Below the most westerly

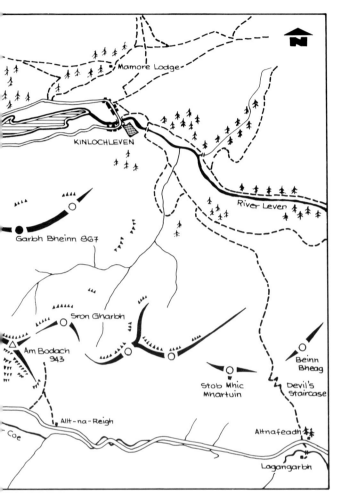

of the two unnamed tops lies a prominent point known as A'Chailleach (*the old woman*) with, as is usual with Gaelic nomenclature of hill-form, Am Bodach (*the old man*) across the corrie.

Garbh Bheinn   (*rough hill*) (867m)

Despite its proximity to Kinlochleven, this hill gives a decided sense of remoteness. Its northern flank is steep and rugged while to the south it is walled in by the Aonach Eagach. It was on Garbh Bheinn that Robert Louis Stevenson, in his novel *Kidnapped*, had David Balfour lie nursing his hunger while Alan Breac brought food up from Caolasnacon.

The easiest approach is by the track on the south bank of the River Leven that turns south up to the reservoir supplying domestic water to Kinlochleven. Above, easy slopes lead to a plateau east of the top. From the farm at Caolasnacon a fine circuit can be made over the knolls on the west ridge and then, via the bealach (530m) to the south, on to traverse the Aonach Eagach and Sgorr na Ciche.

Until 1922 and the completion of the road along the southern shore of Loch Leven — started with the labour of German prisoners-of-war — all transport from the south reached Kinlochleven by boat, and the narrows at Caolasnacon (meaning in Gaelic 'the narrows of Con') needed dredging and the diversion of the silt-carrying Allt Gleann a'Chaolais before a passenger boat of any size could be used. These narrows were not cleared until 1907, and before then the motor-boats in use, often with rowing-boats for extra passengers in tow, could only overcome the full tidal force when empty. Passengers of the day were put off at one end of the channel and had to cross the swampy flats to the other end carrying their rowing boat with them.

The narrow section of the Aonach Eagach between Meall Dearg and Stob Coire Leith

Sgorr na Ciche from Kinlochleven

Beinn a'Chrulaiste *(rocky hill)* (857m)
Meall nan Ruadhag (646m)
Stob na Cruaiche (739m)

To walk this stretch of high ground between the Blackwater and Rannoch Moor gives a taste of remoteness without the heavy going that a crossing of the moor entails. Starting from the Kingshouse, Beinn a' Chrulaiste is easily ascended by its east ridge and on the return it is worth holding due west from Stob na Cruaiche until the path (clearly shown on the OS 1:50 000 map) is found leading from the Black Corries north of the Stob down to the lodge of the same name, (though local people know this group of buildings as the Iron Lodge).

Before the opening of the West Highland Railway, when the Blackwater was a mere scatter of lochans, a drove route crossed these hills taking the lairig between Meall Bhalach and Meall nan Ruadhag. Until a century ago thousands of cattle and sheep crossed this pass each year, but it needs an optimistic eye to find any trace now beside the Allt Chailleach on the south and the Allt nan Fuaran to the north. Further north a path on the east side of the Ciaran Water can be followed almost into the Blackwater. Before the inundation of 1906, it led to the stance at Ciaran between Lochan Inbhir and Lochan na-Salach-Uidhre, all now under the waters of the reservoir.

Rannoch Moor

This moor represents a vast basin scoured out of granite 400 million years old by successive periods of glaciation and now covered by blanket bog broken by an extended waterway draining to the north-east corner. It is hemmed in on all sides by high hills made of rocks more resistant to the forces of glaciation and takes the shape of an inverted triangle having a base made by the high ground running from Beinn a'Chrulaiste to Rannoch Station and sides composed of the railway line and the A82 road.

Bare physical details, however, give little impression of the scenic quality which is perhaps best appreciated in descent from one of the easterly ridges on the Black Mount, from where the great channel winding and stretching from Ba Bridge to Loch Laidon adds greatly to the sense of scale. This same sense of space is to be experienced when crossing the moor — an outing to be reserved for clear weather with dry conditions underfoot or, alternatively, a hard frost in winter. Then the expanse of the moor with its scattering of lochans, knolls, and granite boulders is accentuated by the distant circle of peaks rising abruptly at the moor's edge.

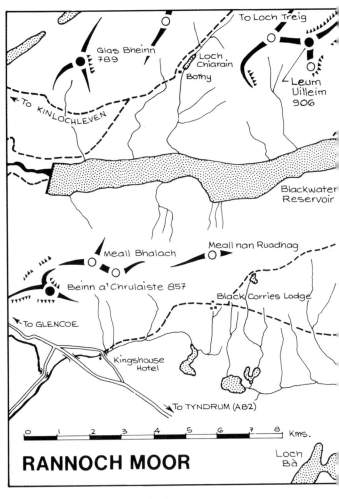

RANNOCH MOOR

To experience a real sense of the moor's remoteness, the line of Loch Laidon and Loch Ba should be followed. Then the flatness of the moor can be appreciated — in 21 kilometres from Ba Bridge to the northern end of Loch Laidon there is a drop of only 44m — though hours of leaping from one tussock to another can make steep ground seem easy going. Following the waterway by canoe has become a popular expedition and, in hard winters, the same route has been followed on skates.

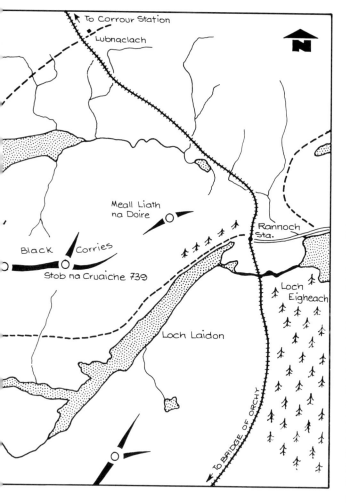

The Blackwater Hills

Leum Uilleim (*William's leap*) (906m)
Glas Bheinn (*grey hill*) (789m)

These two hills are divided by the course of the old drove road from Lochtreighead to the Ciaran Water. Further tracks encircle the northern arc about this area, but despite such easy access promoted further by the presence of Corrour Station at c. 400m close under the north-eastern corrie of Leum Uilleim, the hills are rarely visited.

To ascend Glas Bheinn from Kinlochleven a good path can be followed on the north side of the River Leven, past the site of the prisoner-of-war camp where German soldiers were kept during the First World War, to the dam head. Those travelling across country from the north will find the most gentle incline on Glas Bheinn's north-north-east spine, where 2 kilometres of ridge rise by a mere 30m, allowing one to walk hands-in-pockets and enjoy the fine views to the west.

No more than 2 hours are needed for the easy walk up Leum Uilleim from Corrour Station. The central, indeed almost pivotal position of this top within a great, northern arc of higher hills makes it a grand viewpoint. It holds more snow than its height might suggest.

A path skirts the south-eastern flank of Leum Uilleim from the house at Lubnaclach, now a ruin, but like that beside the Ciaran Water, it disappears into the Blackwater. Beyond to the west the shore of the reservoir offers very rough going only exceeded by that on the opposite shore.

Rannoch Moor, looking towards the Black Mount

PATHS AND WALKS

Altnafeadh to Kinlochleven.   The original track crossing from Glen Coe to Kinlochleven starts at the house of Altnafeadh about 4 kilometres west of the Kinghouse Hotel and at an altitude of 300m. It climbs through an old plantation of small pines and up to a bealach at 550m, then descends to sea-level at Kinlochleven. (9 kilometres).

Kingshouse to Rannoch Station.   A crossing of Rannoch Moor can be made with relative ease by the track between the Kingshouse Hotel and Rannoch Station, with only a 3 kilometre stretch out of the total where the track degenerates into rough going. This is the stretch west of the ruined croft at Tigh na Cruaiche where the traces of a path can be found beside Loch Laidon. (20 kilometres).

Kinlochleven to Corrour Station.   There is still a good path that can be followed from Kinlochleven up to the damhead and along the course of the Allt an Inbhir to Loch Treig. This old droving route then meets the Road to the Isles, which can be followed east and south-east to Corrour Station. (23 kilometres)

CLIMBING

The route worthy of real note on the north side of the glen is the *Clachaig Gully* — an expedition of character containing some fine pitches. Cleaving the hillside so obviously above the Clachaig Hotel, it did not escape the attention of the pioneers and Collie, with Solly and Collier, was the first to make an attempt. Not surprisingly, the month being March (1894), they were turned back by a cascade pouring over the *Great Cave* (pitch 4). What does cause surprise is that men of such ability as Raeburn and later J.H.B.Bell, with their predilection for difficult gullies and their preparedness to tackle loose and vegetated rock, should have left it unclimbed until W.H.Murray, A.M.MacAlpine, J.K.W.Dunn and W.G.Marskell made the first ascent in May 1938.

Facing only a little west of south, the climbing can be on sun-warmed rock and, unlike most guilies, a dry spell will remove most of the drainage water, but leaving always *Jericho Wall* greasy from seepage. Above the Great Cave escape routes are as difficult as the climbing in the gully above and, even lower, they are unattractively vegetated and steep. With a good flow of water coursing down the gully it is an awesome place but the major waterfalls are turned on their right walls and only the *Red Chimney* must be climbed direct.

There is little else worth climbing on these peaks. What is available will be found on the steep southern flanks of Am Bodach. They are mostly gully routes needing a hard winter. All are described in *Glencoe: Rock and Ice Climbs*, by K.V.Crocket, R.Anderson and D.Cuthbertson, published by the Scottish Mountaineering Trust (1992).

On the south-eastern slope of A'Chailleach, a rarely climbed gully, *Red Funnel Gully*, offers a taste of exploration. It starts at c. 500m and though the lower pitches are merely scrambling, there are two long pitches in the upper half that are Very Difficult in standard.

SKI MOUNTAINEERING

Three tours, suitable for very short days, may be mentioned. Starting from Altnafeadh (or any point on the A82 road just to the west) an easy climb leads to Stob Mhic Mhartuin and the broad ridge westwards can be followed, possibly as far as Sron Gharbh. Return by the same way.

Beinn a'Chrulaiste is also a pleasant hill for the ski-tourer, either from the Kingshouse Hotel or Altnafeadh. If starting from Kingshouse, Meall Bhalach can be included in a longer circuit with a fine easy run back to the hotel down the Allt a'Bhalach.

The third short tour is Leum Uilleim from Corrour Station. Either of the two north-east ridges of the hill may make a good ascent route, but the best downhill skiing will almost certainly be found in Coire a'Bhric Beag.

CHAPTER 8

The Mamores

Sgurr Eilde Mor	1008m	231 658
Binnein Beag	940m	222 677
Binnein Mor	1128m	212 663
Na Gruagaichean	1055m	203 652
An Gearanach	982m	188 670
Stob Coire a'Chairn	981m	185 661
Am Bodach	1032m	176 651
Sgor an Iubhair	1001m	165 655
Sgurr a' Mhaim	1099m	165 667
Stob Ban	999m	148 654
Mullach nan Coirean	939m	122 662

A gently rising and extensive moor of great size — as might be the meaning of the name 'Mamore' — seems hardly appropriate to this mountainous ridge stretching some 20 kilometres east to west and throwing out spurs north and south that, even from the valley, are obviously steep and sharp. To walk the length of the ridge in a day makes a splendid outing — long certainly, but with only occasional difficulties to interrupt a steady pace. Kinlochleven makes the most convenient starting point with the estate road to Loch Eilde Mor and the old military road to Fort William providing easy going for the first two hours and for the last, long hour. As three of the main tops are removed from the ridge on northern spurs, the distance for the round trip is greater at about 33 kilometres than a casual glance at the OS map might suggest. However the main ridge does not drop below 745m, and in a westerly traverse reserves its gentlest slopes until the last top. If the eastern outliers of Binnein Beag and Sgurr Eilde Mor are included, the additional 8 kilometres or so, with the extra ascent, make the traverse a very long outing and one that on a short winter's day will be started and finished in darkness.

There is a remarkable network of stalker's paths in the Mamores. Those on the southern flank are of most use to the hillwalker as they penetrate most of the corries and reach the main ridge. In the steeper corries to the north they tend to traverse the corrie walls without reaching either valley bed or summit ridge.

THE HILLS

Sgurr Eilde Mor *(big peak of the hind)* (1008m)
From Kinlochleven a good path crosses the burn draining from the east past the north end of the village and ascends in a northerly direction to connect at c.300m with the Land-rover track running east along the north side of Loch Eilde Mor. (Another path strikes more directly east to a fine waterfall and continues steeply up a spur between a bifurcation of the burn, but higher this path dwindles and it is probably as quick to follow the dog-leg of the first-mentioned. Alternatively, from Mamore Lodge, follow the Land-rover track towards the loch). From the Land-rover track a stalker's path makes a long rising traverse north-east to the lochan beneath Sgurr Eilde Mor's south-western flank. A broad steep ridge runs up from the south-east corner of the lochan, and there are splendid views across to the ridges bounding Binnein Mor's huge east corrie. The spine of the hill runs for 2 kilometres in a north-easterly direction and is paved with distinctive platelets of schist broken by outcroppings of quartz. Here and there are gravelly clearings and, particularly on the western flank, occasional clumps of moss campion can be found in flower from June to August. Being removed from the main chain of the Mamores, there is an extraordinarily open outlook to the east from the summit ridge.

A more gentle ascent and a fine traverse can be made by following the Land-rover track to the spit of land between lochs Eilde Mor and Beag, from where a stalker's path rises north. After 3½ kilometres it reaches a little plateau beneath the mountain's north-east ridge, which is well-defined and easy walking to the top.

Binnein Beag *(little peak)* (940 m)
This conical hill appears to be a rather low outlier of Binnein Mor, but it occupies a commanding position overlooking the watershed between Glen Nevis and the Abhainn Rath. The path system described under Sgurr Eilde Mor offers the easiest approach to the hill and, from the lochan at 730m, the path continues further north after a short descent across the eastern flank of Binnein Mor to a high bealach at 750m with a lochan just beneath. There is no escaping the rough scree slopes that encircle the hill and seem at their longest in the northern arc, but the least rough ground will be found after passing east around the lochan and taking a line due north. Such bad footing do these screes make that it is worthwhile, in approach from Glen Nevis, bearing for the bealach between Binnein Beag and Mor. In its somewhat isolated position above Glen Nevis, the hill makes a fine viewpoint with the huge bulk of Ben Nevis and the sharp outline of its North-east Buttress particularly impressive. Nearer at hand the slender north-east ridge of Binnein Mor is an attractive prospect.

Binnein Mor *(big peak)* (1128m)
For such a large hill, Binnein Mor is not a conspicuous distant feature, although when filled with snow the regular shape of its north-eastern corrie is distinctive from faraway hills to the east. Whilst there are no recognised climbs, the northern ridges offer sporting ascents and, with little exception, the slopes on all sides are very steep. The summit ridge runs north to south and at both ends it divides, thus giving on a map rather the shape of an X.

A straightforward route via the south-eastern ridge uses again the path system described under Sgurr Eilde Mor and the stalker's path leading into Coire an Lochain should be followed to c. 730m where well-engineered zigzags carry one directly north to the top at 219 653 known rather confusingly to those who climb hills rather than look at them as Sgurr Eilde Beag. In winter the ridge ahead is often beautifully corniced and leads easily over a southern top to the final sharp point.

For a traverse of the hill, the north-east ridge makes a most enjoyable scramble exiting steeply onto the summit ridge just north of the cairn, but its winter ascent demands care. At an easier angle is the north-north-west ridge which is an obvious route after a long approach from Glen Nevis. In most winters this ridge carries much snow which tends to form an arete of shallow but regular curvature which is a fine thing to look upon from the Grey Corries to the north. The last spur of Binnein Mor carries the main ridge south-west to Na Gruagaichean.

Na Gruagaichean *(the maidens)* (1055 m)
Few hills of comparable stature can be so little climbed in their own right. Lying so close between the obvious attractions of the ridges thrust out north by Binnein Mor and An Garbhanach, its grace of form and the complexity of its twin tops are only

Binnein Beag from Binnein Mor; the Grey Corries beyond

revealed when approaching along the main ridge. In winter especially the view of the north-west top from the col between the two peaks is breathtaking in the juxta-position of the very steep, eastern slope in the fore-ground against the Alpine grace of the distant Carn Mor Dearg. Both slopes down into the col require care in icy conditions and neither the easy angles of the ridge east and west nor the drawing of the contours on the OS map prepare one for the sharp dip of 70m.

For the ascent of this peak by itself a stalker's path leaves the Land-rover track 1 kilo-metre north-east of Mamore Lodge, climbs up the east side of the Allt Coire na Ba and breaks off right in great zigzags to join the main ridge west of the top. A short-cut west can be made from the last arm of the zigzags but the angle is very steep.

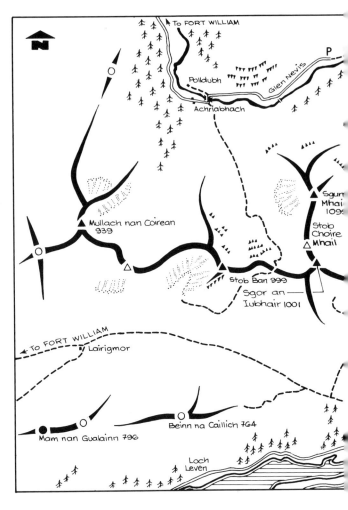

An Gearanach *(the complainer)* (982m)
An Garbhanach *(the rough one)* (975m)
Stob Coire a'Chairn *(peak of the corrie of the cairn)* (981m)

To approach the mountainous ridge formed by these three peaks from the south by way of Coire na Ba above Mamore Lodge is far less repaying than to start in Glen Nevis, from where the north-facing arc made with Am Bodach and Sgurr a'Mhaim makes for a magnificent outing with a strong mountaineering flavour. If they are to be included as part of a traverse of all the Mamore tops, the main ridge must be left at the distinct top of Stob Coire a'Chairn (981m), (not named on the OS 1: 50 000 map).

To reach the northern spurs of An Gearanach from Glen Nevis a path skirts below the buttress to the east of the Steall waterfall and turns up south into the fine

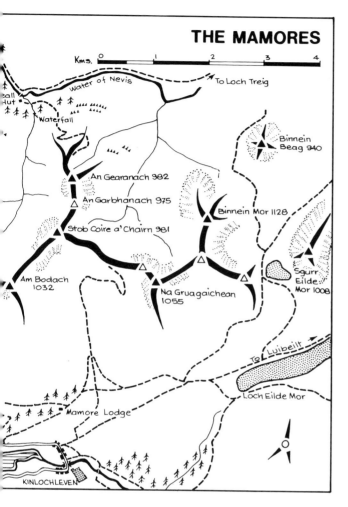

THE MAMORES

V-shaped corrie well named Coire Dubh for the frieze of dark rock on its west wall. The path continues up the east side of the burn to about the 400m level where the glen opens out and where its bed, in late spring, is a mass of blue hyacinth. After crossing the burn the path continues quite clearly and continuously up the west side in long zigzags which lead to the north ridge, and so to the top.

Beyond An Gearanach one can wander hands in pockets until the ridge narrows to an arete that demands care in icy conditions. An Garbhanach falls away to east and west abruptly in rocky slopes, but there is insufficient continuous rock for climbing. The descent of the south ridge of An Garbhanach and reascent to Stob Coire a'Chairn are steep enough to require care in winter.

Am Bodach *(the old man)* (1032m)

This peak is easily reached from the old military road 2 kilometres west of Mamore Lodge, a faint path on the left bank of the burn carrying up to the 750m level in Coire na h-Eirghe, from where zigzags continue to the bealach west of the peak. An alternative for descent is the south-south-east ridge which is sharply defined in its upper 100m, but which lower down becomes interrupted by shelves of quartzite dipping to the south-west with awkward and repeated drops from their lips. A line west-south-west from the col just north of a bump in the ridge at c. 740m — known as Sgorr an Fhuarain — avoids this tiresome ground and leads to the point on the old military road at 172 631 where a good path runs down through the indigenous woods to Kinlochleven school.

Binnein Mor from Stob Coire a'Chairn

The peak has an extensive east face which offers winter mountaineering of an easy standard, while steeper, though short lines will be found in the southern sector. When approaching along the main ridge in winter, its north-north-east ridge is quite steep and short sections can be awkward, particularly when iced.

Sgurr a'Mhaim *(peak of the large rounded hill)* (1099m)
Stob Choire a'Mhail (980m)
Sgor an Iubhair *(peak of the yew)* (1001m)
This is the longest and most significant arm stretching north from the main ridge. In summer it is an exhilarating scramble but in winter conditions, whether of snow or ice, there are two or three steps along the arete between Stob Choire a'Mhail and the main peak where inexperienced climbers might welcome a rope. (William Inglis Clark when traversing the arete in the summer of 1880 had to lower and raise a nervous companion by his coat collar at the steepish bits. The companion was also handicapped in wearing smooth-soled leather shoes).

While the three tops can be reached from Kinlochleven by way of the track mentioned under Am Bodach, it is far more repaying to approach from Glen Nevis where the splendour of An Steall and Sgurr a'Mhaim's eastern corrie can be appreciated. From Steall Cottage a way can be found up the steep slopes to the west of the waterfall, but without prior knowledge this route is not advised for descent.

An Gearanach above Steall waterfall

Once over the lip of the hanging valley, the way to the north-east ridge of Sgurr a'Mhaim is straightforward, but an alternative more in keeping with the expedition is to cross the foot of the eastern corrie, Coire nan Cnamh, to scramble up the east ridge. Whilst the romantic-sounding name of the corrie has the mundane translation of cud-chewing (cnamh), there is the more romantic inference of cattle driven here for summer pasture (remains of shielings is evidence of seasonal transhumance).

An obvious continuation of the ridge is to traverse in a great arc over Am Bodach and An Gearanach, though in winter such a day can take much longer than the map distance would indicate. An easier option for return to Glen Nevis, but just as delightful, is to descend the west ridge of Sgor an Iubhair and then into the glen of Coire a'Mhusgain where an excellent path winds through glacially scoured rocks and lower through indigenous woodland with fine views of the crags on either side.

For a simple ascent of Sgurr a'Mhaim, its north-west ridge provides a straightforward route from Achriabhach in Glen Nevis.

Stob Ban *(white peak)* (999 m)
From Glen Nevis and particularly from the pony track above Achintee, this peak presents a shapely cone, while in certain lights its summit cap of quartzite can look remarkably like snow. However its best aspect is seen from Sgurr a'Mhaim with a north-eastern complex of buttresses and gullies clustered beneath the summit.

Sgurr a'Mhaim, An Garbhanach and An Gearanach from Binnein Mor

The north ridge provides a simple ascent from Achriabhach and, once the steep section at mid-height is passed, the angle is easy enough for one to enjoy the fine views around the compass.

From the old military road about 5 kilometres west of Mamore Lodge the going is much rougher and a pleasanter route can be made by picking up the path between 600 and 700m and following it north-east beneath steep, coggly slopes almost to the bealach, from where the narrow east ridge can be climbed. In the craggy ground south of the east ridge an ice-fall forms in most winters that gives difficult though not serious climbing as escape routes are numerous.

Mullach nan Coirean *(summit of the corries)* (939m)

Suffering by contrast with its more mountainous neighbours to the east, this grassy, easy-angled hill has perhaps the finest views. Its subsidiary top, Meall a' Chaorainn (910m), has a particularly open view down Loch Linnhe, and from the north ridge of the main top the steep slopes of Ben Nevis and those of Sgurr a'Mhaim lend a sense of tremendous scale as they plunge into the rift of Glen Nevis. This north ridge, or its parallel north-north-east spur, is easily reached from Achriabhach where a track leads through the afforestation in long zig-zags. At about the 760m level on the north ridge, just beyond a bump known as Glas Chreag, there is a spring whose waters are cold on the hottest day.

Looking up the north ridge of Stob Choire a'Mhail

Beinn na Caillich (764 m)
Mam na Gualainn (796 m)
These two small hills between Loch Leven and the old military road also provide
splendid views, but are more distinguished for bearing a particularly fine stalker's
path that starts on the old military road about 2 kilometres west of Mamore Lodge
and maintains a stately progress in well engineered zigzags to the top of Beinn na
Caillich. Rather oddly this path, visible from miles away, is not shown in its entirety
on OS maps. Local people consider the first-named hill twice wronged by the
map-maker as it has always been known by Gaelic speakers as A'Chailleach (*the old
woman*) — as usual across a glen from Am Bodach (*the old man*).

PATHS AND WALKS

Glen Nevis to Corrour. The route from Fort William through Glen Nevis to Loch Treig
— and then beyond either north or south — has been in use for centuries and is
considered a right of way. It makes a splendid walk in itself apart from providing
approach in remote settings to the hills north and south of the glen. The West
Highland Line station at Corrour makes the through-route possible inside a day.
There are good paths as far as the old ruined cottage of Steall in the west, and from
Loch Treig to Corrour in the east, but in the central section the track is discontinuous
at best and it is well to remember that where the traces cross the Abhainn Rath just
east of Luibeilt the stepping stones are often under a metre of water.

Sgurr a'Mhaim from the col between Stob Ban and Sgor an Iubhair

The north-east face of Stob Ban

The path through the Nevis gorge is a delight in itself and it is a sobering thought that but for the efforts of a few individuals at the Public Inquiry in 1961, a hydro-electric scheme might well have inundated this magnificent ravine, described by W.H.Murray as a scene of Himalayan character. Clinging to the northern slopes of the gorge, the path winds through mixed woodland of small oak, Scots pine, and birch scrub: it gains little height once into the gorge and runs close enough to the torrent — the meaning of its Gaelic name, Eas an Tuil, is torrent — for the erosive power of the water to be appreciated.

The Water of Nevis retains its strong flow beyond the meadow flats and is not easily forded, but a wire bridge crosses it at 177 685 to Steall Cottage run as a club hut by the Lochaber Mountaineering Club. Within sight and sound of the cottage is the waterfall also known as Steall (pronounced stowl and meaning a deluge, a great quantity of liquid). It has a clear fall of 110m and is believed to have a greater volume than other higher falls in Scotland. During long spells of hard frost the fall does freeze, forming marvellous convolutions of ice pillars, between which further pillars can be seen. In these conditions it has been climbed but each account speaks of water running behind the ice and of a disconcerting increase in volume as height is gained. Steall receives enormous drainage from Coire a'Mhail and is a fitting outflow from one of the finest hanging valleys in Scotland.

Stob Choire a'Mhail from Sgurr a'Mhaim

For such a flat and boggy place, the watershed between the Water of Nevis and the Abhainn Rath is narrow, there being little more than 100 metres between the main watercourses while small tributaries to each are but a few metres apart. Such watersheds have been given the general name of corrom from the Gaelic word cothrom, meaning evenly weighted. The old Gaelic name for this watershed is Moinarmachd, meaning moss of the armour, said to have been derived from the shedding of weapons there by the troops of the Earl of Mar in retreat from the First Battle of Inverlochy. (21 kilometres from the end of the public road in Glen Nevis to Corrour Halt).

A section of the West Highland Way runs between Kinlochleven and Fort William and is well signposted at both ends. Roughly 7 kilometres from Kinlochleven a right of way cuts off to the left, skirts the western flanks of Mam na Gualainn and drops to Callert.

An eastern extension of the old military road between Kinlochleven and Fort William runs from Mamore Lodge to Luibeilt, a distance of about 13 kilometres. Mamore Lodge itself is easily reached by the signposted West Highland Way starting from the school just west of Kinlochleven, or a car can be driven up the unsurfaced road a little further west. The Land-rover track itself runs through grand scenery but it can be extended into a fine hillwalk reaching an altitude of c.700m but avoiding the high tops. A circuit of Sgurr Eilde Mor is made by following the stalker's path starting from the east end of Loch Eilde Mor. Though rough in places and crossing some wet ground, this circuit allows a taste of high mountain scenery.

CLIMBING

Some winter climbs have been made on the high crags that stretch across the north-eastern aspect of Stob Ban. The crags are extensive, steep and offer routes of up to 150m. They are best reached by the path from Achriabhach in Glen Nevis. A fine mountaineering route here is *East Ridge* (Grade II/III) on the North Buttress.

There are a few rock-climbs of indifferent quality high in the north-west corrie of Sgorr an Iubhair.

On the back wall of the east-facing corrie of Sgurr a'Mhaim there is a very clear exposure of folded schist, where there are several hard short rock-climbs.

All these climbs are described in *Ben Nevis: Rock and Ice Climbs*, by S.Richardson, R.Clothier and A.Walker, published by the Scottish Mountaineering Trust (1994).

Across the Water of Nevis and directly opposite to the carpark at the road end in Glen Nevis lies a north-westerly facing crag, Creag Uamh Shomhairle. It achieves a maximum height of 100m, is some 150 metres long and is composed of steep, sound schist. The many rock-climbs here are detailed in *Highlands Outcrops* edited by Kevin Howett and to be published by The Scottish Mountaineering Trust in 1995.

During periods of hard frost, Steall waterfall becomes a winter climb of quality (Grade III).

CHAPTER 9

Ben Nevis and Carn Mor Dearg

Ben Nevis	1344m	166 713
Carn Mor Dearg	1223m	177 722

ACCESS
There are two main points of access, one starting from the A82 and the other from the minor road up Glen Nevis. On the main road the distillery and the golf club provide points of access to the Allt a'Mhuilinn path. The carpark at the golf club is private and not for use by climbers. In Glen Nevis the bridge over the river at the youth hostel gives access to the Achintee path. Car-borne climbers wanting to start from Achintee itself should follow the road on the east side of the river which starts immediately north of the road bridge at Nevis Bridge.

TRANSPORT
Glasgow — Fort William train service.
Glasgow — Fort William bus service.
Both 7 days a week.

ACCOMMODATION
Apart from the accommodation mentioned in Chapter 8 (see p102) at Fort William, SYHA, Steall Cottage and campsites in Glen Nevis, there is the CIC Hut by the Allt a'Mhuilinn. This hut is under heavy demand, and early booking through an affiliated club is needed. A few dry, sheltered sites for camping will be found beside the Allt a'Mhuilinn, roughly 1 kilometre above the dam. The orange summit shelter and two others at 173 714 (Coire Leis) and 158 719 (Carn Dearg North-west) are intended as emergency bivouacs with maximum capacity of eight seated adults. That in Coire Leis is difficult to find in its boulder field and can be entirely covered by snow in heavy winters.

MAP
OS 1:50 000 Landranger Sheet 41

Whether seen from the road side or from other hills at great distance, the height and shape of Ben Nevis are unmistakable. What is not appreciated from either viewpoint is the detached nature of the Ben. Its slopes to the west and south plunge into Glen Nevis, where at Polldubh is produced the longest continuous slope in the British Isles — 1200m at an average angle of over 35 degrees. Then the steep slopes to the east and the northern precipices both drop for 700m and are interrupted only by the slender attachment of the Carn Mor Dearg Arete. Most southern viewpoints do not give a clear impression of the overall steepness of the Ben and only in a narrow corridor to the west-north-west, where the pony track winds its way, does this angle

Carn Mor Dearg and Ben Nevis from Corpach

relent. However from the east and west a proper impression is gained and the popular viewpoint from Banavie shows the aptness of Robert Southey's description 'looking as if it had been riven from the summit to the base, and half of it torn away'.

For some years after attempts began to measure the heights of Scottish hills, other contenders such as Ben Macdui were thought by some to be the highest and though toward the end of the 18th century the Reverend George Skene Keith decided, on the basis of his own and his son's surveys, in favour of Ben Nevis, it was not until 1847 that Ordnance Survey measurements on Ben Macdui finally deposed the latter. Early travellers began making the ascent in the 18th century and in 1818 Keats compared it to the 'task of mounting ten St. Pauls without the convenience of a staircase'; but it was only in 1880 that the citizens of Fort William accorded to Wm.W.Naismith and two friends the accolade of 'first ascent without guides'. From about this date the ascent began to gather popular interest and once the pony track from Achintee to the summit had been constructed in 1883 for the servicing of the Observatory, each summer saw a regular stream of tourists. Ten years later the first proposal was made for a railway to the summit, and various schemes were floated during the following twenty years. Published plans were for 4¾ miles of rack railway with a maximum gradient of 1 in 2.62 on the slopes above the Red Burn.

The establishment of the Observatory and its 20-year life make a fascinating story most engagingly told by Wm.T.Kilgour in his book *Twenty Years on Ben Nevis* (1905).

The Ben Nevis Observatory in winter (c.1903)

To a large extent the Observatory was the child of Clement L.Wragge (depicted in newspapers of the day as the 'inclement rag') who with the support of the Scottish Meteorological Society spent two years in compiling meteorological data with the aim of demonstrating the value of a summit observatory. From 1st June until 1st November, in both 1881 and 1882, he made a daily ascent to the summit starting at 4.00 a.m. and recording *en route* data at several stations. He used the old track from Lochy Bridge — the site of the distillery — that followed above the woods on the eastern side of Allt Coire an Lochain to the Lochan Meall an t-Suidhe, and though this path is shown on the 1877 First Edition of the Ordnance Survey One Inch to One Mile map as continuing to the summit, it must have been rough going above the lochan. His dedication was soon rewarded and the Observatory was opened in October 1883.

Wm.T.Kilgour's book was published with the intention of raising public support for the reopening of the Observatory and is far from being a dry, scientific record. (Determined enquirers should find a copy in the larger reference libraries.) Statistics, however, it did contain and they have a fascination of their own — 240 inches of rainfall in 1898 (extrapolated to give a figure of 240,000 tons of water falling on the summit area); mean annual temperature 31.4 degrees F (for the same 11 year period 47.4 degrees F at Fort William); worst gales, between 80 and 150 m.p.h., recorded from the south-east quadrant; lightning struck the Observatory on several occasions (in June 1895 fusing the telegraph apparatus — now in the possession of the Scottish Meteorological Society — and setting the wainscotting on fire). Even more interesting, though, is the insight given by the chapter entitled 'Some entries from the log' and a random sample indicates something of the personal regret felt by Kilgour at the closure of the Observatory.

1884 Jan. 6th — Everything covered with ice, either solid or crystalline. At 4 h. thermometer box was frozen so fast that it needed a chisel to open it. At 10h., some snowflakes about 1 inch diameter were observed.

Feb 16th — Owing to storm, every observation taken by two observers roped together. At 20 h. as soon as Mr. Omond went outside door of snow porch, he was lifted off his feet and blown back against Mr. Rankin, who was knocked over.

Mar. 1st — Snow porch at outer door is now about 33 ft long, with a rise of about 12 feet in its floor.

1886 Apr. 21st — Meteor as bright as first mag. star seen at 23h. 5 m. It went from Pole Star towards W.N.W. horizon, and left a train about 10 degrees long at a height of about 50 degrees, which remained visible for a second.

1887 Oct. 29th — At 1h. 5m. St. Elmo's Fire was seen in jets 3 to 4 inches long on every point on the top of the tower, and on the top of the kitchen chimney. Owing to the number of jets on each cup of the anemometer, this instrument was quite ablaze. On the kitchen chimney, the jets on the top of the cowl were vertical, and those on the lower edge of same horizontal. While standing on office roof watching the display, the observer felt an electric sensation at his temples, and the second assistant observed that his companion's hair was glowing. At 1 h. 15 m. the accompanying hissing noise ceased, and the fire vanished from every point the same instant.

1888 Sep. 19th — Very fine sunrise. Just before the sun rose, long pink streamers were seen diverging from E. horizon, passing over-head, and converging to W., where a rosy belt topped the earth shadow.

1890 Feb. 20th — The crystals on the anemometer were today fully 7 feet long.

1891 Apr. 13th — Beautiful snow crystals falling in the afternoon; not in any measurable quantity, only a few now and again; are perfect hexagons, some in star and others in glassy disc shape. Most had small motes of dry snow attached to them, and these motes were always on one side only.

1892 Sep. 21st — A Magnificent aurora seen from 20h. till midnight. There were three distinct arches from W. and S. to N.E., with shifting streamers shooting to the zenith.

Though the descent of Tower Ridge on 3rd September 1892 is generally considered to be the first mountaineering venture on the Ben, Wm.W.Naismith reported (SMCJ, I, p221) a discussion in 1889 with the Observatory staff of a climbable gully in the northern precipices, and mountaineering ability among the staff is evidenced by a report in Kilgour's book that 'Mr. Rankin and two others descended the Tower Ridge, crossing The Gap, with a couple of cameras'.

The north face of Ben Nevis

Snow can, and does, fall on any day of the year on the Ben and rarely in recent years has the snowfield at the foot of Observatory Gully completely disappeared. However, whilst 1933 was reported 'to be the first year for a century in which such a snowfield did not last through the summer' (the Observatory staff during the years 1883-1904 had considered it and other drifts to be permanent and, even earlier, observers such as Bishop Pocock [1760], Wilkinson [1787] and Thomas Pennant [1796] spoke of snow lasting throughout the year) Professor Gordon Manley's careful survey (SMCJ, XXX, p4) takes the cautious view that the mean temperature would need to drop by 2 degrees C for 15 years to produce a budding glacier. He goes on to show the unlikelihood of such a sequence and concludes that late snowfall in March and April is the cause of snowfields lasting through the summer.

Like the group of superb cliffs in Glen Coe, Ben Nevis owes its tough andesite to the ancient foundering of a great mass of schist overlaid with thick layers of lava, which were subsequently protected from erosion and now stand proud above the Allt a'Mhuilinn. This durable rock covers an area of about 1.6 kilometres in diameter and extends from Carn Dearg North-west to include the summit area and the great cirque of cliffs above the Allt a'Mhuilinn. It is encircled by a sea of granite that reaches down into Glen Nevis and produces the pink boulders that litter Carn Mor Dearg. Although not as rough in texture as the rhyolite of Buachaille Etive Mor, the

The summit of Ben Nevis at the top of Tower Ridge

rock on the northern cliffs is ideal for climbing, weathering to produce positive features and, on the easier routes such as the main ridges, a good supply of incut holds. Away from the ridges, however, route-finding problems are of a high order and particularly on the great north-west face of North-east Buttress — named the Orion Face by J.H.B.Bell — the easiest line is rarely obvious.

THE HILLS

Ben Nevis *(possibly from an old Gaelic word meaning venomous)* (1344m)
There is no need to make the claim that one's granny could walk up the pony track — she can be seen complete in high-heeled sandals on a clear, summer's day. Before her have trundled wheel-barrows, motor-cycles, a car and even a piano. Recent improvements to the track from Achintee and to the one joining it from the youth hostel have made the ascent to the Lochan Meall an t'Suidhe an easy walk indeed, but beyond, the crossing of the Red Burn and the zigzags above are not suited to sandals. In winter descent the area above the Red Burn deserves a cautious approach as the ground drops away steeply to the left and, unless visibility is good, the crossing point of the deep channel made by the Red Burn is not obvious. Again caution is needed when crossing the summit area in winter, for where the summer path flattens out near the top it veers away from the deep indentation made by

The North-east Buttress

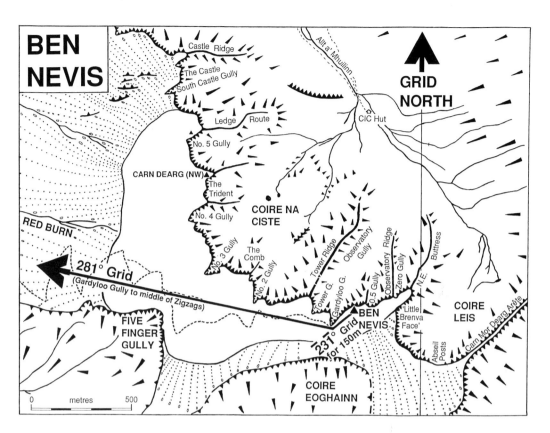

Gardyloo Gully, but in winter there is a tendency to cut across this angle; such a line goes perilously close to the gully whose cornice has been measured as extending 5.2 metres horizontally. Again in winter the descent bearing from the summit of 231 degrees grid for 150m then 281 degrees grid has to be held or there is a danger of walking onto the steep slopes at the top of Five Finger Gully. Winter navigational errors in this area, usually due to strong winds allied to very poor visibility, have led to frequent and usually fatal accidents.

For those seeking a walking route away from the summer crowds on the pony track, the steep slopes immediately above the carpark at the Glen Nevis road end, though lessening little in angle, lead to a fine ridge that gives views west into the enormous bowl of Coire Eoghainn and east to the long ridge of Aonach Mor, while higher, once it runs into the slopes above the Carn Mor Dearg Arete, the splendid complexity of the Little Brenva Face (i.e. the south-east face of North-east Buttress) can be studied. Close under the summit near to the head of this ridge at 167 712, there is a spring that very rarely runs dry.

On a clear day, preferably in winter or under a north-westerly airstream, there is undoubtedly an extensive view from the summit and not even the eye of faith is needed to pick out the Cuillin, the Paps of Jura, or even the Ochils in the south-east.

Carn Dearg Buttress (centre) and Castle Ridge (right)

However, such a view is as nothing compared to the splendour of the great cirque of crags above the Allt a'Mhuilinn and the three hours taken to reach the head of the glen is amply repaid as one wanders ant-like under the glacier-smoothed apron beneath Coire na Ciste, turreted high on the skyline with the Comb and Trident buttresses.

There are three walking routes into the glen of the Allt a'Mhuilinn. The easiest going will be found on the track from Achintee to the Lochan Meall an t'Suidhe, past which to the east faint and boggy paths lead north across the open bealach to a sudden drop. From this point a more easily identified path makes a descending traverse across the steep slopes beneath Carn Dearg's north face. Both other paths converge at a dam across the Allt a'Mhuilinn, the first starting at the southern edge of the distillery and the second 1 kilometre north where a path leads under the railway from the golf clubhouse. Neither path allows access dry-shod with the crucial section occurring a little above the old tramway. The northerly option sports a particularly well developed bog at this point that has swallowed boulders, old railway sleepers and other aids that have been carried up in attempts to avoid knee-deep plunges. While the pony track from Achintee involves the greatest distance, in anything but a drought it is certainly the most comfortable approach.

With the existence of a comprehensive climbers' guide, only those easier routes that are obvious topographical features will be described. From the paths beside the

At the top of the Comb, the Great Tower behind

Allt a'Mhuilinn there is a satisfying complexity to the crags above and many features cannot be seen from this depth. All four main ridges are, however, easily identified in clear weather. Castle Ridge, the first, is directly above the point where the Allt a'Mhuilinn splits in two for a short distance (165 725) and, if the first 100m are avoided to the left by scrambling up the bed of North Castle Gully, its ascent need involve no more than Moderate scrambling. Once past the CIC Hut (the property of the Scottish Mountaineering Club) bouldery slopes rise steeply to the foot of the Douglas Boulder, which forms a shapely cone at the foot of Tower Ridge and is noteworthy as a viewpoint. It can be circumvented by easy scrambling up either its East or West Gully, but both are unpleasantly loose and the obvious ridge overlooking West Gully — South-west Ridge (170m, Moderate) — makes a better route.

Tower Ridge itself is a mountaineering route of great length where difficulties and variety increase with height, but no pitch is harder than Difficult. Views both near and far become more spectacular as one progresses and those on their first visit will see ahead at the Tower Gap a degree of exposure that belies the Difficult grading.

In winter Tower Ridge is a magnificent expedition fully deserving its Grade III designation. It can be very time-consuming and knowledge of the ground from a previous summer ascent is a great advantage. There are three points worthy of mention: starting from Observatory Gully on the craggy slopes to the left of East Gully is usually the quickest approach, particularly if icy conditions prevail. In most conditions the easiest climb- ing will be found to the left of the crest even when there is a steep ice-fall left of the Little Tower. An escape into Observatory Gully can be made by continuing on the level of the Eastern Traverse at the Great Tower, but those then descending, perhaps in darkness, should traverse directly across to the eastern side of the gully to avoid a fall line above the steep ice of Tower Scoop.

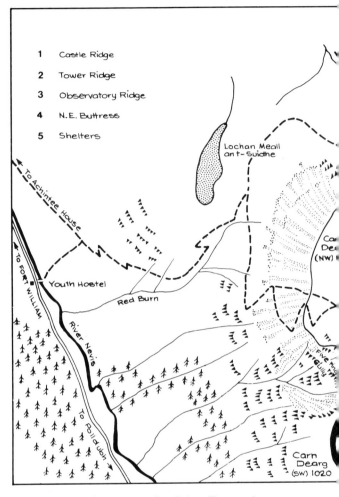

1   Castle Ridge

2   Tower Ridge

3   Observatory Ridge

4   N.E. Buttress

5   Shelters

When the Douglas Boulder has been skirted Observatory Ridge comes into view as a buttress pro- truding out into Observatory Gully and soaring up to taper and flatten into the face. Zero Gully is seen as a deep recess to the left of the ridge and the vast wall to the left again — the Orion Face — imparts a sense of enormous scale. Although they are of roughly the same order of difficulty, the technical standard of some pitches on Observatory Ridge is a little harder than those found on Tower Ridge. Also route-finding is more of a factor on the former and if the easiest line is not found, more pitches of Very Difficult than necessary will be met. Both ridges have their share of debris on ledges and with its higher angle, falling stones, usually moved by human agency, have caused accidents on Observatory Ridge. This route is almost as fine an outing as Tower Ridge and though shorter by 200m, most parties new to the area seem to take longer on it.

The stark and challenging outline of North-east Buttress is unmistakable from the upper reaches of the Allt a'Mhuilinn, as is its First Platform. The most obvious and direct route to the ridge from Observatory Gully — *Slingsby's Chimney* (Moderate, 125m) — has a surprisingly awkward and usually wet pitch at mid-height and *Raeburn's 18 Minute Route* (Moderate, 140m) following the wall north of

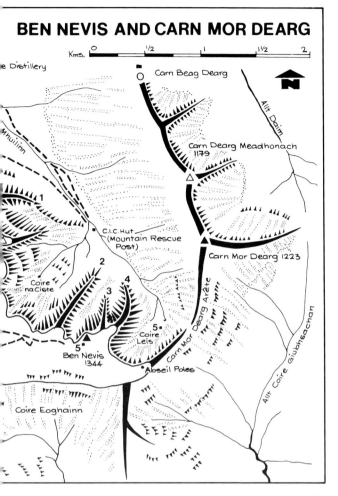

BEN NEVIS AND CARN MOR DEARG

Slingsby's Chimney is pleasanter. Above the First Platform sound, steep rock at Very Difficult standard can be followed by keeping to the right of the broad crest. Most of the ground to the left offers easier and more broken climbing. At the Second Platform the ridge narrows and leads *via* a steep wall to the Mantrap. This short, bulging nose is always awkward and doubly so when wet; it has defeated parties in winter. There is an avoiding movement but as this takes a line to the right of great exposure and involves crossing slabs at Difficult standard, its escape value is dubious and those setting out to climb the Northeast Buttress should consider it as the hardest of the four classic ridges on Ben Nevis.

A good introduction to winter mountaineering and one quickly reached for a day's outing from the carpark beyond Polldubh, will be found in *Bob-run*. Lying in the corner where the Brenva Face turns to meet the Carn Mor Dearg Arete, and starting at a height of over 1000m, it is a natural ice-trap and holds good climbing conditions from December to April. It is often bulging with ice when other straight- forward routes such as the Castle gullies show only sad remnants and it is less prone to avalanche than the easy gullies, though care should be taken in spring when early-morning sunshine floods the top of the Brenva Face and causes stone-fall onto the longer routes of *Cresta* and *Slalom*. In approach from the south, the rim of Coire Leis should be left a little way above the abseil posts and a descending traverse made over steep snow. There are usually two ice-pitches, one at the foot and another above mid-height and, though not a serious route, it can feel extravagant for a Grade II.

Winter descent to the Allt a'Mhuilinn is problematical and a careful study of the topography before a first visit is well worthwhile. The shortest descent and the easiest gully is Number 4 which lies almost 1 kilometre north-west and c. 170m below the summit cairn. This bland statement hides — as usually does the cloud — the left-curving arc that has to be traversed and the confusing terrain where the descent flattens out at Number 3 Gully. However the latter's uppermost slopes are split by a distinctive and flat-headed sheaf of rock and a little beyond, Number 4 should be identifiable by a metal marker post (only very occasionally is this covered by snow). Often a short abseil over an overhanging cornice is worthwhile from this post.

Another descent used as much for continuing along the Carn Mor Dearg Arete as for descending to the Allt a'Mhuilinn also demands careful navigation for it goes close to the convex slope above the headwall of Coire Leis. With its south-eastern exposure, the deep snow cover on this slope is often converted to ice. To reach the Arete a bearing of 130 degrees (true) should be followed for 400 metres from the orange-painted mountain-rescue shelter; then turn due east and further descent soon leads to the flattening at c. 1150m where the line of abseil posts indicates the way down into Coire Leis. Some posts are not secure and others are missing, however in very icy conditions inexperienced parties might be glad of what remains. Certainly all other options for descent into Coire Leis from the Arete are steeper.

Obviously some degree of winter mountaineering experience is necessary for these last two descents to be accomplished with comfort and safety. But it is just as important for those descending by the pony track to have a map and compass and the ability to use them in adverse conditions.

Carn Mor Dearg *(big red hill)* (1223m)
Carn Dearg Meadhonach *(middle red hill)* (1179m)
From the Mamores to the south or when approaching from the north by way of the Allt Daim, the winter view of Carn Mor Dearg is positively Alpine. It forms an elongated, south to north ridge with moderate slopes falling to the Allt a'Mhuilinn but much steeper slopes interrupted by three fine ridges to the east. The southern tail of the hill's spine curls round to form the Carn Mor Dearg Arete, by which it is joined to Ben Nevis. With its great height — 1058m at its lowest — and with its genuinely sharp crest, the Arete often forms a tight-rope of neve and is, in such conditions, an exhilarating outing. Both sides of the Arete fall away very steeply indeed and though no definite lines present themselves, there is winter mountaineering among the crags above Coire Leis and also on the east face. To traverse from Carn Mor Dearg to Ben Nevis on a clear winter's day is an outing unique in the British Isles, for the vast spread of crag between North-east Buttress and Carn Dearg Buttress is perfectly complemented by the slender elegance of the Arete.

The length of the summit ridge is composed of a pink granite and lies within the ring of granite surrounding the Ben Nevis core of ancient lava. Bouldery slopes cover the crest and make the Arete itself in summer — so aptly described by Geikie as 'a

Carn Dearg Meadhonach from the east

mass of ruin, like the shattered foundations of an ancient rampart' — a place for nimble feet.

Most ascents of Carn Mor Dearg are made by way of the Allt a'Mhuilinn, however the hill can be reached from Glen Nevis starting at Old Steall and following the course of the Allt Coire Giubhsachan. This approach leads to the foot of the east ridge which is well-defined and often in winter forms its own arete. There are two other easterly ridges and that leading directly to the summit of Carn Dearg Meadhonach, with a pinnacle near the top, makes a fine winter route.

At various points from the ridge between the two main tops a very long glissade of up to 500m can be made down to the Allt a'Mhuilinn. Frequently in spring the right conditions occur for this exhilarating plunge and, if a lucky course leads into one of the drainage channels, the downward swoop can be as brief as nerve allows.

CLIMBING

Walking up the path beside the Allt a'Mhuilinn (with right and left being as the climber views), the North Wall of Castle Ridge is the first obvious feature. Its scrappy-looking face has yielded some excellent long winter routes and a few rock climbs. From the obvious terrace at about half-height the renowned *Lobby Dancer* (Grade VI,6) follows a prominent groove.

Early morning at the CIC Hut

Beyond Castle Ridge and deeply recessed is *The Castle* (Very Difficult; Grade III) bounded left and right by *South Castle Gully* (Grade I) and *North Castle Gully* (Grade II). The Castle as a winter route is a notorious avalanche risk.

Tucked in to the left of Castle Ridge is the slender Raeburn's Buttress, and the route of that name makes a good mixed winter climb (Grade IV,5). To the left again *Boomer's Requiem* (Grade V,5) is a fine route following the left branch of a gully system.

Next to the left is the huge projecting buttress of Carn Dearg with many long hard rock climbs including classics such as *Bullroar* (HVS) and *Centurion* (HVS), and several equally fine routes in the E1 to E5 class, *Torro* (E2) and *Agrippa* (E5). At the back of The North Wall of Castle Ridge, *Harrison's Climb Direct* (Grade IV,4) is a superb ice climb, while to the left of Carn Dearg's front *Route II Direct* is an equally fine outing in summer and winter (Severe; Grade VI,6). Left again is the obvious ice smear of *The Curtain* (Grade IV,5) probably the most popular ice climb on Ben Nevis.

Beyond Carn Dearg is the huge bay of Coire na Ciste which is bounded to the left by Tower Ridge. The first obvious feature is the deeply recessed *Number Five Gully* (Grade I) an easy winter descent. Above it to the right is Number Five Gully Buttress with an easy descent route in summer, *Ledge Route* (Moderate), although route-finding is not straightforward. The gully wall of this buttress has several rock

Evening descent from the summit to the Carn Mor Dearg Arete

climbs ranging from Severe to E1. Moving left again, next are the Trident buttresses and *Number Four Gully* (Grade I). The latter provides the easiest winter descent from the plateau. On South Trident Buttress an excellent rock climb can be made by linking *1944 Route* (Severe) and *Pinnacle Arete* (Very Difficult). There are several harder rock climbs and some middle-grade winter routes on the three Trident buttresses.

Next left is Creag Coire na Ciste which is a winter crag only with routes mainly in the middle grade. It is noted for the size of its cornices. Beside it is the deep recess of *Number Three Gully* (Grade I) and then Number Three Gully Buttress with its abutting Sioux Wall. On the latter are some fine hard rock climbs, *The Knuckleduster*, *Last Stand* and *Sioux Wall* (all HVS) and on the former one of the best winter routes at Grade III, Number Three Gully Buttress, and two excellent harder routes in Two Step Corner (Grade V,5) and Thompson's Route (Grade IV,4).

The classic Green Gully (Grade IV,4) separates *Number Three Gully Buttress* from The Comb which has one of the harder mixed winter routes in *Tower Face of the Comb* (Grade VI,6), surprisingly first climbed in 1959. Another classic gully, *Comb Gully* (Grade IV,4) lies to the left of Comb Buttress, and then the steepest of the easy gullies is *Number Two Gully* (Grade II).

Reaching the summit of Ben Nevis at the top of Observatory Ridge

Next is Number Two Gully Buttress which contains several hard winter routes and one good route at Grade III. The rock here is not ideal for rock climbing.

Beyond is the long flank of Tower Ridge seamed by three classic winter routes, *Glover's Chimney* (Grade III,4) leading to the Tower Gap, *Italian Climb* (Grade III) and *Vanishing Gully* (Grade V,5). Moving round the Douglas Boulder leads into the very open Observatory Gully. At its head lies Gardyloo Buttress with its intimidating winter line, *Smith's Route* (Grade V,5).

Moving round onto the eastern flank of Observatory Gully, from which most routes lead up to the crest of North-East Buttress, the first feature is Indicator Wall where there are some of the hardest modern winter routes which involve climbing on thin ice. Examples are *Stormy Petrel* and *Albatross* (both Grade VII,6). At the left edge of Indicator Wall is an easier but enjoyable winter route in *Good Friday Climb* (Grade III).

Observatory Buttress is the next feature and the rock climb of that name is an enjoyable Very Difficult whilst the winter ascent is much more serious at Grade V,5. On the east wall of the buttress there is one fine rock climb, *Rubicon Wall* (Severe) and two very hard modern winter routes, *Match Point* (Grade VI,6) and *Point Blank* (Grade VII,6).

Next left is the famous winter line of *Point Five Gully* (Grade V,5). On the wall beyond there are two good winter routes, *Galactic Hitchhiker* (Grade VI,5) and *Hadrian's Wall Direct* (Grade V,5).

This wall butts against the very prominent Observatory Ridge, and the route of that name makes a fine climb both in summer (Very Difficult) and in winter (Grade IV,4). In the south-east corner beside Observatory Ridge lies another famous winter route, *Zero Gully* (Grade V,4). To its left is the major feature of The Orion Face which abounds in long hard climbs. A selection includes the excellent rock climb, *Slav Route* (Severe), which makes a very long winter route (Grade VI,5), *Journey into Space* (Grade VII,6), *Orion Direct* (Grade V,5) and *The Long Climb* (VS).

As the flank loses height, the Minus Face appears with several hard summer and winter lines, pride of place going to *Minus Two Gully* (Grade V,5), known as the best of the Nevis gullies.

Next occurs the easy gully of *Slingsby's Chimney* leading to the First Platform, and on the buttress below the First Platform Raeburn's Route is a particularly clean and sustained rock climb (Severe).

Round on the south-east face of North-East Buttress — The Little Brenva Face — there are some middle-grade winter routes, notably *Cresta* (Grade III). *North-East Buttress* (Very Difficult in summer and Grade IV,4 in winter) itself makes a fine mountaineering expedition.

All the winter and summer climbs are described in *Ben Nevis: Rock and Ice Climbs*, by S.Richardson, R.Clothier and A.Walker, published by the Scottish Mountaineering Trust (1994). Low-lying climbs in Glen Nevis — mainly on the crags above Polldubh — will be described in *Highland Outcrops* to be published by the same publisher in 1995.

References

Twenty Years on Ben Nevis, Wm.T.Kilgour (Ernest Press 1985)

Climber's Guide to Ben Nevis, G.G.MacPhee (SMC 1936 op).

This edition contained the complete summit panorama in four folding sections, originally drawn by James E. Shearer in 1895.

Climber's Guide to Ben Nevis, J.R.Marshall (SMC 1979 op).

Mountaineering in Scotland, W.H.Murray. Diadem Compendium edition, 1982.

A Progress in Mountaineering, J.H.B.Bell (op).

The SMC Journal in the last 100 years has hundreds of notes, references, and articles about Ben Nevis. The following is a personal selection.

Vol. III, p323. *Hospitality in the Observatory after the second ascent of North-east Buttress.* Wm.Brown.

Vol. V, p45. *Hospitality at 8.30pm. New Year 1898 in the Observatory.* '16 hours on the Ben', W.I.Clark.

Vol. V, p87. Note on a winter climb on the west face of the Carn Mor Dearg Arete.

Vol VI, p213. *The Observatory Ridge*, H. Raeburn. First ascent (solo) 1901.

Vol. VII, p. 195. *From Sea to Summit*, H. Raeburn. A fine article that mentions in passing the first, solo ascent of Observatory Buttress.

Vol. IX, p153. *A Scottish Ice Climb*, H. Raeburn, The first ascent in 1906 of Green Gully.

Vol. XXI, p200. *Zero Gully*, J.H.B.Bell. Article describing an ascent combining Slav Route and Zero Gully, and an indication of what winter climbing standards were in 1936.

Vol. XXII, p367. *A Ben Nevis Constellation of Climbs*, J.H.B.Bell. A summary of the author's outstanding exploration of the Orion Face.

Vol. XXVII, p107. *Modern Scottish Winter Climbing*, J.R.Marshall. A definitive summary at the time — 1962.

Vol. XXX, p4. *Scotland's Permanent Snows*, G. Manley.

CHAPTER 10

The Aonachs and the Grey Corries

Aonach Mor	1221m	193 730
Aonach Beag	1234m	196 715
Stob Choire Claurigh	1177m	262 739
Stob Coire an Laoigh	1115m	240 725
Sgurr Choinnich Mor	1095m	227 714
Stob Ban	977m	266 724
Cruach Innse	857m	280 763
Sgurr Innse	808m	290 748
Stob Coire Easain	1116m	308 730
Stob a' Choire Mheadhoin	1106m	316 736

ACCESS
From the north via the minor road between Spean Bridge and Insh on the south side of the River Spean.
From the south via the Glen Nevis road.

TRANSPORT
Glasgow — Fort William train service stopping at Tulloch, Roybridge and Spean Bridge.
Glasgow — Fort William bus service.
Local bus service, June — September, Fort William — Polldubh.
Local bus service Fort William — Spean Bridge.

ACCOMMODATION
Hotels, guesthouses and bed and breakfast at Fort William, Spean Bridge and Roybridge.
Climbers' hut at Steall, Glen Nevis (Lochaber Mountaineering Club).
Caravan and camp sites at Inverroy and Roybridge.
Self-catering chalets at Roybridge.
Youth hostel in Glen Nevis.
Bothies at Lairig Leacach (283 737), Staoineag (295 678) and Meanach (268 685). These are small cottages which only provide simple shelter for small parties.

MAP
OS 1:50 000 Landranger Sheet 41

Lying between Glen Nevis and Glen Spean, these hills form to Ben Nevis a lower ridge stretching eastwards, with one deep gap at the Lairig Leacach, to the boundary formed by Loch Treig. Most of the Grey Corries are built of the same quartzite that gives such distinctive whiteness to the bare summits of the Mamores, and thus the name Grey Corries, but the northerly spurs do not form quite such sharp aretes as those in the Mamores. The great forest of Leanachan to the north restricts access in this arc, but an excellent track through the Lairig Leacach is compensation to the north-east, and the forest can be penetrated from the west at Torlundy. Still on the northern fringes there are two fine rivers, the Cour and the Spean, which are both worthy of visits in their own right. While the first can be followed in descent from the hills, (and is described later), the Spean deserves a half-day, preferably in spring or autumn for appreciation of the deciduous woodland along its southern shore.

Access to these hills from Glen Nevis involves, with the exception of Aonach Beag, both great distance and rough ground, though a camp near the watershed or use of Steall Cottage makes the traverse of all the tops between the Lairig Leacach and Aonach Beag feasible. For those planning use of the West Highland Line — and the station at Spean Bridge is convenient for approach to the Lairig Leacach — there is a useful adjunct in the summer bus service (June-September only) plying between Fort William and Polldubh (phone 0397-2373 for details).

THE HILLS

Aonach Mor *(big ridge)* (1221m)
Aonach Beag *(little ridge)* (1234m)
Somewhat overshadowed in their proximity to Ben Nevis, these hills have a pleasant air of seclusion for those who wander into their vast eastern bays. In spring the series of corries beneath Aonach Beag and Aonach Mor's southern shoulder are a wonderland where great snowfields push snouts into the corrie-beds and form moraines, where burns spout over ice-falls in the ravines that have been scored deeply into the lower cliffs, and where ranks of *roches moutonnées* point their striae north-east. On the headwalls masses of rock occur apparently haphazardly, sometimes as isolated buttresses beneath the cornice rim and less often as ridges reaching up to breach it, but all of mountaineering interest and mainly composed of compact rough schist.

Aonach Mor is of greater bulk than its higher neighbour, and thus its Gaelic name given before the advent of the Ordnance Survey. With the snow-gathering ground of the extensive summit plateau the eastern corries of Aonach Mor hold snow throughout most years. It is claimed that Roybridge railway station is the only one in Britain from which snow can be seen all year round. Great quantities of snow also last into most summers in the open corrie to the north containing the Allt an t-Sneachda (*burn of snow*), although local people know it as Coire nan Geadh (*corrie of the goose*) from the shape of the snow remnants that forms in most summers. This is the site of the development of mechanised skiing uplift completed in 1990, since when it is now impossible to climb this hill from the north without being aware of the intrusion. The development caters for 3500 people with a gondola, chairlift and tows, and has a considerable visual impact. For those with insufficient time to follow the long southern approach, there is a good footpath from the ski slope carpark, which can be followed round at the 640m level to the north-north-west edge of the northern slope, which leads easily to the summit plateau. Alternatively, from the carpark, tracks wind south-south-west through the forest and into the glen of the

Aonach Beag from Ben Nevis

Allt Diam. This glen leads to the bealach between Aonach Mor and Carn Mor Dearg, and then up a steep slope east to Aonach Mor's south ridge.

Despite its great area, the summit plateau of Aonach Mor is a ridge clearly defined by very steep slopes falling on both sides throughout its 2 kilometre length. In thick weather, and particularly under snow, its featureless character is confusing and finding both the bealach for continuation south onto Aonach Beag and the only safe winter descent — from 192 722 west to the bealach under Carn Mor Dearg — needs careful compass work.

When climbing Aonach Mor from the north, return over Stob an Cul Choire and its northern top, Tom na Sroine (918m), which are in effect a north-eastern arm of the larger hill, makes a pleasant circuit, though in icy conditions descent of Aonach Mor's east ridge demands some mountaineering technique if not a rope. The bealach at the foot of this ridge is a spectacular place. Facing south, the ground drops away steeply into An Cul Choire above which towers the outline of Aonach Beag's North-east Ridge while closer at hand a steep slope sweeps up toward the summit plateau and a narrow, rocky arete is immediately above on the left.

The ridge between Stob an Cul Choire and Tom na Sroine is narrow and the steeper ground beneath the crest to the south and east develops into crags which as the ridge turns north become very steep indeed. From the bump on the ridge known as Stob Coire an Fhir Dhuibh a wall of schist stretches for perhaps 1 kilometre but rarely attains more height than 100m.

Descending north from Tom na Sroine, there is a small dam across the Allt Choille-rais at the forest edge. Less than 100 metres lower a new Land-rover track winds down through the afforestation to the line of the old tramway. From there the ski development carpark is quickly reached.

Joined to its neighbour Aonach Mor at a high bealach of c.1050m, Aonach Beag has nevertheless a different and more complex form. It differs also in being composed mainly of ancient schists whereas Aonach Mor falls within the great circle of granite surrounding Ben Nevis. A straightforward

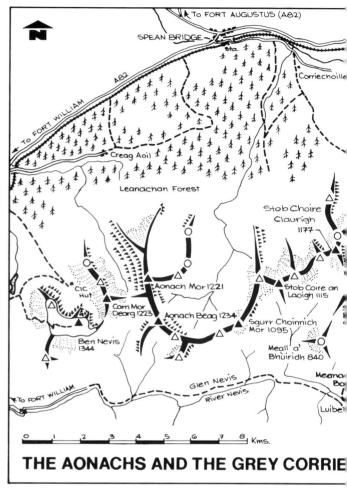

THE AONACHS AND THE GREY CORRIE

ascent can be made from Glen Nevis turning up north at the ruin of Old Steall where a bridge crosses the Allt Coire Giubhsachan. Above, open slopes lead north-east to the series of tops, starting with the sharp cone of Sgurr a' Bhuic so prominent in views from the east, and continuing over the twin tops of Stob Coire Bhealaich. Parts of this ridge are steep enough to require care when icy conditions prevail, and its upper part including the summit plateau builds out enormous cornices above the north-eastern face.

The mountaineering potential on Aonach Beag was recognised almost a century ago by Norman Collie who recommended its North-east Ridge to William Naismith. Naismith very properly made the first ascent in winter (April 1895) with Maclay and Thomson, for it is under these conditions that the ridge becomes a fine expedition (Grade III, 460m). Not least of its attractions is its remoteness, and the approach

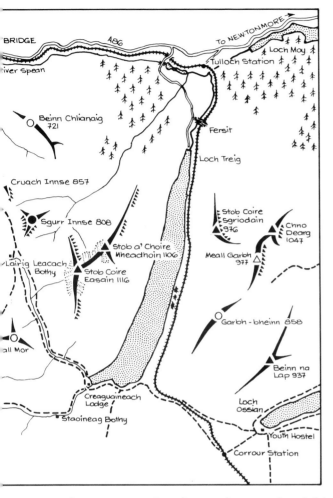

from upper Glen Nevis of over three hours makes the sight of another party a rare occurrence. In its later stages this approach has confused and even confounded many parties for, in poor visibility, picking a good line across the corrie to find the foot of the ridge is no easy matter.

From Old Steall it is quicker to follow the line of the path east for 2 kilometres before striking north to the bealach just west of Sgurr Choinnich Beag. (Traversing the southern slopes of Sgurr a'Bhuic over ground seamed by deep drainage channels is exasperatingly slow). If a clear view can be had from the bealach a terrace will be discerned traversing the corrie at the 700m level, i.e 30m beneath the level of the bealach, but the ridge itself is not properly seen from this point. In thick weather a better policy is to descend 100m from the bealach and take a line north-north-west across three burns, the second and third of which are ravine-like. At the fourth burn the North-east Ridge is immediately above. The apparent map distance of 2 kilometres across the corrie is no measure, and unless conditions are good both underfoot and overhead, a minimum time of one hour should be expected.

The scale of this north-eastern face can only properly be studied and appreciated from the head of the tortuous glen from which flows the burn with three names, first Allt a'Chul Choire, then lower Allt Coire an Eoin, and lastly The Cour. A similar but more distant viewpoint is Stob Coire Easain. From this angle the aptness of the Gaelic name An Aghaidh Gharbh (*the rough face*) is very clear, as is the climbing potential. The routes described in *Ben Nevis: Rock and Ice Climbs* waited 80 years before Collie's recommendation was taken up once more.

Stob Choire Claurigh

Stob Choire Claurigh *(claurigh is probably from the Gaelic clamhras, brawling or clamouring)* (1177m)
Stob Coire an Laiogh *(peak of the corrie of the calf)* (1115m)
Sgurr Choinnich Mor *(big peak of the moss)* (1095m)
Stob Ban *(white peak)* (977m)
With the accompanying tops to the first three-named Munros, there are ten distinct peaks on this ridge running about 8 kilometres from north-east to south-west. However the quantity flatters to deceive, for very little height is lost in a traverse. Once on Stob Choire Claurigh, in a westerly direction the lowest bealach falls beneath 914m only between Sgurr Choinnich Mor and Beag, and all the tops can be traversed in the course of a summer's day. However, unless one has a camp near the Glen Nevis watershed, this fine hillwalk is probably best enjoyed when travelling through the hills, for the distance involved in a round trip from either Corriechoille to the north-east or from Glen Nevis to the south is over 30 kilometres.

From Corriechoille, reached either from Roybridge station and the bridge over the River Spean 1½ kilometres east, or by the single-track road from the Spean Bridge Hotel (so fine is the river scenery, the Scots pine and the broad-leaf woodland along this stretch of road, that it seems a pity to drive it), the old drove road runs up the eastern margin of the Leanachan Forest and through the Lairig Leacach. (This ancient track is a right of way). There is a locked gate just north of the old tramway

Stob Coire na Ceannain

but the track beyond is negotiable only by four-wheel drive vehicles. At the southern limit of the forest easy slopes lead up to Beinn Bhan and over the minor top of Stob Coire na Gaibhre to Stob Choire Claurigh, but this approach, though pleasant enough, bypasses the finest feature at this end of the ridge which is the double-storied corrie looming above the Lairig Leacach. Particularly in winter this great amphitheatre with an almost perfectly circular lochan nestling in the upper bowl is a delightful place. On the eastern and southern headwall there will be very steep snow slopes but terrain at an easier angle leads south-east to the summit of Stob Coire na Ceannain, from where the quality of this winter approach continues with the narrow ridge, often an arete of snow or ice, to Stob Choire Claurigh. Beyond the main summit the ridge undulates and twists gently to the final and appropriately sharp cone of Sgurr Choinnich Beag.

While the terrain makes for easy going, there is one point on the ridge deserving of great caution when fresh snow lies thick on the crest. Low on the north-east ridge of Sgurr Choinnich Mor, at 231 720, there are quartzite pavements at low angle, rent by a series of crevices parallel to the direction of the ridge, wide enough to admit a human body, and deep enough to cause serious injury. When snow-free these fissures are obvious, but when snow has masked them completely — as does happen — it is well to keep to the eastern side of the crest.

Fine though this long ridge is, with spectacular views of Ben Nevis towering above the great wall of Aonach Mor and Beag, merely to traverse the tops is to miss some of the hidden qualities that lie to the north. And hidden they are for the distant main road behind the expanse of the Leanachan Forest allows neither close view nor obvious access. The hub from which the northern spurs and corries are reached is Coire Choimhlidh. Either the old tramway or a Forestry Commission Land-rover track (starting at Corriechoille) leads to a dam across the Allt Choimhlidh above the forest. From there one looks up to the twin northern spurs of Beinn na Socaich and Sron an Lochain enclosing Coire a'Mhadaidh with its spectacular headwall of black crags. While appearing attractively steep, these crags must class as the most rotten and loose in Scotland. During a foray in 1886 by a party of botanists who penetrated the recesses of these crags, a member of the rearguard who had served in the trenches with the Naval Brigade was heard to shout 'confound it! This is worse than the cannon balls in the Crimea; unless we remove beyond the elevation of our friends we shall get killed'. His companion on the day went on to report 'As we were speaking, a large piece of rock came past me down a perpendicular rent. which covered me with dust as it went past, filling the air with sulphurous odour. This caused so much alarm that a retreat … over dangerous loose rocks, had to be accomplished at a pace which astonished my companions as well as myself … I am afraid some unparliamentary exclamations accidentally escaped the lips of some unclerical members …' The incident was rationalised and even justified — a mental adjustment familiar to most climbers — on the basis of discovering a new station for *saxifraga rivularis* and the first find for fifty years of *saxifraga caespitosa* (true). Almost a century later the place is unchanged, though in a hard winter and on a day of deep frost, the deeply recessed gullies make fine ascents. Attractive snow climbs of an easier nature also lead from the corrie to the ridge of Beinn na Socaich.

Above 850m, the narrow confines of the three northern corries between Beinn na Socaich and Stob Choire Claurigh are great snow gatherers and mountain skiers can enjoy long traverses between the corries and the main ridge, which is accessible by way of hidden corridors.

On a long summer's day a most worthwhile descent to the north is that from Sgurr Choinnich Beag down over the serried ranks of *roches moutonnées* beneath An Aghaidh Gharbh and alongside the twistings of The Cour's limestone bed. This 5-kilometre stretch of water is a paradise of waterfalls and swimming pools of deep green water. The watercourse cuts through miniature gorges, turns through innumerable angles and from a final constriction at the corrie mouth bursts forth in a magnificent cascade. A little below this point, where there is a dam and a pipe-line, a clearing on the west bank beside the forest leads down to a bridge and the old tramway.

If descending from the Grey Corries into the Leanachan Forest late in the day, it is well to have a clear idea of the route to be followed. There is a multiplicity of tracks confusingly alike, not all of which are shown on the OS 1:50 000 map.

Stob Ban from the Lairig Leacach bothy

In an area of remote peaks, Stob Ban is particularly awkward of access. Approach from the main ridge of the Grey Corries involves a descent of 300m and a reascent over scree of the most unstable kind, while, if starting from Glen Nevis or from Corrour railway station the peak is perhaps best taken as one incident in a through-route. Probably the most interesting way to include it in a traverse of the Grey Corries is to cross the Lairig Leacach from the north and take to the north-east ridge beyond the bothy. From the bealach to the north of Stob Ban there is a curious giant's staircase of quartzite that spills down east for about 150m. It makes an interesting ascent to the bealach.

Stob Coire Easain *(peak of the corrie of the little waterfall)* (1116m)
Stob a'Choire Mheadhoin *(peak of the middle corrie)* (1106m)
These two hills, usually known collectively as the Easains, are easily climbed from the north by the 9-kilometre long north-east ridge, starting from the road to Fersit at the north end of Loch Treig. The return can be varied by descending the north-western corrie, Coire Easain Beag, between the two peaks and following down the course of the Allt Laire.

However, the convenient siting of the railway stations at Corrour and Tulloch allows a very pleasant traverse with the better views in a south to north direction when the Grey Corries, the Aonachs and Ben Nevis unfold as one progresses along the excellent path to Lochtreighead. Once beyond Creaguaineach Lodge it is worth-while to follow the path on the north side of the Allt na Lairig for 1 kilometre both to enjoy the gorge between Creag Ghuanach and Creagan a' Chaise and to avoid the hummocky ground on the latter top. (Those with the time on a clear evening would profit from a walk up Creag Ghuanach which is perfectly placed for views of the peaks on both sides of Glen Nevis and of Buachaille Etive Mor through the narrows of Gleann na Giubhsachan).

No climbing has been recorded on these two hills, though directly beneath and east of Stob a'Choire Mheadhoin lies a steeply-walled corrie with schist crags high on the south wall. With their north-easterly aspect, these crags may be worth a winter visit.

Sgurr Innse *(peak of the meadow)* (808m)
Cruach Innse *(hill of the meadow)* (857m)
Despite its relatively minor stature, Sgurr Innse is prominent from great distances. Its barrel-like form is instantly recognisable from Buachaille Etive Mor. As the distant view suggests, both Sgurr and Cruach Innse are steep and rocky, but the Sgurr far outweighs its higher neighbour in this respect. Both hills can be traversed in a short day from the Lairig Leacach, but for those without rock-climbing experi-ence the only comfortable descent of the Sgurr is down a north-westerly shelf. In fact Sgurr Innse belies its formidable appearance as its crags are too broken for much continuous climbing and only one route has been recorded on the south-western aspect.

WALKS AND PATHS

A little-used single-track tarmac road runs from Spean Bridge to Corriechoille and a footpath continues beyond Insh. Footbridges cross the river ½ kilometre east of Roybridge and also at the Glenspean Lodge Hotel. Between these two bridges and further east there is a series of waterfalls on a grand scale.

Part of the old drove route, 'The Road to the Isles', runs south from Corriechoille to the head of Loch Treig. Beyond there it continues to Corrour station — a distance of about 25 kilometres. The scenic quality of this route is splendid and the railway offers the luxury of returning in comfort to one's starting point.

CLIMBING

There has been a remarkable development of climbing, nearly all winter snow, ice and mixed routes, on the Aonachs in recent years. While for almost a century the North-east Ridge of Aonach Beag was the only climb of note, now there are nearly a hundred routes, some of them among the hardest in the area.

On Aonach Mor there are many routes up to 150m long in Coire an Lochain on the east face of the mountain. There are climbs of all grades from I to VI. The approach may be made from Leanachan Forest up the Allt Choille-rais, or more

On the cliffs of Stob Coire an Laoigh

*The ascent of Beinn na Socaich to Stob Coire Easain, looking towards Aonach Beag whose
North-east Ridge rises directly above the climber*

easily (for those with skis) up the lifts and tows of the Aonach Mor ski system to the
top of the highest tow from where there is a short walk 150 metres on 185 degrees
grid to the top of Easy Gully, which gives the best descent through the cliffs into the
corrie. Beware of the cornice. Not advised in bad visibility.

The West Face of Aonach Mor has four long, fairly easy winter routes above the
Allt Daim.

On Aonach Beag, in addition to the North-east Ridge, there are several hard
winter routes on the north flank of this ridge above An Cul Choire, and other long
climbs on Stob Coire Bhealaich and An Agaidh Gharbh — the wild east face of the
mountain.

The West Face of Aonach Beag at the head of Coire Giubhsachan provides more
hard winter lines, and on one of its cliffs, the Raw Egg Buttress, two E-grade rock
climbs are the only recent summer climbs in the area.

Details of all these routes are described in *Ben Nevis: Rock and Ice Climbs* by S.
Richardson, A.Walker and R.Clothier, published by the Scottish Mountaineering
Trust (1994)

SKI MOUNTAINEERING

The traverse of Aonach Beag and Aonach Mor from Glen Nevis to the Leanachan Forest, or vice versa, has for long been a classic ski tour in the Lochaber mountains. The development of the downhill ski system on Aonach Mor has possibly increased the popularity of the tour when done from north to south.

The Grey Corries are magnificent ski mountains, and the traverse from Stob Choire Claurigh to Stob Coire Easain is not difficult (in good visibility) as the ridge is nowhere narrow or steep enough to cause problems. The broad north-facing ridges of Beinn Bhan and Beinn na Socaich at the two ends of this traverse give easy skiing, but the best downhill running at the end of the day will almost certainly be found in Coire Choimhlidh, a great white arena where the many shallow gullies hold snow well.

The long north-east ridge of Stob a'Choire Mheadhoin and Stob Coire Easain (Loch Treig) gives an easy ski ascent and there is plenty of scope for downhill runs on the north-west flank of this ridge down to Coire Laire.

All the ski tours in this area are described in *Ski Mountaineering in Scotland* edited by D.J.Bennet and W.Wallace, and published by the Scottish Mountaineering Trust (1987).

CHAPTER 11

Ben Alder to Rannoch

Carn Dearg	941m	418 661
Sgor Gaibhre	955m	444 674
Beinn Pharlagain	868m	448 642
Ben Alder	1148m	496 718
Beinn Bheoil	1019m	517 717
The Fara	911m	598 844

ACCESS
From Rannoch and Corrour railway stations. From the B846 road at Rannoch station and the west end of Loch Rannoch. From the A9 road at Dalwhinnie. All approaches entail long walks. The north-eastern route involves about 17 kilometres to reach the foot of Ben Alder.

TRANSPORT
Train Glasgow — Fort William calls at Rannoch and Corrour stations daily.
Train Edinburgh — Inverness calls at Dalwhinnie daily.
Express coach service daily Edinburgh and Glasgow to Inverness calls at Pitlochry and may set down at Dalwhinnie on request.
There is a bus service between Pitlochry and Kinloch Rannoch, Monday - Friday (tel. 0796-472290) and another between Kinloch Rannoch and Rannoch Station, Monday — Saturday (tel. 0882 632348).

ACCOMMODATION
Hotels at Dalwhinnie and Rannoch Station.
Youth hostel at Loch Ossian. (Booking is advised)
Bunkhouse at Corrour Halt (Tel 0397 85236).
Bothies at Culra Lodge (523 762) and Benalder Cottage (499 680). Not available during the stalking season and only suitable for small parties at other times. Both bothies are on the Ben Alder estate; enquiries about use to the Head Stalker (tel 052 82 224).

MAPS
OS 1:50 000 Landranger Sheets 41 and 42

Despite having two railway lines adjacent to it — the West Highland Line to Rannoch and Corrour and the Inverness Line to Dalwhinnie — this area has a greater sense of remoteness than any other in the Central Highlands. There are no public roads within the area and the only two roads near its margins — the B846 to Rannoch Station, and the A9 — are at great distance from the hills. The boundaries are Loch Ericht, the West Highland Line and, to the north, a less straightforward line that

Loch Ossian youth hostel, looking towards the Bealach Dubh and Ben Alder

follows Loch Ossian and the Uisge Labhair to cross the Bealach Dubh and then to veer north by Loch and River Pattack; thus including the wedge of land between that river and the A9. Within lies Ben Alder, fascinating in its variety of corrie and ridge and with a definite air of inaccessibility adding to its attraction. All the tops in the western half are most conveniently reached *via* the West Highland Line and a start from the isolated Corrour Halt adds to the refreshing aura of remoteness that attaches to these hills.

THE HILLS

Carn Dearg *(red hill)* (941m)
Sgor Gaibhre *(goat's peak)* (955m)
Meall na Meoig of Beinn Pharlagain *(hill of whey {pharlagain perhaps grassy hollow})* (868m)
A traverse of these tops from Corrour Halt to Rannoch Station, i.e. between the morning and afternoon trains, makes a splendid outing. Views both far and near — of Binnein Mor and Binnean Beag's sublime outline, of the great stretch of Rannoch Moor, and of Strath Ossian's U-shaped trench — are particularly satisfying from Carn Dearg, whose slopes are at an angle easy enough to walk with hands in pocket. Indeed the whole round of these tops is characterised by the easy going which, when not under snow, is on carpets of moss and sedge, amongst which occasional clumps

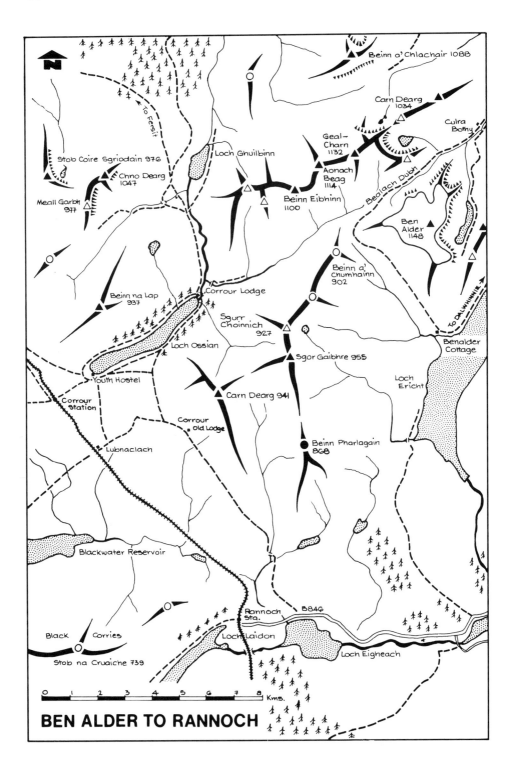

BEN ALDER TO RANNOCH

of moss campion blend into the muted colours. Carn Dearg's broad, western flank is traversed by a good path — 'The Road to the Isles' — which commences immediately south of the youth hostel at Loch Ossian. This path leads eventually to Rannoch Station passing on the way the ruin of Corrour Old Lodge. As can be surmised from the substantial granite walls, the Old Lodge was a fine building, but once the railway line was installed, a new lodge was built at the eastern end of Loch Ossian. For some time the Old Lodge was used as an isolation hospital, and no more isolated site can be imagined, but once this use ceased it lay empty until its roof was removed to avoid the pointless payment of rates.

In descent from Beinn Pharlagain the above-mentioned track can be met at the bridge over the Allt Eigheach, from which a line can be taken south-west over the moor for the railway track. However such a short cut is advisable only when dry conditions prevail underfoot for some of the bogs hereabout are truly dangerous and extremely difficult to detect even when not snow-covered. Particularly is this the case a little to the north on the moor beneath Carn Dearg's southern outpost, Sron Leachd a'Chaorrainn, where the author witnessed one unfortunate descend very quickly to his thighs — amusing enough when there was sufficient man-power for extraction, but with possibly fatal consequences for the solo walker.

In winter vast herds of deer gather in the corrie between the long southern ridges (Coire Eigheach) and on its slopes beneath the Mam Ban. The very names for these hills, Corrour Forest and Rannoch Forest, are used in the sense, adopted from mediaeval times, of open ground peopled with deer.

For those walking through the hills to the east there is an obvious continuation over Sgor Choinnich (927m), Meall a'Bhealaich (862m) and Beinn a' Chumhainn (902m) with the latter providing a fine view through the Bealach Dubh to the north-east and into Coire a'Charra Bhig to the north.

Ben Alder *(from the Alder burn, which may be from the Gaelic alldhobhar meaning rock water)* (1148 m)

Like Ben Nevis, the great bulk of this hill is instantly recognisable from great distances. Its steep slopes above the Bealach Dubh to the north and above the Bealach Beithe to the east distinguish it from the west and south, while from Dalwhinnie and the Drumochter Hills the snow-holding properties of its Garbh Choire are very apparent in winter. All approaches are long, though by the shortest it is possible to make the ascent inside a summer's day. This shortest route starts from Corrour Halt and follows the track along the southern shore of Loch Ossian until a bridge behind Corrour Lodge leads to a path winding north of a wood and across flats to a substantial bridge over the Uisge Labhair. What path there is beside this burn lies on the north bank and in the usual wet conditions the 9 kilometres to the Bealach Dubh make heavy going. Before two thirds of this distance have been covered, Ben Alder's west ridge, by which the ascent is best made, swoops down and the burn is easily crossed through the alluvial spreads that have been carried down from Coire a'Charra Bhig. Those following this route and planning to climb the hill in between

Ben Alder and Sgor Iutharn (right) from the Allt a'Chaoil-reidhe near Culra Lodge

trains will have little time to explore the vast summit plateau of almost 4 square kilometres above 1000m or to soak in the extensive view. With its central position in the Highlands, it wants only a clear day for other peaks at great distance to be picked out, for example the lowly West Lomond in Fife can be seen in the gap between Schiehallion and Carn Mairg, and the upper cone of Sgurr Mor in the Fannaichs stands out above Creag Meagaidh — at 96 and 112 kilometres respectively.

Other approaches involve considerable distances that require an overnight stop in the hills. From Dalwhinnie a good track runs for 14 kilometres beside Loch Ericht, leaving it at Ben Alder Lodge to veer west to Loch Pattack. This track is barred by locked gates, but these are negotiable with a bicycle. From a point roughly 2½ kilometres west of the Lodge a boggy path crosses the moor to hug the eastern side of the Allt a'Chaoil-reidhe, passing Culra Lodge on the other bank, and eventually climbs to the bealach between Beinn Bheoil and Ben Alder. Leaving the path ½ kilometre before reaching Lochan a'Bhealaich Beithe, rough slopes of boulders and heather lead west to the Short and Long Leachas; both of these ridges provide natural mountain routes of Moderate standard, while the corries between and to the south have steep headwalls. Of the two, the northernmost, the Long Leachas, has the better situations and in good winter conditions its narrow upper part is an exhilarating scramble.

Those seeking a walking route without the need to use hands for progress should cross the Allt a'Chaoil-reidhe by the bridge just north of Culra Lodge and follow the track to the Bealach Dubh, beyond which the path continues south-west skirting the western flanks of Ben Alder. 1½ kilometres beyond the Bealach Dubh the west ridge can be gained and followed easily to the summit.

Again using the West Highland Line, a start can be made from Rannoch Station where 2 kilometres east along the B846 the 'Road to the Isles' turns in a northerly direction. Before reaching the Allt Gormag an indistinct path starts in a north-easterly direction at 435 599 and grows ever fainter as it skirts the north of Lochan Sron Smeur. Beyond the lochan only traces of the path occur and there are 3 kilometres of rough going in an easterly direction, skirting south of recent afforest-ation and north of Lochan Loin nan Donnlaich, before a good track heading north is joined at 479 617. This second track — an ancient route shown on Roy's Map of 1755 — commences at the west end of Loch Rannoch and, being shorter and without the interruption affecting the other approach, may be preferable, particularly to those arriving by car.

A bus service between Kinloch Rannoch and Rannoch Station meets the north-bound, morning train and saves 11 kilometres of road walking for those wanting to use the continuous track. However the first path has advantages in the moorland area between the two lochans which is rich in bird-life (herons seen feeding at the easterly lochan, both redshanks and greenshanks seen, grey wagtail and dippers also) which in spring makes the path through the glacial breach occupied by Lochan Sron Smeur the more interesting.

Beyond the junction a view of great splendour steadily unfolds with the length of Loch Ericht stretching into the distance. Above it, scarped slopes to the east and the unrelenting angle of those to the west beneath Sron Coire na h-Iolaire are redolent of the glacier that oversteepened these walls, down-cutting by as much as 400m. Beneath the bridge over the Cam Criochan slabs of pink granite form summer swimming pools that in spring flood are invisible, for this burn drains a vast shelf of saturated peat to the east of Sgor Gaibhre and Sgor Choinnich. Once over the bridge the track dwindles to a path skirting afforestation, past which it fades altogether. For the next 2 kilometres one wanders through an idyllic setting of Scots pine forming open woodland, that is crowned by the view through the trees of Ben Alder and Sron Coire na h-Iolaire. Alder Bay and Benalder Cottage add a hint of peace to heighten the grandeur of this scene.

At one time this corner held a small community and the diligent searcher will find rickles of stone amongst the bracken. When this hamlet died is not known, but it must have been long before the pre-war inundation of the track along which pony-carts used to be driven from Dalwhinnie. The raising of the water level took place when Loch Ericht was dammed and its waters impounded to feed the turbines of the Grampian Electricity Supply Company, which in the 1930s was the first Scottish producer of hydro-electric power for public consumption.

Above the bay a faint path leads up north to the Bealach Breabag, and an ascent of roughly 300m brings easy slopes to the left that lead on to a southerly ridge of Ben Alder. Higher still the ridge bends north-west, flattens, and becomes better defined, skirting the rim of the Garbh Choire that in most winters carries enormous cornices.

In summer Ben Alder's huge summit plateau is a fascinating place. Both ptarmigan and dotterel breed amongst the wilderness of granite boulders and moss campion favours the gravelly clearings along the western slopes. Then the subarctic climate promotes the phenomenon known as stone polygons, associated with perma-frost, where frost action extrudes stones into an occasionally recognisable pattern. When these extrusions do occur with regular form, there will be a central area of small stones surrounded by a polygonal wall of larger stones. This outer wall can appear as a startlingly symmetrical design. With time enough for a careful search, examples can be found on the flat ground west of the cairn. One such was measured at 130cm diameter with the larger stones having a maximum dimension of 23cm.

In winter, when even the excellent track from Dalwhinnie can take hours of toil through deep snow, Ben Alder shares with the deeper recesses of the Cairngorms a quality of genuine remoteness. When winter storms blow there, and they seem as fierce in the long glens as on the top, the strongest party will be taxed.

Beinn Bheoil *(hill of the mouth)* (1019m)
Sron Coire na h-Iolaire *(nose of the eagle's corrie)* (955m)
This long spine of a hill has a splendid position cut off abruptly to the east by Loch Ericht and to the west by the trench containing Loch a'Bhealaich Bheithe. Its summit ridge carries clear evidence in granite erratics of the thickness of the ice that flowed north from the Rannoch ice-cap and ground out these two trenches. On the moor to the north one of these erratics is so nicely balanced on a plaque of schistose rock — itself planed by glacial action — that it can be rocked with one hand. Climbed from the north there are splendid views across to the Short and Long Leachas jutting out into the moor, while further south the great eastern wall of Ben Alder is in full view. The bealach between these two hills is a good position from which to study the South Buttress of the Garbh Choire. Sron Coire na h-Iolaire is well-named as both eagles and hen harriers have been frequently sighted quartering the ground below this top. Descent west from the bealach between the two hills is down steep slopes of boulder and scree.

The Fara *(properly Am Faradh — the ladder)* (910m)
The last top in this area lies in the north-east corner and is very accessible from Dalwhinnie. There can be few hills with such a great length of ridge above 800m and roughly 7 kilometres are spent walking on the easiest possible ground between The Fara and its far-flung outliers Meall Cruaidh (896m) and Meall Leac na Sguabaich (843m). The continuous view to the south-west is superb: the great through routes

of An Lairig and the Bealach Dubh, the full length of Loch Ericht, and the corries and ridges of Aonach Beag and Ben Alder. Its great length would save The Fara from ever being described as nondescript, but views from its ridge lift it quite out of the ordinary.

Also out of the ordinary is the great rift of Dirc Mhor (*the great slash*) that cuts into The Fara's northern flank. It was first brought to the attention of mountaineers by the landscape artist Colin Phillip and Harold Raeburn was quick to investigate. He found a remarkable cleft of 400ft depth, with savage cliffs on either side but finer on the east and floored with a jungle of boulders and an abundance of ferns making the holes between the boulders difficult to see. Curiously there is no record of a second visit by Raeburn, though he recommended it; however the description stands and while the defile is easily enough reached by following the Allt an t-Sluic for 5 kilometres almost to its head, progress along its bed is necessarily slow and cautious.

PATHS AND WALKS

A leisurely stroll in remote surroundings can be had on the Land-rover track that encircles Loch Ossian from the railway station at Corrour. For many the delightfully picturesque situation of the wooden youth hostel (once a boat house) on a promontory at the head of the loch makes it the best of its kind in Britain — and of a wider field judging by the number of Continentals who return year after year. Some come to wander the hills but many have further interest in the flora and fauna, which in the latter case has great variety for such high land. With the mixed woodland of indigenous birch and a variety of mature, exotic conifers — the latter planted with fringes of hardwoods and flowering shrubs of azalea and rhododendrons under the plan of a forestry pioneer, Sir John Stirling Maxwell — providing food and shelter, there is an attractive mix of bird-life. Many of the common waders and passerines breed in the area, and several ducks, game birds and birds of prey can be seen. Over 100 different species have been observed about the loch and the surrounding hills: golden plover keening over the slopes of Carn Dearg, heron fishing the shallows at the east end of the loch, redpoll, twite, siskin and other finches feeding in trees, and the distinctive mew of the buzzard is often heard, again over Carn Dearg.

When Sir John Stirling Maxwell bought Corrour Estate in 1890, only the birch wood on the southern shore of the loch provided shelter, but a year later he had started his experiments with the noble fir, larch, western hemlock and with the eventual groundrock of afforestation in Scotland — the sitka spruce. A memorial to this pioneer can be seen on a plaque inset in a granite boulder at the east end of the loch.

At this same east end of the loch, or better still walking down beside the Uisge Labhair, there is a disturbing sense of something awry in the landform. Some may wonder at the sluggish meander of the River Ossian and the way it cuts through almost a lip of ground; others puzzle at the sudden turn north of the straight-coursed

The northern and eastern corries of Ben Alder

Uisge Labhair. It is considered that at one time the Uisge Labhair drained into Loch Ossian and that the two flowed on into the Loch Treig basin. Later glaciation deepened Strath Ossian so that it captured the Uisge Labhair and left morainic material to block Loch Ossian's western outlet.

The walk around Loch Ossian can be lengthened by leaving the train at Rannoch and following the 'Road to the Isles' which starts 2 kilometres east of the station on the B846 road.

Many of the lochans on the fringe of Rannoch Moor have a plentiful stock of small brown trout. Loch na Sheallaig 1 kilometre south of the youth hostel is one such case. For those spending some time in the area, a fishing rod would be almost as useful as a Primus stove.

Alder Bay can be reached from the east end of Loch Ossian but the path from there to the Bealach Cumhann is very poor and the overall distance is considerable, about 12 kilometres. Once over the bealach the path does improve.

A Land-rover track runs 15 kilometres from Dalwhinnie to Loch Pattack and a long cycle ride could be made by following another track north to Kinloch Laggan, then returning to Dalwhinnie by the main roads.

CLIMBING

Only during the last few years has winter climbing been recorded on Ben Alder and its rock features are, with one exception, lacking in a sufficiency of continuous and clean crag. This exception lies in a large, complex crag of quartz-feldspar facing east and north-east above the southern end of Lochan a'Bhealaich Bheithe. It is known as the South Buttress of the Garbh Choire and three routes have been recorded.

However in winter its eastern corries and huge north face offer superb mountaineering. In the westernmost corner of Garbh Choire a straightforward gully of Grade I standard makes a pleasant route while to its right an obvious ramp trends rightward up the open face to finish on steeper ground — the easiest line hereabouts would be of Grade II standard. Further right still the headwall steepens yet more, and in Garbh-choire Beag one 300m Grade III route has been done up the centre of the headwall in the left-hand side of the corrie.

On the north side of Ben Alder a hanging-valley indents deeply into the summit plateau, beneath a shallow depression separating the top above Garbh-choire Beag from the summit plateau. At the back of this corrie two snow gullies of Grade I standard are easily found. Further west a great open face of rock looms above the path to the Bealach Dubh and has retained an enigmatic air despite the attention of several explorers. A good view of the face can be had from the south-western slopes of Sgor Iutharn (unnamed on OS 1:50 000 Sheet 42, 490 743), and from this viewpoint a series of diagonal weaknesses can be seen. One winter route at Grade IV has been made near the middle of this face. At the north-east end of this face lies Maiden Crag (498 734) where three Grade V routes of over 250m length have been made.

Ben Nevis: Rock and Ice Climbs, by S.Richardson, R.Clothier and A.Walker, published by the Scottish Mountaineering Trust (1994) contains all the route descriptions for Ben Alder.

SKI MOUNTAINEERING

The traverse of Carn Dearg, Sgor Gaibhre and Beinn Pharlagain from Corrour Halt to Rannoch Station is a fine long tour of no difficulty, and The Fara gives a good short day from the A899 road 1 kilometre north of Dalwhinnie. The most attractive objective, Ben Alder, involves such a long approach from any direction that good snow cover on the low ground is essential if a long walk carrying skis is to be avoided. Loch Ossian youth hostel, if available in winter, is the best base for this long tour.

References

Undiscovered Scotland W. H. Murray, Diadem Compendium 1982 (for a paean to Ben Alder in Chapter 19).

CHAPTER 12

Loch Ossian to Loch Laggan

Stob Coire Sgriodain	976m	356 744
Chno Dearg	1047m	377 741
Beinn na Lap	937m	376 696
Beinn Eibhinn	1100m	449 733
Aonach Beag	1114m	458 742
Geal-Charn	1132m	470 746
Carn Dearg	1034m	504 764
Beinn a'Chlachair	1088m	471 781
Creag Pitridh	924m	488 814
Geal Charn	1049m	504 812

ACCESS
From Corrour and Tulloch stations. From Dalwhinnie and from the A86 at Kinloch Laggan and the bridge at Luiblea (433 830).

TRANSPORT
Glasgow — Fort William train service stopping at Corrour and Tulloch.
Perth — Inverness train stopping at Dalwhinnie.
Express coach service Glasgow and Edinburgh to Inverness may set down passengers at Dalwhinnie on request.

ACCOMMODATION
Hotels and guest houses at Dalwhinnie, Laggan and Spean Bridge, with caravan hire at the latter place.
A small bunkhouse at Corrour station (tel 0397 85236), a youth hostel at Loch Ossian and a bothy at Culra. The Blackburn bothy beside the River Pattack was burnt to the ground in 1993.
There are two club huts in the area — Jock's Spot on the A86 midway between Laggan and Newtonmore owned by the JMCS (Edinburgh Section); and the Raeburn Hut on the A889 midway between Dalwhinnie and Laggan owned by the Scottish Mountaineering Club.

MAPS
OS 1:50 000 Landranger Sheets 41 and 42

The hills in the interior of this area share with Ben Alder a decided air of remoteness, and even those relatively accessible from Loch Laggan have a sense of being cut off by the barriers of Lochan na h-Earba and the two Binneins, Shuas and Shios. Three lochs form pronounced boundaries — Laggan, Treig and Ossian — with the great divide between Ben Alder and Aonach Beag and the River Pattack closing the ring. Enclosed within are the awesome glacial trench of Strath Ossian, a fine crag on Chno Dearg and a complement of stalkers' hill paths and estate tracks greater than in any other area of the Central Highlands. Again, as with Ben Alder, the sense of remoteness is preserved by use of the West Highland Line to Corrour Halt, although there are three points of access from the Spean-Laggan valley, and, Dalwhinnie makes another, more distant starting point.

THE HILLS

Stob Coire Sgriodain *(peak of the corrie of the scree)* (976m)
Chno Dearg *(appears on early maps as cnoc dearg, red hill)* (1047m)
Meall Garbh *(rough heap)* (977m)
These three hills make a natural round from Fersit, while for an extra 3 kilometres one can include the intriguing Garbh-bheinn in the traverse from Corrour Halt to Tulloch Station.

The northern slopes of Stob Coire Sgriodain make heavy going over bouldery ground, though *roches moutonnées* and glacially-scoured slabs provide distraction and there is a splendid view from the top with the fiord-like Loch Treig curving west at its head and leading the eye to Binnein Mor and Beag. There are two other distinct tops to the south-east before a longer descent to the dip in line for Meall Garbh. This dip appears to gather unusually deep drifts of snow and, in poor visibility, is broad enough to be confusing as is its proximity to the dip between Meall Garbh and Chno Dearg, only 20m above.

Chno Dearg offers its own fine view across the flats holding Loch Ghuilbinn and backed by Beinn a'Chlachair, while behind again is the prominent gap occupied by Lochan na h-Earba and the diminutive cone of Binnein Shuas. Easy slopes lead north for the return to Fersit, but it is worthwhile keeping due north and turning to the east of Creag Dubh (607m) partly to meet the path from Strath Ossian, but more to see the double rampart of terminal moraines that starts just above the path and curves round to follow the edge of the forest and the course of the Allt Loraich.

The traverse of these tops from Corrour to Tulloch follows the old drove route alongside the railway and turns up onto Garbh-bheinn at the foot of the Allt Luib Ruairidh. There is little or no trace here of the stance that once catered for the drovers who had brought their cattle and sheep over 13 kilometres or so of difficult ground from the previous night's lodging under Sgurr Innse. Garbh-bheinn is notable for the multitude of perched blocks that litter its long south-west ridge and give rise to its Gaelic name — the rough hill; and, in an area where fine views abound, that to the west toward the head of Glen Nevis is outstanding. This route is recommended as a ski tour, going in a northerly direction as the northern slopes of Chno Dearg carry a quantity of snow unusually large for their altitude.

Fersit is a backwater that appears little affected by the adjacent massive works of man in the dams at Loch Treig and Loch Laggan. The single-track road to it winds

Stob Coire Sgriodain, with the Easains beyond, from Chno Dearg

through hummocky ground crossing the Spean, the Allt Laire, and the River Treig in little more than 3 kilometres. The few houses mingle with straggling Scots pine, and birch follow the Allt Laire down to the road. Nevertheless it is not difficult to imagine the enormous forces that once went to make the general shape of this idyllic corner. For 10 000 years ago a glacier, large enough to have down-cut the fault-line now occupied by Loch Treig by 550m, was forcing its great bulk through the constriction now straddled by the dam. In retreat this glacier left some classic examples of deposition in the cones of sand and gravel clustered about the road-end, and it carried some boulders of Rannoch granite as far as Tulloch. Where the road climbs from Inverlair Bridge, there is one of the clearest examples known in Scotland of those melt-boles left by stranded masses of ice. In Gaelic it is called Slochd a'Mheirlich (*the robber's pit*) and it is easily seen at the side of the road at 337 801.

Lochs Treig and Laggan were dammed in the 1930s to provide water-power for the turbines of the British Aluminium Company and a 24-kilometre tunnel now carries water from both lochs beneath the hills to Fort William. The damming of Loch Treig raised the high-water level by 10m, potentially inundating the old railway track, and an extensive section complete with a tunnel (at 347 764) had to be relaid higher up the hillside.

Beinn na Lap *(mottled hill? {lap means a defective spot in a colour})* (937m)
Few hills in such a remote setting can be so easily climbed from a railway station. Leaving the train at Corrour Halt, the old drove route follows beside the railway to the foot of the south-westerly slopes at an altitude of 400m, and above it a ridge carpeted with dwarf vegetation and at the easiest of angles leads to the top. Like other hills about the head of Loch Treig, there is a fine outlook and the contrast between the mountainous ridges to the west and the flat expanse of Rannoch Moor to the south deserves a clear day for its appreciation.

From the top a long, low-angled ridge leads north-east over platelets of quartzite and above the profound cut to the north-west of a major fault-line that continues through Lochan na h-Earba. This extraordinary feature runs an almost geometrically straight course through the hills and rises only 50m in the 4 kilometres between the Ossian flats and the tiny Lochan Ruigh Phail at its highest point. Where the ridge drops into the flats west of Strathossian House the underlying rock changes to granite as can be seen in the burn where good pools for swimming are ringed with boulders of pink and cream granite. Return from such a crossing is easily made by the excellent tracks through Strath Ossian and along the north side of Loch Ossian. The vast shelf of high ground to the east of the summit, containing Loch na Lap, should be avoided as it is a waste of poorly drained peat-hags.

Strath Ossian's pronounced U-shape, so indicative of glaciation, is perhaps best appreciated from the hills, and to walk its length in poor weather can seem a dreary stretch. However, from the bed of the strath it is still easy to picture the Ossian Glacier grinding north and polishing the two granite crags — both known as Creagan nan Nead — on either side at the mouth of the strath. Of these two crags, that to the east forming a nose above Strathossian House has been investigated and the climbing reported as poor; that on the west wall might better repay exploration, but neither would provide climbs of any length nor match the quality of the adjacent crag on Chno Dearg.

Beinn Eibhinn *(delightful hill)* (1100m)
Aonach Beag *(little ridge)* (1114m)
Geal-Charn *(white hill)* (1032m)
Sgor Iutharn (1021m)
Carn Dearg *(red hill)* (1034 m)
These hills form one long and elevated ridge between Strath Ossian and Loch Pattack set at such great distance from both road and rail that they are not easily accessible for a day's outing. However, a fast-moving party not meeting any delaying factor such as fresh snow, can make the ascent of the three western tops in the 10 hours between trains from Corrour. At least 38 kilometres would be involved in such a rush, leaving no time to explore the corries and ridges to the east and perhaps needing Wm.W.Naismith's regimen of 'young men eating their pieces on the move'. The south-westerly route onto Beinn Eibhinn is straightforward until the

confusing area between the main summit and two minor tops — Mullach Choire nan Nead (921m; 431 734) and Meall Ghlas Choire (922m; 438 729) — neither of which is named on OS 1:50 000 Sheet 42. There is, however, no mistaking the almost square section of the narrow window (Uinneag a'Ghlas Choire) between the last-named top and Beinn Eibhinn.

Another long approach, but one recommended for the views into the shapely northern corries, starts from the concrete bridge at Luiblea (433 830) 8 kilometres east of the Laggan dam. A forestry track starts there and runs through to Strath Ossian, but a path on the east of the Amhainn Ghuilbinn should be followed. This leads across Meall Ardruigh to Lubvan and thence up the course of the Allt Cam to the foot of Aonach Beag's north-north-west ridge. Either it or a

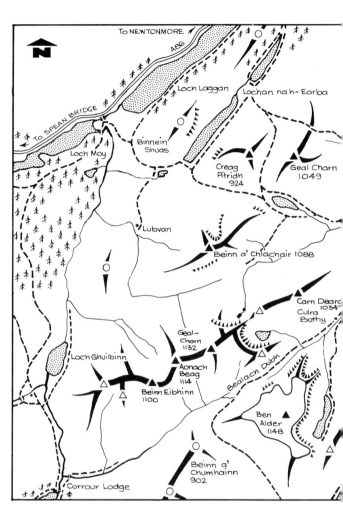

parallel ridge to Beinn Eibhinn makes a pleasant route, and in good winter conditions an easy snow climb with a steep finish may be had from the corrie enclosed between the two ridges (Coire a'Charra Mhoir). The north ridge of Geal-Charn steepens to a nose at the plateau rim and while it can be circumvented, the avoiding line for descent is not easily found in poor visibility from the featureless plateau. In winter those without experience of snow and ice climbing would probably not be comfortable in descending by this route.

There are some ideal camping sites along this approach, but the flats at the head of the Allt Cam are subjected to strong winds.

The third and longest approach is that by the estate tracks leading to Loch Pattack from either Dalwhinnie or Kinloch Laggan, and a traverse of the tops from this

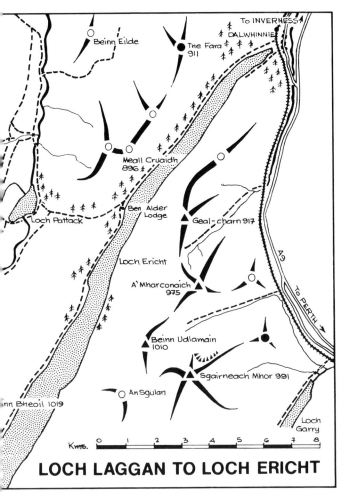

LOCH LAGGAN TO LOCH ERICHT

junction makes a fine winter expedition. To walk in beside the Pattack is the pleasanter route with fine waterfalls at Linn of Pattack and, a little beyond at a bridge, there is an abandoned channel worn out of solid rock. From a large shed south of Loch Pattack a boggy path leads south-west, and after 4 kilometres a bridge across the Allt a'Chaoil-reidhe should be crossed. Those favoured with a clear winter's day will see ahead the route up Sgor Iutharn, a sharp ridge known as the 'Lancet Edge' that is narrow enough to require care. Steep ground sweeps down on either side of the ridge and the view left to the hanging valley on Ben Alder's north face, and right to Loch an Sgoir fed by a tracery of waterfalls is very fine indeed.

By contrast the ground between Sgor Iutharn and Geal-Charn is easy going and the latter's summit plateau is surprisingly extensive and well irrigated by snow-fields that last into summer. Comp- osed of mica-schist and producing luxuriant summer grass, this top is favourite grazing for deer.

Returning north-east from Geal-Charn in poor visibility, it is worthwhile taking a careful bearing for the steep, narrow ridge leading down to the saddle known as Diollaid a'Chairn. Many parties trend too far right and follow a parallel ridge until they find themselves peering down the crags above Loch an Sgoir.

Carn Dearg can seem anti-climactic after such interest, but in poor weather there is a tendency for it to be free of cloud when its massed neighbours to the west have allowed no view.

Geal-Charn from Carn Dearg

Binnein Shuas from Lochan na h-Earba

Beinn a'Chlachair *(stone-mason's hill)* (1088m)
Geal Charn *(white hill)* (1049m)
Creag Pitridh *(meaning uncertain, perhaps from the surname Petrie)* (924m)
Another natural grouping is formed by the hills between Lochan na h-Earba and An Lairig but, in this case, one that is readily accessible from the A86 to the north. Nearest access is by the bridge at 432 830 from where a path joins the estate track to Lochan na h-Earba. A hill path continues from the west of the lochan to a bealach central to the three hills and overlooking a bleak stretch of water to the east — Loch a'Bhealaich Leamhain. This path, as with most in the Ardverikie Forest, is well engineered and still fairly well drained. It makes better walking than the northern flank of Beinn a'Chlachair which in its lower half can be very wet. As the Gaelic name — stone-mason's hill — suggests, the hill is littered with boulders, which on the east-north-east shoulder and on the upper cone are frequently of regular proportions. The shoulder terminates sharply to the east in a schist crag above the loch, but it appears too broken and loose for climbing. Also disappointing in climbing terms, though impressive from a distance, is the northern corrie.

A further path leads to the bealach between Creag Pitridh and Geal Charn. It branches from the main path between the hills at the apex of a long zigzag, engineered to avoid a gully beneath the south-west nose of Geal Charn. Even with the presence of this path, the bealach is a confusing place in thick weather. The path actually ascends the western slope of Geal Charn and remains 20m above and 200 metres east of the bealach before dropping quite sharply to the north.

Geal Charn, once more conveniently known — in view of its namesake across the An Lairig — as Mullach Coire an Iubhair, is largely composed of lime-rich mica-schist and produces some rare Alpines on craggy ground protected by its steepness from grazers and also from the rapacity of that other plunderer — the Victorian collector. Purple saxifrage blooms hereabout in early spring and Alpine hawkweed has also been seen. The hills of the Ardverikie Forest seem also to have a particularly rich and varied crop of lichens, and at one time dyers of tweed produced some of their less common colours (known as 'crottles' from the Gaelic word crotal) from lichen gathered on these hills.

For those returning to Kinloch Laggan, the narrow north-east spur of Geal Charn descending over Sron Garbh provides a splendid route with a little scrambling low down and leads to another good path descending to the Pattack.

Binnein Shuas (746m)
Lying between Loch Laggan and Lochan na h-Earba, and almost forming a peninsula, is a strip of land carrying Binnein Shuas and Binnein Shios. Both hills offer outstanding views up and down the length of the Spean — Laggan valley and both are easily reached by their south-west ridges. Binnein Shuas carries a major crag of pegmatite on its east face which lay unexplored until the 1960s. It now has a host of excellent rock-climbs. This crag is blessed with largely sound rock and, being at such low altitude, offers comfortable climbing when the high mountain cliffs are out of condition.

PATHS AND WALKS

In the Ardverikie Forest, south of Loch Laggan and west of the River Pattack, there is a network of Land-rover tracks offering low-level walks, and easy access to the hills, particularly if a cycle is used. Access to this network is at two places only — Kinloch Laggan to the east and the bridge at Luiblea (433 830) to the west. One obvious circular walk goes from Luiblea along the track to Lochan na h-Earba and onwards to its north-east end, then north through the forest to Loch Laggan and finally back to Luiblea along the shore of this loch. (22 kilometres).

CLIMBING

Two crags in this area give climbing of contrasting character. The east face of Binnein Shuas is a steep and exposed wall giving excellent rock climbing, and Creagan Coire nan Cnamh on the east face of Meall Garbh (the southern top of Chno Dearg) has been explored to give about 20 winter routes, mostly of easier grades.

On Binnein Shuas the finest route, and one that sees far more ascents than any other, is *Ardverikie Wall*, a superb Severe on impeccable exposed rock. A complete description of this and other routes will appear in *Highland Outcrops* (1995) to be published by the Scottish Mountaineering Trust.

On Creagan Coire nan Cnamh, after the early discovery of two rock climbs in the 1960s, all subsequent new routes have been in winter, most of them pioneered by climbers at the Joint Services Training Centre based at Tulloch.

The climbs on this crag are described in *Ben Nevis: Rock and Ice Climbs* by S.Richardson, R.Clothier and A.Walker and published by the Scottish Mountaineering Trust (1994).

SKI MOUNTAINEERING

There are several good tours in this area. Stob Coire Sgriodain and Chno Dearg make a good round from Fersit (south of Tulloch station). Beinn na Lap is good skiing terrain but rather a short day from Corrour Halt and is best combined with Chno Dearg to give a good traverse from Corrour to Tulloch. Beinn na Lap's north-north-east ridge is narrow and can develop large cornices.

Creag Pitridh, Geal Charn and Beinn a'Chlachair provide a more difficult tour starting from the bridge at Luiblea (433 830).

Another very long tour is that over Carn Dearg, Geal-Charn, Aonach Beag and Beinn Eibhinn. This is a traverse that might best be done in early spring when the days are long, and there is still enough snow on the tops and ridges, but long walks in and out will probably be needed. A start and finish at Luiblea is probably best, and a bicycle as far as the ruined Lubvan bothy would be helpful.

Ardverikie Wall

CHAPTER 13

Drumochter

Geal-charn	917m	597 783
A'Mharconaich	975m	604 763
Beinn Udlamain	1010m	579 740
Sgairneach Mhor	991m	599 731
Beinn Mholach	841m	587 655
Beinn a'Chuallaich	892m	684 618
Stob an Aonaich Mhoir	855m	537 694
The Sow of Atholl	803m	625 742
Meall na Leitreach	775m	639 703

ACCESS
From the A9 north of the Drumochter Pass and from Dalnaspidal. From the B846 at Killichonan, Annat and Kinloch Rannoch. Also from the B847 between Trinafour and Kinloch Rannoch.

TRANSPORT
There is a bus service between Pitlochry and Kinloch Rannoch, Monday to Friday (tel 0796 472290) and the express coach service from Glasgow and Edinburgh to Inverness calls at Pitlochry and may set down at Dalnaspidal given prior warning.

ACCOMMODATION
Hotels at Rannoch Station, Kinloch Rannoch and Dalwhinnie. Guesthouses at Dalwhinnie and Kinloch Rannoch.

MAP
OS 1:50 000 Landranger Sheet 42

This small group of hills lies in the south-eastern corner of the Central Highlands and with its heather-clad eastern slopes and flat rolling plateau seems more akin to the Cairngorms. However the Scottish 'Khyber Pass' of Drumochter (Druim uachdar — *the highest ridge*) acts as a dividing line, and the watershed of Scotland is appropriately not far north where the rivers Pattack and Mashie drain the same hill but then turn west and east respectively. Another boundary is the great length of Loch Ericht and, looking on the slopes dropping steeply into the loch beneath Geal-charn, it is easy to imagine the depth of the glacier that gouged out the fault line here to give the loch a depth of 150m.

Looking across Loch Ericht from Geal-charn to Ben Alder

To the south the northern shore of Loch Rannoch and the road from Bridge of Ericht to the A9 form the base of a triangle containing few distinctive hills but a great southern area of bad-lands where the ground rises and falls imperceptibly over a waste of hummock, bog and meandering burns.

The Pass of Drumochter, bleak and treeless, is a gloomy place in anything but the best of weather, however there is interest in the litter of glacial moraines at the entrance to Coire Dhomhain and also at Dalnaspidal. At the latter place the glacier flowing north from the Loch Garry basin, as Geikie tells us, 'split upon the summit of the Pass and sent one branch into Glen Garry, the other into Glen Truim'. In most winters, with its height, drifting snow closes the road to traffic, but this same height offers reliable mountain skiing and in the 1970s encouraged investigation into the installation of ski-lifts. Early drovers must have found the pass, if not the most hostile in terms of height, the most congested, for two major routes from the north and the north-west converged there. Bishop Forbes in 1723 found eight droves, totalling 1200 beasts, at the Dalwhinnie stance, another drove covering a mile's length in the Pass itself and a further drove of 300 grazing at the head of Loch Garry.

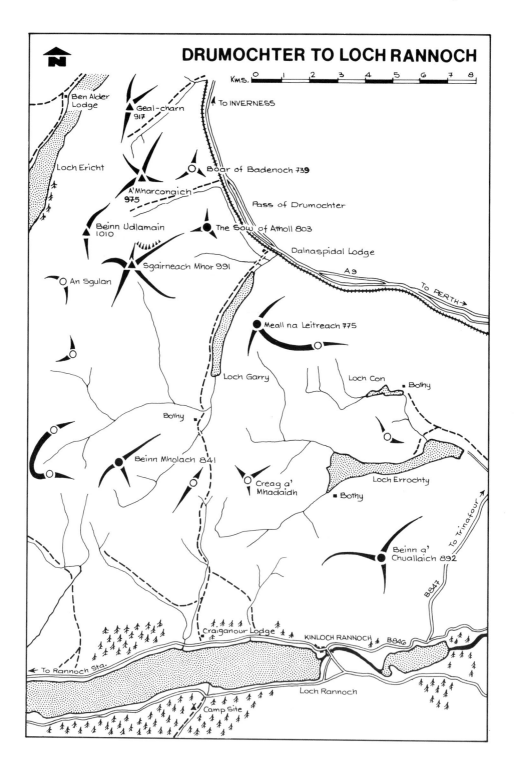

DRUMOCHTER TO LOCH RANNOCH

Kms. 0 1 2 3 4 5 6 7 8

Ben Alder Lodge

Geal-charn 917

TO INVERNESS

Loch Ericht

Boar of Badenoch 739

A'Mharcongich 975

Pass of Drumochter

Beinn Udlamain 1010

The Sow of Atholl 803

Dalnaspidal Lodge

Sgairneach Mhor 991

A9

TO PERTH →

An Sgulan

Meall na Leitreach 775

Loch Garry

Loch Con

Bothy

Bothy

Beinn Mholach 841

Creag a' Mhadaidh

Loch Errochty

Bothy

Beinn a' Chuallaich 892

To Trinafour

B847

Craiganour Lodge

KINLOCH RANNOCH

B846

← To Rannoch Sta.

Loch Rannoch

Camp Site

THE HILLS

Sgairneach Mhor *(big stony hillside)* (991m)
Beinn Udlamain *(gloomy mountain)* (1010m)
A'Mharconaich *(the horse place)* (975m)
Geal-charn *(white hill)* (917m)
The Sow of Atholl (803m)

These hills are gathered in the northerly corner of the area, and with their easy terrain and a starting point at 450m above sea-level they can be traversed easily in a day. For such a round the best starting point is near the summit of Drumochter at the entrance to Coire Dhomhain, from where an obvious circuit winds over Sgairneach Mhor, Beinn Udlamain and A'Mharconaich and is faulted only by the need to turn north for the ascent of Geal-charn and the retracing of steps back over A'Mharconaich. Navigation is also straightforward with the small exception of a series of dog-leg movements between Sgairneach Mhor and Beinn Udlamain, but the clear drawing on OS 1:50 000 Sheet 42 make these obvious.

Both the Sow of Atholl (803m) and the Boar of Badenoch (738m) are easily included in this round, and north of the bealach between the former and Sgairneach Mhor there is a fine gorge that provides a scramble on a dry summer's day.

In an area where heather grows in profusion, the Sow is singular in having the only site in Scotland of the Norwegian blue heather (*Menziesia*). But perhaps the most notable feature of these hills is the view that they provide of the Ben Alder massif, and in this respect Geal-charn has the edge. It can be reached quickly from Balsporran Cottages by a path that carries through thick heather on the north side of the Allt Coire Fhar. From this path a group of giants seem to be marching parallel along the skyline above, but they are nothing more than a series of cairns 2m high. If return is made to the north and over Creagan Mor, it is well worth diverting west to the edge of Creag Dhubh, from where the great length of Loch Ericht and the vast corries of Ben Alder and its neighbouring Geal-Charn provide one of the finest views in Scotland.

Meall na Leitreach *(hill of slopes)* (775m)

This hill forms a long level ridge on the south-east side of Loch Garry, into which its west slopes drop steeply. It can be climbed easily in the space of an afternoon from Dalnaspidal. It is best to follow the track to Loch Garry before crossing the bridges to reach the foot of the north ridge.

Beinn Mholach *(shaggy mountain)* (841m)

South of the pass at Dalnaspidal Lodge where, sadly, there is no longer a railway station, an ancient track, shown on Roy's Map of 1755, runs alongside Loch Garry and through to Loch Rannoch. Apart from being a pleasant long-distance walk, it offers the only reasonable access to Beinn Mholach in the heart of a waste-land. Meall na Leitreach above Loch Garry can also be included in this route, but between its southern spur, Sron nam Faiceachan, and the bridge over the Allt na Duinish, there

Stob an Aonaich Mhoir from Benalder Cottage across Loch Ericht

is 1 kilometre of marsh that can be very wet. At the southern end of the track the east fork leading to Annat should be taken, as the other fork runs through the private grounds of Craiganour Lodge. A hillock between these forks carries an exposure of intrusive igneous rock known as Creagan Odhar that runs for 1 kilometre in a remarkably straight line and shows the predominant grain of the rock in this area.

Stob an Aonaich Mhoir   *(peak of the big crest)*   (855m)
West of the Garry to Rannoch track there is an area which, particularly in its southern half, will attract only the confirmed seeker of solitude. Its featureless plateau of tussocky bog is cut by shallow glens and meandering burns, and carries some extensive plots of afforestation, the most recent of which are not shown on the OS 1:50 000 Sheet 42. They cover a triangle between Loch Rannoch, the Killichonan Burn and the Aulich Burn. One path runs from Killichonan to Coire Bhachdaidh Lodge on Loch Ericht and further west a private road runs from Bridge of Ericht to the lodge and to the power station 1 kilometre to its north.

The remote hill Stob an Aonaich Mhoir can be reached by either path or road, but both involve a minimum distance of 28 kilometres and rough, wet going on the path. However, use of a bicycle on the tarred road from Bridge of Ericht reduces the time to a reasonable level since one can cycle to a height of 650m and to within 1 kilometre of the summit.

A'Mharconaich from Sgairneach Mhor

Beinn a'Chuallaich *(hill of the herding)* (892m)

Unlike the other hills in the southern half of this group, Beinn a'Chuallaich is easily ascended. From the roadside 3 kilometres east of Kinloch Rannoch an easy stroll by way of the south ridge leads to the top. In the north a more varied climb starts west of Trinafour from the road on the south-west side of the Errochty Water. Steep slopes clad with indigenous woodland lead south-west to Loch na Caillich above which is a craggy spur, Meall nan Eun.

PATHS AND WALKS

Dalnaspidal Lodge to Annat (Loch Rannoch). There is one through route beside Loch Garry from Dalnaspidal to Annat on Loch Rannoch, which is shown on Roy's Map of 1755. On the western side of Loch Garry experiments are being carried out with indigenous hardwood planting, which might in time alter the barren appearance of the loch's shoreline. It is a good step of 18 kilometres and there is a 2-kilometre section beyond the head of Loch Garry which will be waterlogged after wet weather. Similarly after rain, fording the Allt Shallainn near Duinish can be impossible. The bridge shown 700 metres upstream on the OS 1:50 000 map had been swept away in 1993.

CLIMBING

There is a series of short crags on a southern spur of Beinn a'Chuallaich. They are known as Craig Varr and can be reached in five minutes from a point on the road 1 kilometre east of Kinloch Rannoch. Twelve routes of from 30m to 50m length, and varying from Very Difficult to Very Severe, have been recorded and will be detailed in *Highland Outcrops* to be published by the Scottish Mountaineering Trust (1995).

The remote crag of Creag Dhubh overlooks Loch Ericht 4 kilometres west of Balsporran Cottages (from where the approach is made). It has been explored in recent winters and some hard ice routes climbed.

SKI MOUNTAINEERING

The traverse of the four Munros west of the Pass of Drumochter is a very fine tour. The high starting and finishing altitude ensures minimal carrying of skis, and the skiing is interesting without being difficult. If a start is made from Balsporran Cottages, climbing Geal-charn first, it is possible to avoid walking back along the A9 at the end of the day by, having skied north-east from Sgairneach Mor down to Coire Dhomhain, climbing 100m to cross the col between A'Mharconaich and the Boar of Badenoch to ski down the Allt an Tuirc.

Far to the south, Beinn a'Chuallaich is a good short ski tour. The eastern corrie usually holds snow well, so the ascent can best be made from the B847 road at a point due east of the summit of the hill.

References

Robert Forbes Journal, J. B. Craven's 1886 edition.

The Scenery of Scotland, A. Geikie (op), 1901.

Scottish Mountains on Ski, M. Slesser.

Ski Mountaineering in Scotland, edited by D.J.Bennet and W.Wallace (SMT) 1987

CHAPTER 14

The Loch Laggan hills:
Creag Meagaidh and Glen Roy

Creag Meagaidh	1130m	418 875
Carn Liath	1006m	472 903
Stob Poite Coire Ardair	1053m	429 889
Beinn a'Chaorainn	1052m	386 851
Beinn Teallach	915m	361 860
Beinn Iaruinn	800m	296 900
Carn Dearg (Gleann Eachach)	815m	349 967
Carn Dearg (north of Glen Roy)	768m	357 948
Carn Dearg (south of Glen Roy)	834m	345 887

ACCESS
From the A86 at Aberarder Farm for Creag Meagaidh. Tulloch Station for Beinn Teallach and Beinn a'Chaorainn. The minor road from Roybridge up Glen Roy for the Parallel Roads and the Carn Deargs.

TRANSPORT
Glasgow — Fort William train stopping at Tulloch and Roybridge.

ACCOMMODATION
Hotels, caravan rental and campsites at Roybridge. There is an open bothy, Luibchonnal, at the head of Glen Roy.

MAP
OS 1:50 000 Landranger Sheet 34

This vast area is contained within a triangle made between the Great Glen, Glen Spean and the Corrieyairack Pass. Inside these margins there are more than twenty hills over 600m and five over 900m. Practically the only low ground is that of the great cut of Glen Roy which sweeps in a north to east arc of about 21 kilometres from Roybridge to its watershed. On both lower and high tops the terrain is complex and navigation demanding.

Creag Meagaidh from Coire Ardair

THE HILLS

Carn Liath *(grey hill)* (1006m)
Stob Poite Coire Ardair *(peak of the pot of the high corrie)* (1053m)
Creag Meagaidh *(bogland rock)* (1130m)
When seen from a distance the plateau-like nature of the Creag Meagaidh range is
the overriding impression and it is only from close at hand that one can appreciate
the mountainous nature of the great corries. Similarly only first-hand experience will
give an idea of the confusing twists to the ridges radiated by Creag Meagaidh which
in plan is somewhat akin to a Catherine-wheel. Allied to these curving arms and
deeply-cut corries, a summit plateau of greater extent than is immediately clear from
a 1:50 000 map makes Creag Meagaidh one of the most confusing hills, in navigational terms, in the Central Highlands. Piloting off the top in a winter storm is a
more than usually serious business, as is evidenced by the number of parties who
spend an unplanned night out at the head of Glen Roy. (That most devoted of
mountaineers Wm.W.Naismith was quoted as remarking to Wm.Douglas, while
they were groping their way to the summit, that 'if he had at that moment to choose
between mountaineering and golf, then the former would go by the board': SMCJ,
Vol. V, p126.)

Meall Coire Choille-rais

A traverse of all the tops from Aberarder Farm is a splendid outing of reasonable length and if started over Carn Liath gives ample opportunity to gaze at the unique architecture of Coire Ardair's headwall. Beyond Stob Poite Coire Ardair (unnamed on the OS 1:50 000 Sheet 34) a sharp turn south drops steeply into The Window — a key feature in winter descents after climbs in Coire Ardair, but one not found without the most careful of compass work. Very large cornices form on the ridge leading south-east from The Window, these mark the rim of the Inner Corrie — that is, the right-hand (north) flank of Coire Ardair, which is further recessed and on an upper level to the main face.

The summit itself is oddly removed from the hub on a south-west ridge, and those on their first visit approaching from the south-east or north-east in anything but perfect visibility may doubt the presence of higher ground beyond the large cairn at 424 878. In descending east over Puist Coire Ardair and Sron a'Choire (1001m) (repeatedly misprinted as 'Ghoire' on OS maps), there are fine downward views into Coire Choille-rais and then over to the cliffs of Coire Ardair. It is a 3-kilometre diversion from the Puist to walk south-west to the twin tops of An Cearcallach and to retrace one's steps *via* Meall Coire Choille-rais.

An ascent of Creag Meagaidh alone can be made quickly, and with the best chance of finding the summit cairn in thick weather, up the long south ridge, but the first kilometre or so above Moy is up very rough and badly drained ground.

Coire Ardair and its cliffs make an already interesting hill one to rank with Ben Nevis and Lochnagar in the quality of its winter climbing. Indeed until the end of the last century the name 'Coire Ardair' was used by local people to cover the whole range (Mrs. Grant in her *Letters from the Mountains* refers to the range as 'lofty Corryarder'). While the cliffs can be viewed from various points on the surrounding horseshoe, the greatest impression will be made on those approaching by the path from Aberarder Farm. A little beyond the farm the path veers uphill and carries through the fringe of a fine birch wood — one of the few large stands of regenerating birch at such an altitude in the Central Highlands. (This birch wood was in a seriously degraded state due to over-grazing and there was no natural regeneration until the Nature Conservancy Council

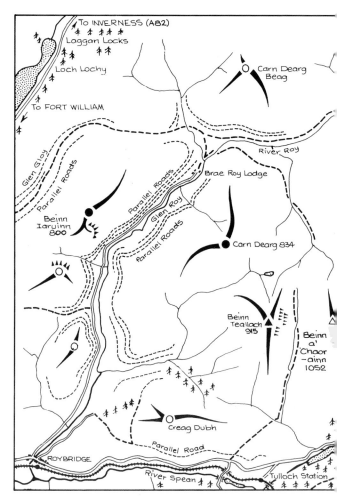

bought the Aberarder Forest and fenced off the woodland to permit regeneration. The whole of lower Coire Ardair is now a National Nature Reserve.)

From the last trees the remarkably ordered structure of buttresses and posts (gullies) comes into view and gives an added impression of grand scale. The three main posts and their accompanying pillars are all serious winter routes of 400m length, though tolerance of vegetated rock, avoidance of which was not a primary concern to Raeburn and J.H.B.Bell whose priorities were exploration, must accompany any approach to rock climbing on the very steep mica schist. J.H.B.Bell observed that apart from their steepness, these crags possessed two habits inimical to the rock climber — 'they form a fertile subsoil for lichens and other vegetation, and they abound in undercut faces and ledges which thin out and peter away into nothingness'. Bell's friend Wedderburn put it succinctly when he remarked that 'the faces would almost appear to be easier if they were turned upside down'.

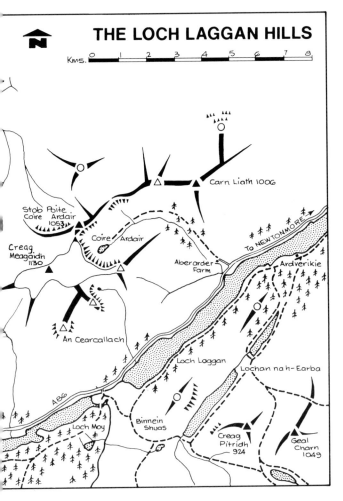

THE LOCH LAGGAN HILLS

Kms.

Carn Liath 1006

Stob Poite
Coire Ardair
1053

Coire Ardair

Creag
Meagaidh
1130

To NEWTONMORE

Aberarder
Farm

Ardverikie

An Cearcallach

Loch Laggan

Lochan na h-Earba

Loch Moy

Binnein
Shuas

Creag
Pitridh
924

Geal
Charn
1049

Throughout the history of climbing on Creag Meagaidh there have been repeated accounts, in impressive and more than coincidental numbers, of avalanches: Raeburn, J.H.B.Bell and W.H.Murray all had experience of the rushing snows beneath the chutes of the Posts and in modern times the frequency of reports increases. Explanation can be found in Coire Ardair's marginal position — open to the severity of the Continental weather systems and yet prone to the sudden thaws from the south-west. Additionally, its enclosed corrie beneath the extensive summit plateau holds vast accumulations of snow.

In most winters Creag Meagaidh's corries and deeply incised glens harbour great reservoirs of snow and none more so than the south facing glen of the Moy Burn. For mountain skiers this makes a fine run, which with its dog-leg course can provide 6 kilometres of ski-ing down to the peat-bogs above Moy.

Beinn a'Chaorainn *(hill of the rowan)* (1052m)
This hill has the form of a south-north spine with three distinct tops, and is joined to Creag Meagaidh in the north-east at a high bealach of 820m (Bealach a'Bharnish). The centre top is the highest by a bare 2m and throws down to the east a narrow ridge that makes a fine winter ascent. Recent afforestation covers the width of the southern approach and it is worthwhile using the forestry track that commences half a kilometre east of the Laggan dam wall at Roughburn. From the point where the track turns east and then west it is better to turn west around the spur of Meall Clachaig and then north through a firebreak. If good winter conditions prevail the long detour east on the track through the forest in order to reach the Allt na h-Uamha is worthwhile for the quality of the east ridge.

Beinn a'Chaorainn from Luiblea

The Parallel Roads of Glen Roy

The Post Face of Creag Meagaidh

Beinn Teallach *(forge hill)* (915m)
The forestry track from Roughburn makes for a straightforward approach and the left turn should be followed west to the burn. However, there is now no footbridge over the Allt a'Chaorainn which takes enormous drainage. If in spate, its east bank will need to be followed for some way before a safe crossing can be made to reach the mountain's south ridge. Above, the ridge offers easy going though there are steep northern and eastern corries beneath the summit. From this top there is a splendid view down the length of Loch Treig which is very fiord-like in its character. A traverse on to Beinn a'Chaorainn involves a drop of just 300m and the two hills make an easy round on a summer's day.

Carn Dearg, north of Glen Roy *(red cairn)* (768m)
Carn Dearg, Gleann Eachach *(red cairn)* (815m)
Carn Dearg, south of Glen Roy *(red cairn)* (834m)
Beinn Iaruinn *(iron hill)* (800m)
Ascent of these four tops, grouped around the head of Glen Roy, has a special interest, for few people can fail to be intrigued by the Parallel Roads clearly seen on both sides when driving up the glen. Beinn Iaruinn and the three Carn Deargs are approached most easily from the public road reaching Brae Roy Lodge. The more northerly pair of Carn Deargs make a pleasant round from Turret Bridge with a good track running into the open mouth of Glen Turret, above which a 'parallel road' at

350m can be followed north into Gleann Eachach. If the northernmost top is ascended first — by way of Teanga Mhor (*the great tongue*) — then descent from the sister peak south-south-west will provide (weather permitting) a particularly clear view of the Parallel Roads.

Beyond Turret Bridge a second bridge crosses the Roy and offers the best approach to the southernmost Carn Dearg over knolly ground.

Very steep slopes of grass and heather lead directly to Beinn Iaruinn from the bridge at the foot of Coire an t-Seilich: a more easy-angled slope up the north-east ridge starts beyond Turret Bridge.

The origin of the Parallel Roads was first correctly proposed by the Swiss glaciologist Louis Agassiz in 1840; before that time Fingal of Gaelic legend was confidently asserted as the ancient engineer. Later in the 19th century T.F.Jamieson carried out a great deal of research and the general definition that he gave in 1863 remains little altered. The roads are in fact strands or terraces remaining from lakes impounded by the great glaciers from the Treig basin, Ben Nevis and further west, that met in Glen Spean. Such clear terraces remain because these lakes were formed during the last period of glaciation in Scotland. This last ice age began its retreat 10 000 years ago.

As can be seen from the clear drawing on Sheet 34 of the OS, there are three distinct altitudes for the terraces and these represent the three water-levels maintained between the uncovering of successively lower outlet-bealachs as the glaciers retreated and the ice-dams lowered. Again the Ordnance Survey show on their Sheet 34 these outlets — marked as cols: that at 410 943 marks the upper level of 350m, when the conglomeration of glaciers in the Spean Valley spread east beyond the present Laggan Dam and pushed ice-lobes halfway up Glen Roy; that at 337 835 marks the first stage in retreat when the dam across Gleann Glas Dhoire was breached and an outlet of 326m was created east into the Spean Valley. The 'road' marked 261m and 262m represents a further stage of glacial retreat when the ice dam impounded one great lake filling Glen Roy and the Spean/Laggan Valley.

Those wishing to read more about the Parallel Roads will find a clear summary by J.B.Sissons in a booklet published by the Nature Conservancy Council. A more detailed paper by the same author can be found in *Transactions of the Institute of British Geography, New Series* 4 (1) 1979.

CLIMBING

Creag Meagaidh is second only to Ben Nevis in the area covered by this guidebook for the scale, seriousness and difficulty of its winter climbing. Due to the very vegetated nature of the cliffs of Coire Ardair, there is no summer climbing. On the other hand, there is a wealth of winter climbing, much of it of very high standard, and the the serious nature is compounded by the reputation which the mountain, and Coire Ardair in particular, has for avalanches.

On the approach up the path to Coire Ardair the main features of the cliffs can be seen. Prominent are two big gullies sloping up from right to left. The left-hand one is *Raeburn's Gully*, the right-hand one is *Easy Gully*. Both are trade routes, the latter a possible descent route if conditions are safe and there is a clear view down the gully. Between these two gullies is Pinnacle Buttress, and on its face, seamed by three narrow gullies, are several superb routes of Grade IV to VII, some as long as 450m.

To the right of Easy Gully is the main headwall of Coire Ardair, called the Post Face. Its most prominent features are the three Posts, or gullies, which give the best known of Creag Meagaidh's climbs. *Centre Post* in the middle of the face is possibly the most famous route in Coire Ardair, having lost none of its reputation since the first ascent by J.H.B.Bell and C.M.Allan in 1937. This great face is bounded to the right by the slanting shelf of *Staghorn Gully*, another Bell and Allan route of character.

Rather hidden on this approach to the mountain, as it lies in an upper corrie to the right of Staghorn Gully, is the Inner Corrie. In this high recess there are many more excellent winter climbs from Grade II to V. The col at the head of the Inner Corrie is The Window, and a kilometre to its north-west is the the corrie of Loch Roy.There are two crags in this corrie, with a variety of routes from Grade I to V, but the long distance to reach it and the fact that one may walk past the finer climbs of Coire Ardair *en route*, have preserved it from popularity.

There is a comprehensive listing of all routes on Creag Meagaidh in *Ben Nevis: Rock and Ice Climbs* by S.Richardson, R.Clothier and A.Walker, published by the Scottish Mountaineering Trust (1994).

SKI MOUNTAINEERING

The classic tour on these mountains is the circuit of Coire Ardair from Aberarder. The best way is anti-clockwise, starting with a steep ascent of Carn Liath. Then there is a long easy traverse along the broad ridge to Stob Poite Coire Ardair followed by a steeper run down to The Window and the final climb to Creag Meagaidh. The return is best made eastwards along the ridge to Sron a'Choire from where there is often a superb run, still eastwards, down a fine snow-holding corrie above Aberarder.

The long corrie of the Moy Burn is an alternative and shorter ski route to Creag Meagaidh, with good skiing on the high snowfields at its head. Further west Beinn a'Chaorainn and Beinn Teallach are both good ski mountains, and they can be combined in a fine circular traverse

These tours are described in *Ski Mountaineering in Scotland*, edited by D.J.Bennet and W.Wallace, and published by the Scottish Mountaineering Trust (1987).

CHAPTER 15

Monadh Liath and the Corrieyairack

A'Chailleach	930m	681 042
Carn Sgulain	920m	684 059
Carn Dearg	945m	635 024
Geal Charn	926m	561 988
Geal-charn Mor	824m	837 124
Carn an Fhreiceadain	878m	726 071
Carn na Saobhaidhe	811m	600 145
Meall an h-Aisre	862m	515 000
Gairbeinn	896m	460 985
Corrieyairack Hill	896m	429 998
Carn a'Chuilinn	816m	416 034

In any guide treating topography with anything wider than a singular bias toward distinctive hill-form above 900m, this enormous tract of high land, making up perhaps a quarter of the total area of the Central Highlands, would deserve several chapters. However, the fact is that relative to all other areas in this guide, the Monadh Liath can best be described as featureless. Certainly there are few summits over 900m and these are clustered in the south-east corner, while to the north extensive high moorland of blanket peat-bog between 700 and 800m is broken only by long, deeply-cut glens. Extensive carpets of grey woolly hair moss cover the higher ground but the corries above Glen Banchor are rich in the dwarf plants of alpine lady's mantle, tormentil and alpine cinquefoil.

So featureless is the northern moorland and so many are the Carn Deargs and the Carn Saobhaidhes that six-figure grid references are more than usually needed. The limits of the area have been taken as the Corrieyairack Pass and Spey Valley in the south and the Great Glen and the A9 to the west and east respectively.

Wade's route across the Corrieyairack was no innovation — it had been in use much earlier by drovers and was shown on a map dated 1725 (in the British Museum). Its hard surface was detested by the former users whose cattle fared badly on the hard stones lacking gravel infill. (Later Thomas Telford, aware of just this problem, was to insist on a minimum of 14 inches of gravel on his own roads). It was completed in 1731 and so well were the twelve zigzags beneath the summit surveyed

ACCESS

For the bulk of these hills Glen Banchor and the road from Laggan towards the Corrieyairack Pass offer the best access. The two eastern outliers are best reached from the A9 south of Aviemore and the one western outlier from Fort Augustus.

TRANSPORT

Train: Perth — Inverness daily; stations at Newtonmore, Kingussie and Aviemore.
Bus: Perth — Inverness daily; calls at Aviemore. Fort William — Inverness, Monday to Saturday; calls at Fort Augustus. Inverness — Whitebridge, Monday to Saturday.
Without the use of a car, reaching places convenient for the hills in this area would need a bicycle to supplement the train and bus services.

ACCOMMODATION

For an area of its size there is a narrow choice of centres from which to operate. In the east there are hotels and guesthouses at Newtonmore, Laggan, Kingussie and Aviemore, with youth hostels in the latter two places. In the west Fort Augustus, with hotels and guesthouses is the only convenient centre for accommodation.
There are four club huts. Jock's Spot owned by the JMCS (Edinburgh Section) lies between Laggan and Newtonmore. The Raeburn Hut owned by the SMC lies on the A889 between Dalwhinnie and Laggan. Milehouse (LSCC) and Mill Cottage (MCofS) are both near Kincraig.

MAPS

OS 1:50 000 Landranger Sheets 34 and 35

that their course is still in existence today. Two of Wade's bridges have also withstood two and a half centuries and appear very much as they did 100 years ago: they are at Garva Bridge and at the crossing of the Allt Coire Uchdachan. However, a little beyond the latter bridge the roaring flood coursing down the the Allt Lagan a'Bhainne took away first the original bridge and then a replacement of 1932 installed with funds from the Scottish Rights of Way Society. The current Bailey bridge was constructed by the Royal Engineers in 1961. Countless feet have crossed the Corrieyairack but one user whose feat must vie with the devotion of Clement Wragge and his daily ascent of Ben Nevis, is the minister of Laggan whose courtship with the eventual Mrs Grant toward the end of the 18th century involved a return journey of about 90 kilometres, as she lived in Fort Augustus.

From the Great Glen a track starts through indigenous woodland 200 metres west of Ardachy Lodge and keeps close to the burn past the fine series of waterfalls on the Culachy Burn. In the east the Corrieyairack road has a tarmacadam surface from Laggan on the A86 to Melgarve and a car driven this far gives good access to some of the lesser hills.

While it is feasible to walk over all the Monadh Liath Munros in one long day, such an outing should be reserved for the end of a drought, as there are long intervening distances over peat hag. This long round would also miss some of the best features to be found in the southern glens and corries.

The east side of the Corrieyairack Pass near Melgarve

THE HILLS

A'Chailleach *(the old woman)* (930m)

This hill is easily reached from Newtonmore and a car can be driven for 2 kilometres up the road leading north-west from the village to the mouth of Glen Banchor. This unexpectedly open strath steeply contained on one side by the northern wall of Creag Dhubh and on the other by a series of spurs, is a sheltered and fertile sanctuary for both birdlife and for men's cattle. Mrs Grant, when married to her Laggan minister, recorded in her collected letters (*Letters from the Mountains*, 1801) the 'nomadic flitting' early each summer to shielings above Glen Banchor. Then in early spring oystercatchers, curlews, lapwings and sandpipers will be seen in unusual numbers.

Beside a plantation of conifers at the end of the public road there is space to leave cars and beyond the track leads west across the Allt a'Chaorainn to the Allt Fionndrigh where it turns north and runs up the glen for 3 kilometres. Where the track dwindles to a path and crosses the burn, a steep nose drops from the north-east and ascent of 200m leads to easier going across Geal Charn (891m) and on to A'Chailleach. Views from this ridge across the Spey valley to the Cairngorms are particularly fine. Return can be varied by descending the open slopes due south, veering south-east lower down to follow a burn past a bothy (687 023). Then cross the Allt a'Chaorainn at 693 018 and follow a track down to Glen Banchor.

The Allt a'Chaorainn below A'Chailleach

Carn Sgulain *(hill of the basket)* (920m)

There is an obvious continuation north to this hill from A'Chailleach with descent between the two of only 100m. This route can then be continued to make a circuit around the head of Glen Banchor's northern feeders, however Carn Sgulain is moated by a series of peat hags that contain in their trenches especially glutinous mud. The westerly route from Carn Sgulain continuing over Meall a'Bhothain (909m) and Carn Ballach (920m) is featureless and the fence posts that mark the old district boundary between Carn Ban (942m) and Carn Sgulain are a welcome aid to navigation in thick weather.

Carn Dearg *(red hill)* (945m)

The highest of the 'red hills' in the Monadh Liath, it is the culminating point on a high ridge carrying other tops, sharply defined to the south and ending at Carn Macoul (800m), and merging with the high moorland to the north at Carn Ban. The track through Glen Banchor follows the River Calder and has bridges across both tributaries from the north — the Allt Fionndrigh and Allt Ballach — so leading to the flats beneath Carn Macoul's south-east nose. This gives a steep ascent for 200m and leads to a fine ridge and two natural circuits of some variety hinging on the stony top of Carn Ban.

The first turns west over the barely perceptible top of Snechdach Slinnean (919m). This was one of the tops of most dubious value entered in Sir Hugh Munro's list. Its highest point was once claimed to be under water — there is a tiny lochan at the summit — and, appropriately, it is no longer named on the OS 1:50 000 map. The route then turns south to descend over the shapely cone of Carn Leth-choin (843m). An evening wander down the latter's east ridge with bars of sunshine flooding through Glen Banchor's southern wall is a memorable experience.

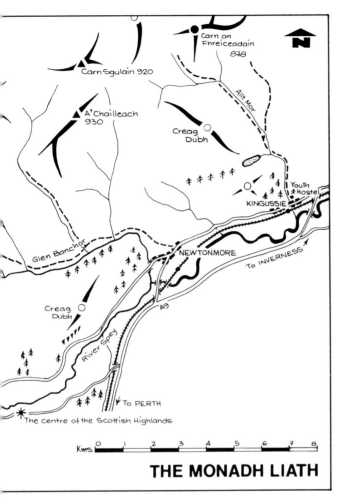

Carn an
Fhreiceadain
878

Carn Sgulain 920

A'Chailleach
930

Allt Mor

Creag
Dubh

Youth
Hostel

KINGUSSIE

Glen Banchor

NEWTONMORE

To INVERNESS

Creag
Dubh

River Spey

A9

To PERTH

The centre of the Scottish Highlands

Kms. 0 1 2 3 4 5 6 7 8

THE MONADH LIATH

The alternative is to turn north-east from Carn Ban and follow the ridge crest around Glen Ballach to Carn Ballach. From there a broad southerly ridge leads to a steep slope down Meall na Ceardaich (870m) to reach a path turning north-east down into the glen of the Allt Fionndrigh. Once across the burn the path develops into a good track.

Directly beneath Carn Dearg's summit cairn a buttress drops steeply for 100m, and though the mica-schist is not continuous enough for worthwhile rock-climbing, a steep shallow gully splits the east-facing buttress. In good winter conditions this gully is a hard ice route. The best approach is by the track up the east bank of the Allt Fionndrigh and over the bealach between Creag Liath (745m) and Meall na Ceardaich (870m). Once over the bealach turn north-west maintaining height along a terrace to the head of the glen. Unless the valley bed is covered in deep old snow, any attempt to cross diagonally to the buttress will waste time and temper through a maze of peat hags.

Geal Charn *(white hill)* (926m)

The long trench of Glen Markie separates Geal Charn from the other Monadh Liath tops. It is best approached by the road from Laggan up the River Spey. From Laggan the motorable road to Crathie and on to the Corrieyairack Pass is a picturesque approach winding through farmsteads and beside the infant Spey, with heavily wooded tors hemming in the strath. One of these tors carries the prehistoric hill fort of Dun-da-Lamh, which is in a truly commanding position. It can be approached by a forestry track leading from the road bend south of the bridge over the Spey just before the dam wall.

Looking west from Geal-charn Beag

To climb Geal Charn a track runs north up Glen Markie from the dam wall. This track was once an alternative drove road to that of the Corrieyairack and crossed the plateau at 830m by the course of the Allt nam Beith to descend then to Loch na Lairige and Sronlarig Lodge. Glen Markie is incised along a fault line that continues north of the plateau along the course of the Abhainn Cro Chlach. In Glen Markie's higher reaches there is a ravine that makes an entertaining summer scramble.

The path up Glen Markie continues for about 10 kilometres almost to its head, crossing the burn east of Geal Charn. This crossing is *en route* for the fine corrie above Lochan a'Choire, the headwall of which is a steep crag beneath Geal Charn. The gully near the centre of this crag makes a straightforward winter ascent amongst splendid scenery leading up to Uinneag a'Choire Lochain.

After heavy rain the Markie Burn can be unfordable and an alternative approach then is from 4 kilometres west of Crathie at Sherramore, where a track leads north onto the open hillside. At 550m it is worthwhile veering right to look into the curious trench of An Dirc Mhor. Higher still there is an ice-carved window, Uinneag a'Choire Lochain, between the southern top, Beinn Sgiath (887m) and the summit.

Geal-charn Mor   *(big white hill)*   (824m)

An easy approach can be made from Lynwilg on the A9 two kilometres south of Aviemore. A good track from the northern end of the hamlet runs west through the

Carn an Fhreiceadain from A'Chailleach

fine indigenous woods and can be followed up to its highest point at 700m. From here Geal-charn Mor is just over 1 kilometre to the south-west. There is an Ordnance Survey cairn on the summit that commands a good view down Glen Feshie and across to the Cairngorms.

Carn an Fhreiceadain *(watcher's {lookout's} cairn)* (878m)
There is an easy approach to this hill by an excellent track that reaches 750m on the south ridge. This ancient track, shown on Roy's Map of 1755, follows the course of the Allt Mor from the centre of Kingussie and continues across the moor to upper Strath Dearn. Once past Carn an Fhreiceadain the path fades and only traces remain across Bruach nan Imirichean and down the Allt Glas a'Charbaid.

Carn na Saobhaidhe *(cairn of the den, fox lair)* (811m)
This is one of the tops scattered over the northern waste of the Monadh Liath that fall within the list of hills devised by J.Rooke Corbett. None is completely in the hinterland, but this hill will require a true devotion to Corbett's list since for either northern or western approaches there is a distance of about 28 kilometres for the round trip. The hill could be reached from Strath Dearn to the north-east but even Corbett, who was a powerful walker, might have considered such a length of approach as gilding a rather wan lily. Both western and northern routes start from the B862/B851 road between Fort Augustus and Strath Nairn. For those not

travelling by car there is a bus service from Inverness through Strath Nairn to Whitebridge on the River Foyers. This service runs Monday to Saturday all year round.

The western route starts at Bunkegivie at the foot of Loch Mhor and follows the track on the north side of the River E for 9 kilometres to a ruin under a false Carn na Saobhaidhe (602m). A further 5 kilometres on slopes at very low angle lead to the top, from where the prospect around the compass is of featureless moor and peat hag.

The northern route uses the private road running south to Dunmaglass Lodge and then up a track along the Allt Uisg an t-Sidhein, and has the merit of a good track to within 2 kilometres of the top.

Meall na h-Aisre   *(hill of the defile)*   (862m)
Gairbeinn   *(rough hill)*   (896m)
Corrieyairack Hill   *(hill of the rising glen)*   (896m)
These three hills lie close together and north of the Corrieyairack road between Garva Bridge and the road summit. From each there is wide view south to the Creag Meagaidh range, which appears vast enough but shows no evidence of its mountainous corries. In clear weather Ben Nevis is surprisingly prominent. The first and most easterly, Meall na h-Aisre, is best reached from Garva Bridge where the stand of Scots pine complements the solid grace of Wade's double-arched bridge. A good path starts from the west side of the bridge and crosses then recrosses the Feith Talagain within the first kilometre. Above, open slopes lead north over a satellite at 844m and then north-west to the OS cairn.

Gairbeinn is an easy climb from the Corrieyairack road 1½ kilometres west of Melgarve. From it there is an attractive traverse to Corrieyairack Hill, with a fine view down onto Loch an Aonaich Odhair from the north-west shoulder of an intervening top — yet another Geal Charn (876m). The return from Corrieyairack Hill leads south past the site of an ancient well at 424 985 beside the old road.

Carn a'Chuilinn   *(cairn of holly)*   (816m)
The most westerly of the Monadh Liath and decidedly the most interesting, this hill is best reached by a path leaving the A862 a little over 3 kilometres from Fort Augustus at 402 091 and soon reaching a good track. After 3½ kilometres the track turns through 180 degrees to cross the Allt Doe and at this point a path cuts off south. When this path runs out under steeper slopes it is worthwhile bearing south-south-east to a subsidiary top at 781m from where Carn a'Chuilinn stands out as a bold craggy mass immediately above a tangle of lochans to the south. From Carn a'Chuilinn's summit the view is unusually extensive. To the west the eye can follow the length of Loch Garry out to Knoydart, and to the north a desolation of knob and lochan country now patched with acres of conifers runs above the great trench of Loch Ness. Even though it involves very rough going, the circuit from Carn a'Chuilinn to Coire Doe *via* the well-named Garbh Choire *(rough corrie)* at the head

of Glen Tarff is strongly recommended to those with a taste for hidden corners and wild craggy ravines.

Indeed it is the glens that provide the most memorable features in the northern area which is a classic example of a dissected plateau left by glaciation. Though exploration of them is not mountaineering, it does provide insight into the mountains and is the ideal place for the use of a bicycle. The longest glen, Strath Dearn, writhes into the heart of the high moor and, with a little licence, could be considered to breach the plateau spine up the the the course of the Abhainn Cro Chlach. A well maintained road runs as far as Coignafearn, where numerous spurs have been planed off leaving steep noses above the flat bed of the glen in which the River Findhorn has cut its way through thick glacial gravels. All about the road end are shielings bearing the prefix to their names of 'Coig' which signifies a measure of land, usually a fifth from the old Celtic custom of dividing land. Higher in the glen, the ruins of crofts show that cultivation must have been taken to altitudes unthinkable today.

On a much lesser scale two glens to the west are worth a visit. At Whitebridge on the A862 the glen occupied by the River Fechlin twists south-east to Loch Killin. This stretch of water is hemmed in by steep slopes, those to the east dropping precipitously into the loch and those to the west just allowing room for the track that continues to Sronlarig Lodge and can be followed through to Laggan — though there are 6 kilometres over the plateau spine with little trace of the old drove route before the southern Glen Markie is reached.

Further north, Conagleann lies 2 kilometres east of Loch Mhor and this narrow cleft has a fine granite crag with good rock-climbing on its western flank. The crag is most quickly reached by the track from the B862 to Wester Aberchalder. Conagleann is one of the many fine features on the shelf that runs along the east side of Loch Ness, and those with the leisure to wander on a bicycle through the numerous lanes will find a variety of loch and glacially-scoured crag.

Loch Ness occupies the site of a wrench-fault first formed some 300 million years ago that has been scoured out to a depth of 160m for much of its 37-kilometre length. This wrench-fault is still unstable, minor tremors being recorded in the area during this century. Earlier, in 1775, a major disturbance to the waters of the Great Glen were associated with the same earth movement that devastated Lisbon. Robert Southey in his *Journal of a Tour in Scotland in 1819* recounts how the waters were driven 200 yards up the River Oich and overflowed the banks to a height of 30 feet. Great movements along the line of this fault in ancient times have been shown by demonstrating that granite at Foyers on Loch Ness and at Strontian, 105 kilometres south, were once part of the same geological unit. Loch Ness was also the subject of a prophecy by the Brahan Seer (Coinneach Odhar) who about 1650 promised that 'full-rigged ships will be seen sailing eastwards and westwards by the back of Tomnahurich', i.e. from Inverness into the Great Glen. In the 1820s when the Caledonian Canal was completed, his prophecy came to pass.

The ascent to Carn Dearg at the head of Gleann Ballach

CLIMBING

Only a few minutes from the main road (A86) and equidistant between Newtonmore and Laggan there is a major crag, Creag Dubh. It has a pastoral setting above birch woods, lochans and the infant Spey. Creag Dubh has over 100 routes of up to 140m in length. The rock is schist, broken with bands of quartzite, and most of the routes are at or above the Very Severe standard. Facing south-east and with a relatively low altitude, climbing is often possible when the high crags are wet and cold. Route descriptions will appear in *Highland Outcrops* to be published in 1995 by the Scottish Mountaineering Trust.

Far up Glen Banchor, above the remote Loch Dubh on the south-west side of Carn Dearg, is Loch Dubh Crag. Two Grade IV routes have been made on this crag.

SKI MOUNTAINEERING

The Monadh Liath is ideal country for ski touring, particularly Nordic style. A wide range of tours, long and short, can be made virtually anywhere across these hills. The most popular of these include A'Chailleach from Glen Banchor, Geal Charn from Glen Markie, Carn an Fhreiceadain from Kingussie (one of the earliest ski tours recorded in the SMCJ) and Geal-charn Mor from Lynwilg. The circuit of A'Chailleach, Carn Sgulain and Carn Dearg is an excellent longer day.

Two of these tours are described in *Ski Mountaineering in Scotland* edited by D.J.Bennet and W.Wallace and published by the Scottish Mounatineering Trust (1987).

References

Letters from the Mountains   Mrs Grant 1801

Journal of a Tour in Scotland in 1819   Robert Southey

The prophecies of the Brahan Seer   Alexander Mackenzie: 1st ed 1877

APPENDIX I

Gaelic Place Names

One may walk and climb for years in the Scottish hills without any knowledge of Gaelic, or its pronunciation, and not feel the need of it. But a little insight into the Gaelic nomenclature of hill-forms will at least enrich one's knowledge of the environment, and can provide significant information, as in the case of Allt a'Mhuilinn (*burn of the mill wheel*), when one can be sure that during spring-melt or after heavy rain such a burn will run like a mill-race and will not be forded easily. The avoidance of the more dissonant mispronunciations will help when seeking information from local people. A very brief and selective glossary together with an indication as to the most glaring pitfalls in pronunciation, is given below. Those fortunate enough to live in Scotland can hear the 'clatter of Gaelic voices' as Ruthven Todd so well described it, on the VHF waveband on any evening of the week and, to especial advantage on Sunday afternoons when Gaelic services, with a primordial ring to their chanted responses, are broadcast on VHF by BBC Radio Scotland.

One of the characteristics of Gaelic nomenclature is the existence in the language of single words for hill-forms which, in English, could only be described by a multi-word phrase. An example is the noun 'druim' which might be briefly translated as a long, whale-back ridge, and such descriptive names for hill-forms are far more numerous than in English. But the Gaels never hesitate at using poetical groupings and nothing could be more descriptive than the Gaelic name for the dipper- 'Gobhainn dubh-a'Chladaich' meaning the blacksmith of the shingle. In another vein there are curiosities illustrating a close familiarity with topography — Binnein Shuas and Binnein Shios in the Ardverikie Forest offer an example. The basic meaning for shuas is above (one) and that for shios is downwards (from one) with these two directions often referring to the flow of a burn and with their meanings extended to allow use of shuas for west and shios for east. A glance at Sheet 42 of the OS 1:50 000 will emphasise the point. However, depending upon the predominant direction of the drainage in an area, the two words can be allotted to other opposing compass points! When trying to relate Gaelic names to contour shapes on the map, it can be helpful to remember that such names were given by people living and working on the lower slopes and rarely if ever from the higher vantage points.

In the following glossary, the phonetic script is from a key by Iain and Iseabail MacLeod from their glossary of Gaelic which is included in *Munro's Tables* published by the Scottish Mountaineering Trust (1990). It is based on English spelling and it is therefore impossible to give other than a rough approximation of the Gaelic sounds, which are very different from those of English. This difficulty is compounded by the variety of Gaelic pronunciation from region to region — there being no 'received' Gaelic. For instance Gaelic speakers in the Laggan area will say 'bellach', whereas across the Great Glen in Kintail 'byalach' is nearer the mark.

However the key should enable the user to pronounce the names in such a way that they would be at least intelligible to a Gaelic speaker. Note that the script is based on the standard Scottish pronunciation and not on standard Southern English (for example, *day* and *road* have simple vowels and not diphthongs.

Vowels

a	as in the	Y	as in by	ow	as in howl
a	as in tap	o	as in top	ö	approximately the
aa	as in father	oa	as in road		sound in French
ay	as in day	aw	as in bawl		*oeuf* or German
ee	as in deed, weak	oo	as in pool		*Österreich*
i	as in tip	ou	as in our		

Consonants

Most of the consonants represent approximately the same sounds as in English, e.g.

g   as in get
s   as in sit
ch   as in loch
gh   has no equivalent in English; it is voiced ch (i.e. pronounce ch using the vocal chords).

y   as in yet
^   indicates a slight y sound after a consonant
bold   indicates the stressed syllable.

ban — white, pale (baan)
beag — little (bayk)
breac — speckled (brechk)
buidhe — yellow (**boo**ya)
cas — steep (cas)
dearg — red (**dyer**ak)
dubh — black (doo)
fada — long (**fat**a)
fionn — white, bright (fyoon)
garbh — rough (**gar**av)

geal — white (**gyal**)
gearr — short (gyar)
glas — grey, green (glas)
gorm — blue (**gor**am)
labhar — loud (**lav**ar)
liadh — grey (**lyee**a)
mor — large (moar)
odhar — dun-coloured (**ou**ar)
riabhach — brindled or striped (**ree**avach)

adharcan — lapwing (o**ghar**kan)
ba — cattle (baa)
beith — birch (bay)
caorach — sheep (plural) (**kor**eech)
caorunn — rowan (**kor**an)
cat — wild-cat (caht)
coille — wood (**kil**ya)

damh — stag (dav)
darach — oak (**dar**ach)
eilidh — hind (**ayl**'t^)
feadag — plover, whistler (**fed**ak)
fraoch — heather (fröch)
gabhar — goat (**gow**ar)

giuthas — pine (**gyoo′**as)
iolaire — eagle (yi′lara)
madadh-ruadh — fox (**mat**agh-**roo**agh)
roid — bog-myrtle (rot^)

achadh — field, often of parkland
    nature (**ach**agh)
airidh — sheiling (**aa′**rea)
blar — cleared space, field (blaar)
both — but (bo)
clach — stone (klach)
dail — field, usually by water (daal^)
eas — waterfall (es)
fas — deserted place (faas)

aonach — ridge (**ön**ach)
bealach — a narrow pass (**byal**ach)
bidean — pinnacle (**beet**yan)
binnean — high, conical hill (**beeny**an)
cioch — breast, breast-shaped hill
    (**kee**ach)
ciche — genitive of cioch (**keech**a)
coire — cauldron (**kor**a)
creachan — rocky surface with no
    vegetation, especially on a summit
    (**kray**chan)
lairig — a broad pass (**laa**rik)

tarmachan — ptarmigan (also eun
    fionn) (**tar**ama**cha**n; ayn fyoon)
trilleachan — oystercatcher, sandpiper
    (**treel** yachan)

feith — vein; sinuous stream (fe)
gort — enclosure; standing corn
    (gawrsht)
leis — leeward (laysh)
luib — bend, as in a stream; a little
    glen (**loo**eeb)
muileann — mill (**mool**an)
sneachd — snow (shnyachk)
uinneag — window (oonyak)

leacach — bare summit or side of a hill
    (lyechkach)
leathad — broad slope (lyehat)
mam — large, round hill (maam)
meall — a mound (myowl)
monadh — a range; heathy moor
    (**mon**agh)
sgor and sgurr — a sharp, steep hill
    (skor and skoor)
sron — a nose; a promontory from a
    hill (srawn)
stob — a sharp point (stop)

Pronunciation

Frequently when a word takes the genitive case or the feminine gender an 'h' is inserted after the first consonant, e.g. fuaran — fhuaran, muileann — mhuillin, mor — mhor, beag — bheag, druim — dhruim. In pronunciation mh and bh, when initial letters, sound like the English v, and fh and dh are most often aspirated. When the definite article takes the form 'an t-', it makes a following 's' silent as in Allt an-t-Sneachd — pronounced Alt an Trachka. A useful reference work is that produced by the Royal Scottish Geographical Society in 1957 — *A Glossary of Gaelic and Scandinavian elements used in places names on Ordnance Survey maps*. Another is Professor W.J.Watson's *The Celtic Place Names of Scotland*. Both are out of print but should be available in a reference library.

Hill Names and Meanings

The following list attempts to give the meanings of the hill names mentioned in the guide. Gaelic spellings, as in the guide itself, are those of the Ordnance Survey.

A'Chailleach: *the old woman (wife).*
Allt a'Mhuilinn: *burn of the mill.*
A'Mharconaich:*the horse place.*
Am Bodach: *the old man.*
An Garbhanach: *the rough ridge.*
An Gearanach: *the complainer.*
An t-Sron: *the nose.*
Aonach Beag: *little ridge.*
Aonach Dubh: *black ridge.*
Aonach Eagach: *notched ridge.*
Aonach Mor: *great ridge.*
Beinn a'Bheithir: *hill of the thunderbolt.*
Beinn a'Bhuiridh: *hill of roaring (stags).*
Beinn a'Chaoruinn: *hill of the rowan tree.*
Beinn a'Chlachair: *stone-mason's hill.*
Beinn a'Chochuill: *hill of the cowl.*
Beinn a'Chuallaich: *hill of herding.*
Beinn Bheoil: *hill of the mouth (of Ben Alder).*
Beinn Ceitlein: *hill of concealment*
Beinn Chumhainn: *narrow hill.*
Beinn Eibhinn: *delightful hill.*
Beinn Eunaich: *fowling peak.*
Beinn Fhada: *long hill.*
Beinn Fhionnlaidh: *Finlay's hill.*
Beinn Iaruinn: *iron hill.*
Beinn Maol Chaluim: *Calum's bare hill.*
Beinn Mhic-Mhonaidh: *hill of the son of the moor.*
Beinn Mholach: *shaggy hill.*
Beinn nan Aighenan: *hill of the hinds.*
Beinn Teallach: *hill of the forge.*
Beinn Trilleachan: *hill of sandpipers.*
Beinn Udlamain: *gloomy hill.*
Ben Alder: *hill of rock and water.*
Ben Cruachan: *hill of peaks or stacks.*
Ben Starav: *stout hill with small head.*
Bidean nam Bian: *peak of the bens.*
Binnein Beag: *little hill.*
Binnein Mor: *big hill.*

Buachaille Etive Beag: *little herdsman of Etive.*
Buachaille Etive Mor: *great herdsman of Etive.*
Caisteal: *castle.*
Carn a'Chuilinn: *cairn of the holly.*
Carn an Fhreiceadain: *cairn of the watcher.*
Carn B(e)allach: *cairn of the pass.*
Carn Ban: *white cairn.*
Carn Beag Dearg: *little red cairn.*
Carn Dearg: *red cairn.*
Carn Dearg Meadhonach: *middle red cairn.*
Carn Easgann Bana: *cairn of the white eels.*
Carn Liath: *grey cairn.*
Carn Mor Dearg: *big red cairn.*
Carn na Laraiche Maoile: *cairn of the bare site or ruin.*
Carn na Saobhaidhe: *cairn of the fox's den.*
Carn Sgulain: *cairn of the basket.*
Chno Dearg: *red hill*
Clach Leathad: *stony slope.*
Creach Bheinn: *hill of prey or spoil.*
Creag Dubh: *black rock.*
Creag Mhor: *great crag.*
Cruach Innse: *stack of the meadow.*
Diollaid a'Chairn: *saddle of the cairn.*
Drochaid Glas: *grey bridge.*
Fara, The (G. faradh): *ladder.*
Fraochaidh: *place of heather.*
Gairbeinn: *rough hill.*
Garbh Bheinn: *rough hill.*
Geal-Charn: *white cairn.*
Geal-Charn Mor: *big white cairn.*
Gearr Aonach: *short ridge.*
Glas Bheinn: *grey hill.*
Glas Bheinn Mhor: *big grey hill.*

Leum Uilleim: *William's leap.*

Mam Coire Easain: *moor or plateau of the corrie of the waterfalls.*

Mam na Gualainn: *plateau of the shoulder.*

Meall a'Bhuiridh: *hill of the roaring (stags).*

Meall an t-Snaim: *hill of the knot.*

Meall Cruidh: *hill of the hardness.*

Meall Cuanail: *seaward-looking hill (cuan — ocean).*

Meall Dearg: *red hill.*

Meall Garbh: *rough hill.*

Meall na h-Aisre: *hill of the defile.*

Meall na Leitreach: *hill of slopes.*

Meall nan Eun: *hill of the birds.*

Meall an t-Suidhe: *hill of the sitting.*

Meall Corranaich: *hill of the bracken corrie.*

Mullach Coire an Iubhair: *top of the corrie of the yew tree.*

Mullach Coire Choille-rais: *top of the corrie of the shrub wood.*

Mullach Coire nan Nead: *top of the corrie of the nests.*

Mullach nan Coirean: *top of the corries.*

Na Gruagaichean: *the maidens.*

Poite (Poit) Coire Ardair: *pot of the high corrie.*

Puist Coire Ardair: *post of the high corrie.*

Sgairneach Mhor: *big rocky hillside.*

Sgor Choinnich: *Kenneth's peak.*

Sgor Gaibhre: *peak of the goats.*

Sgor Iutharn: *hell's peak.*

Sgor na h-Ulaidh: *peak of the hidden treasure.*

Sgorr nam Fiannaidh: *peak of the Fianns.*

Sgor an Iubhair: *peak of the yew tree.*

Sgorr Bhan: *white peak.*

Sgorr Dhearg: *red peak.*

Sgorr Dhonuill: *Donald's peak.*

Sgurr a'Bhuic: *peak of the buck.*

Sgurr a' Mhaim: *peak of the pass.*

Sgurr Choinnich Beag: *little mossy peak.*

Sgurr Choinnich Mor: *big mossy peak.*

Sgurr Eilde Beag: *little peak of the hind.*

Sgurr Eilde Mor: *big peak of the hind.*

Sgurr Innse: *peak of the meadow.*

Sne(a)chdach Slinnean: *snowy shoulder-blade.*

Sron an Isean: *nose of the gosling.*

Sron Coire na h-Iolaire: *nose of the eagles' corrie.*

Sron Garbh: *rough nose.*

Sron Garbh Choire: *nose of the rough corrie.*

Sron nan Giubhas: *nose of the firs.*

Stob a'Bhruaich Leith: *peak of the grey brae.*

Stob a'Choire Leith: *peak of the grey corrie.*

Stob a'Choire Mheadhoin: *peak of the middle corrie.*

Stob a'Choire Odhair: *peak of the dun corrie.*

Stob a'Ghlais Choire: *peak of the grey corrie.*

Stob an Aonaich Mhoir: *peak of the big ridge.*

Stob an Cul Choire: *peak at the back of the corrie.*

Stob an Fhuarain: *peak of the well.*

Stob Ban: *white peak.*

Stob Choire Dhuibh: *peak of the black corrie.*

Stob Coir'an Albannaich: *peak of the corrie of the Scotsman.*

Stob Coire Altruim: *peak of the nursing corrie (hinds with calves).*

Stob Coire a'Chairn: *peak of the stony corrie.*

Stob Coire Easain: *peak of the corrie of the waterfalls.*

Stob Coire an Fhir Dhuibh: *peak of the corrie of the black man.*

Stob Coire an Laoigh: *peak of the corrie of the calf.*

Stob Coire Bhealaich: *peak of the corrie of the pass.*

Stob Coire Dheirg: *peak of the red corrie.*

Stob Coire Gaibhre: *peak of the corrie of the goats.*

Stob Coire Leith: *peak of the grey corrie.*

Stob Coire nam Beith: *peak of the corrie of the birch trees.*

Stob Coire na Ceannain: *peak of the corrie of the headland.*

Stob Coire nan Lochan: *peak of the corrie of the lochans.*

Stob Coire Raineach: *peak of the corrie of the ferns.*

Stob Coire Sgreamhach: *peak of the scabby corrie.*

Stob Coire Sgriodain: *peak of the scree corrie.*

Stob Dearg: *red peak.*

Stob Diamh: *peak of the stags.*

Stob Dubh: *black peak.*

Stob Garbh: *rough peak.*

Stob Ghabhar: *peak of the goats.*

Stob na Broige: *peak of the shoe.*

Stob na Doire: *peak of the copse.*

Tom na Sroine: *hill of the nose.*

Uinneag a'Ghlas Choire: *window of the grey corrie.*

APPENDIX II

Selected Bibliography

Mountaineering
Avalanche Enigma, Colin Fraser, Murray.

The ABC of Avalanche Safety, ed. La Chapelle, obtainable from Glenmore Lodge.

Mountain Leadership, Eric Langmuir, Scottish Sports Council.

Scottish Mountains on Ski, Malcolm Slesser, West Col. (op)

Always a Little Further, Alastair Borthwick, Diadem, 1987.

A Progress in Mountaineering, J.H.B.Bell (op).

Mountaineering in Scotland and Undiscovered Scotland W.H.Murray, Diadem compendium, 1982.

A Climber's Guide to Ben Nevis, G.G.MacPhee, (SMC) (op).

A Climber's Guide to Ben Nevis, J.R.Marshall, (SMC) 1979 (op).

Ben Nevis: Britain's Highest Mountain, Ken Crocket, (SMT) 1986

Ben Nevis: Rock and Ice Climbs, by S.Richardson, R.Clothier and A.Walker, (SMT) 1994

Ski Mountaineering in Scotland, D.J.Bennet and W.Wallace, (SMT) 1987

Glen Coe: Rock and Ice Climbs, by K.V.Crocket, R.Anderson and D.Cuthbertson, (SMT) 1992

Highland Outcrops (SMT) 1995

Early Travellers
Recollections of a Tour Made in Scotland A.D. 1803, Dorothy Wordsworth, (James Thin) 1974.

Letters from the Mountains; 1773-1807, Mrs. Anne Grant of Laggan (op).

Journal of a Tour in Scotland in 1819, Robert Southey (op).

Prospects and Observations on a Tour in England and Scotland in 1785, Thomas Newte (op).

Journal , (Rev. J.B.Craven's edition), Bishop Robert Forbes (op).

Weather
Climate and the British Scene, Gordon Manley, (Collins Fontana) 1962.

Britain's Weather: Its Workings, Lore and Forecasting, David Bowen, (David and Charles) 1973.

Flora and Fauna
The Highlands and Islands F.Fraser Darling and J.Morton Boyd, (Collins) 1964.

A Herd of Red Deer, F.Fraser Darling, (O.U.P.) 1969.

Landform
The Scenery of Scotland, A.Geikie (op).

Geology and Scenery in Scotland, J.B.Whittow, (Penguin) 1979.

British Regional Geology-Scotland: The Grampian Highlands, G. Scott Johnstone, (HMSO) 1966

History
Montrose, John Buchan, (Nelson) 1928.

The Drove Roads of Scotland, A.R.B.Haldane, (Edinburgh University Press) 1968.

New Ways through the Glens, A.R.B.Haldane, (Nelson) 1962.

The Prophecies of the Brahan Seer, A.Mackenzie, (Golspie) 1970.

Novels and General
Kidnapped, Robert Louis Stevenson.

The New Road, Neil Munro, (Blackwood).

Children of the Dead End, Pat MacGill, (Caliban) 1982.

Twenty Years on Ben Nevis, Wm.T.Kilgour, (Ernest Press) 1985.

The High Tops of Black Mount, Marchioness of Breadalbane, (Blackwood, op) 1935.

The Path by the Water, A.R B.Haldane, (Nelson, op) 1944.

Scottish Hill and Mountain Names, Peter Drummond, (SMT) 1992

APPENDIX III

Climbers' Huts

The following list summarises the climbers' huts in the area covered by this guidebook.

As a general rule these huts are available to members of clubs which are members of the Mountaineering Council of Scotland (MCofS) and the British Mountaineering Council (BMC), and also to individual members of these two organisations and other groups of bona fide climbers.

The normal procedure is for club members to make bookings through their club secretaries unless arrangements have been made for them to book directly. Individual members of the MCofS and BMC may make bookings direct to hut custodians.

The following information purposely does not include the names and addresses of the custodians of huts, as these are liable to change and such information quickly becomes out of date. The MCofS compiles a Scottish Hut List which includes the names and addresses of custodians. This list is regularly updated and supplied to secretaries of member clubs.

Clashgour. Glasgow University Mountaineering Club.
Near Victoria Bridge, Bridge of Orchy, 1½ kilometres west of Forest Lodge at 256 425.
Accommodation 6

Blackrock Cottage. Ladies Scottish Climbing Club.
Near Kingshouse Hotel, on the south side of the A82 road on the access road to the White Corries Chairlift at 268 530.
Accommodation 10.

Lagangarbh. Scottish Mountaineering Club.
Near Altnafeadh on the A82 road 4 kilometres west of Kingshouse Hotel at 221 560.
Accommodation 20.

Inbhir-fhaolain. Grampian Club.
In Glen Etive 1 kilometre south-west of Dalness at 158 508.
Accommodation 12.

The Smiddy, Glen Etive. The Forventure Trust.
On the north side of the Glen Etive road 1 kilometre before its end at Loch Etive at 115 455.
Accommodation 14.

Waters Cottage. Fell and Rock Climbing Club.
In Kinlochleven village.

Alex. MacIntyre Memorial Hut. BMC and MCofS.
On the north side of the A82 road adjacent to the Creag Mhor Hotel,
Onich at 046 612.
Accommodation 16.

Manse Barn. Lomond Mountaineering Club.
On the south side of the A82 road adjacent to the Onich Hotel at
032 613. Accommodation 10.

CIC Hut. Scottish Mountaineering Club.
Situated on the north side of Ben Nevis beside the Allt a'Mhuilinn at
167 722.
Accommodation 18. Bookings are considered from parties of more
than 2 and less than 9 persons.

Steall Cottage. Lochaber Mountaineering Club. (JMCS Lochaber
Section).
Situated in Glen Nevis 1½ kilometres beyond the end of the public
road at 177 683. Access by footpath and wire bridge over the River
Nevis.
Accommodation 15.

Raeburn Hut. Scottish Mountaineering Club.
Situated beside the A889 road between Laggan and Dalwhinnie at
636 909.
Accommodation 15.

Jock's Spot. JMCS Edinburgh Section.
Situated on the north side of the A86 road midway between Laggan
and Newtonmore at 667 947.
Accommodation 16.

Milehouse. Ladies Scottish Climbing Club.
Situated 1½ kilometres south of Kincraig beside the B970 road at
839 043.
Accommodation 9.

Mill Cottage. Mountaineering Council of Scotland.
Near Feshiebridge on the north side of the B970 road at 846 047.
Accommodation 14.

INDEX

Aberarder Farm 177, 178, 183
Abhainn Cro Chlach 189, 190, 193
Abhainn Rath 111, 115
A'Chailleach (Glen Coe) 95, 101
    Red Funnel Gully 101
A'Chailleach (Monadh Liath) 184, 186
Achintee Farm 103, 121
Achriabhach 110, 115
Achtriochtan 82
Alder Bay 153
Allt Ballach 188
Allt Cam 162
Allt Ceitlein 39
Alltchaorunn 50, 52, 53
Allt a'Chaoil-reidhe 152, 163
Allt a'Chaorainn 181, 186
Allt a'Chul Choire 139
Allt Coire Chreachainn 25
Allt Coire an Eoin 139
Allt Coire Ghlais 25
Allt Coire Giubhsachan 129, 138
Allt Coire na Larach 44
Allt Coire a'Mhusgain 109
Allt Coire Uchdachan 185
Allt Cruachan 22
Allt Daim 137, 146
Allt Dochard 43
Allt Fionndrigh 188, 189
Allt Gormag 153
Allt Gruiniche 22
Allt Hallater 40, 41
Allt Lagan a'Bhainne 185
Allt Laire 160
Allt nan Meirleach 45
Allt Mheuran 35, 38, 41
Allt a'Mhuilinn 124
Allt-na-Reigh cottage 93
Allt Toaig 47, 49, 50
Allt Uisg an t-Sidhein 192
Altnafeadh 94, 100
An Aghaidh Gharbh 146
Am Bodach (Glen Coe) 92
Am Bodach (Mamores) 107
A'Mharconaich 171, 174
An Cearcallach 177
An Garbhanach 106
An Gearanach 106
An t-Sron 82, 83
Aonach Beag (Lochaber) 136, 146, 161
Aonach Beag (Ben Alder) 166

Aonach Dubh 82, 90
Aonach Dubh a'Ghlinne 65, 84
Aonach Eagach (Glen Coe) 91, 92
Aonach Eagach (Stob Ghabhar) 47
Aonach Mor (Lochaber) 136, 144
Aonach Mor (Stob Ghabhar) 50
Ardverikie 166
Ardmaddy 41, 44
Aulich Burn 172
Aviemore 191

Ba Bridge 49, 50, 98
Ba Cottage 52
Ba, River 49
Bealach a'Bharnish 179
Bealach Breabag 154
Bealach Cumhann 156
Bealach Dubh 149, 157
Bealach Fhionnghaill 66, 87
Bealach Fuar-chathaidh 53, 57
Ben Alder 1, 151, 157
    Bay 153
    Cottage 148, 153
    Lodge 152
    Long Leachas 152
    Short Leachas 152
Beinn nan Aighenan 40
Beinn Bhan 141, 147
Beinn a'Bheithir 67
Beinn Bheoil 154
Beinn Bhreac 59
Beinn a'Bhuiridh 20, 21, 25
Beinn na Caillich 111
Beinn Ceitlein, Stob Dubh 53
Beinn Chaorach 37, 45
Beinn a'Chaorainn 179, 183
Beinn a'Chlachair 165, 166
Beinn a'Chochuill 29
Beinn a'Chrulaiste 97, 101
Beinn a'Chuallaich 173, 174
Beinn Chumhainn 151
Ben Cruachan 21, 22
Beinn Eibhinn 161, 166
Beinn Eunaich 31
    Black Shoot 31, 33
Beinn Fhada 82, 86
Beinn Fhionnlaidh 63
Beinn Iaruinn 181
Ben Inverveigh 33
Beinn na Lap 161, 166

Beinn Larachan 32
Ben Lora 60
Beinn Lurachan 31, 32
Beinn nan Lus 41, 45
Beinn Maol Chaluim 86, 87
Beinn Molurgainn 59
Beinn Mheadhonach 59
Beinn Mhic Chasgaig 52
Beinn Mhic-Mhonaidh 32
Beinn Mholach 171
Ben Nevis 121, 130
    Bob-run 127
    Castle Ridge 125, 130
    Mantrap 127
    No. 3 Gully 128
    No. 4 Gully 128, 131
    North-east Buttress 126
    Observatory Ridge 126, 133
    Orion Face 133
    Polldubh Crags 133
    Pony Track 116, 121
    Red Burn 121
    Tower Ridge 125
    Zero Gully 126
Beinn Pharlagain 149, 157
Beinn Sgiath 190
Beinn Sgulaird 60, 72
Beinn na Socaich 142, 147
Ben Starav 35, 45
Beinn Suidhe 32, 36
Beinn Teallach 180, 183
Beinn Toaig 50
Beinn Trilleachan 63
    The Chasm, of 63
Beinn Udlamain 171
Bidean nam Bian 82
    Church Door Buttress 83
    Flake Route 83
    Diamond Buttress 83
    Dinnertime Buttress 82
Binnein Beag 104
Binnein Mor 104
Binnein Shuas 165, 166
Blackburn bothy 158
Black Corries 97
Blackrock Cottage 46, 55
Blackwater Reservoir 97
Boar of Badenoch 171
Bridge of Ericht 172
Bridge of Orchy 1, 33, 44
Buachaille Etive Beag 81
Buachaille Etive Mor 76, 88
    Chasm, The 79
    Collie's Climb 76

    Curved Ridge 78
    Great Gully 79
    North Buttress 78
    Raven's Gully 79, 88
Bunkegivie 192
Calder, River 188
Cam Chriochan 153
Caolasnacon 95
Carn Ballach 188, 189
Carn Ban 188, 189
Carn a'Chuilinn 192
Carn Dearg (Ben Alder) 157, 161, 166
Carn Dearg (Corrour) 149
Carn Dearg (Monadh Liath) 188, 189, 194
Carn Dearg (south of Glen Roy) 181
Carn Dearg (north of Glen Roy) 181
Carn Dearg (Gleann Eachach) 181
Carn Dearg Meadhonach 128
Carn Dearg, NW 130
Carn an Fhreiceadain 191, 195
Carn Liath 176
Carn Macoul 188
Carn Mor Dearg 128
Carn na Saobhaidhe 191
Carn Sgulain 188, 195
Castles Farm 30, 31
Chno Dearg 159, 166
Ciaran 97
Clachaig Gully 101
Clach Leathad 51
Clashgour 44, 46, 47, 49, 55
Coe, River 86
Coignafearn 193
Coileitir Farm 35, 37, 38, 45
Coire Ardair 177, 178
Coire Ba 46, 56
Coire na Ba 106
Coire nam Beith 82
Coire na Caime 36
Choire Chat 28
Coire a'Charra Bhig 151
Coire a'Charra Mhoir 162
Coire Choimhlidh 142, 147
Coire na Ciste 124
Coire Cloiche Finne 80
Coire Dhearg 36
Coire Dhomhain 171, 174
Coire Doe 193
Coire Dubh 65
Coire Eigheach 151
Coire na h-Eirghe 107
Coire Eoghainn 123
Coire Gabhail 82
Coire Leis 127

Coire nan Lochan 86
Coire a'Mhadaidh 142
Coire Pollach 52
Coire na Tulaich 80
Conagleann 193
Corriechoille 140, 144
Corrieyairick Hill 192
Corrieyairack Pass 184
Corrour Lodge 151
Corrour Old Lodge 1
Corrour Station 1, 91, 99, 100, 111, 144, 148, 149, 155, 158
Cour, The 139, 142
Creach Bheinn 59
Creagan a'Chaise 144
Creagan Coire nam Cnamh 166
Creag Dubh (Glen Etive) 72
Creag Dubh 194
Creag Ghorm 67
Creag Ghuanach 144
Creag Liath 189
Creag Meagaidh 176, 177, 182, 183
    Easy Gully 183
    Raeburn's Gully 183
Creagan nan Nead 161
Creag Pitridh 165, 166
Creag Uamh Shomhairle 115
Creaguaineach Lodge 144
Creise 51
Cruachan, Falls of 21
Cruach Innse 144
Culra Bothy 152
Culra Lodge 148, 152

Dalmally 1, 19, 20, 25
Devil's Ridge 108
Diollaid a'Chairn 163
Dirc Mhor 155
Drochaid Ghlas 25
Dun-da-Lamh 189
Dunmaglass Lodge 192

Easains, The 143
Elleric 61, 71
Etive Slabs 72

Falls of Cruachan 21, 26
Fara, The 154, 157
Fersit 159, 166
Fionn Ghleann 84
Fort Augustus 192
Fort William 117
Fraochaidh 67

Gairbeinn 192
Garbh Bheinn (Glen Coe) 95
Garbh-bheinn (Loch Ossian) 159
Garbh Choire (Ben Alder) 151, 154, 157
Geal-Charn (Ben Alder) 161, 165, 166
Geal-charn (Drumochter) 171
Geal Charn (Laggan) 166
Geal Charn (Monadh Liath) 189, 190, 195
Geal-charn Mor (Monadh Liath) 191, 195
Gearr Aonach 82, 84, 90
Glas Bheinn 99
Glas Bheinn Mhor 41
Glen Banchor 186, 188
Glen Ceitlein 37, 43, 50
Glen Creran 61, 71
    Caving 71
Gleann Fhaolain 84
Glen Kinglass 40, 44
Gleann Leac na Muidhe 64, 84
Glen Liver 30
Glen Markie 190
Glen Nevis 104, 111
Glen Noe 19, 23
Glennoe Farm 23, 30, 41
Glen Orchy 32
Glen Roy 175, 176, 181
Glen Salach 59
Glen Spean 144
Glen Strae 19, 32
Glen Tarff 193
Glen Ure 61
Glenure House 61
Gorton 91
Grampian Club 34, 59, 74
Grey Corries 140

Inbhir-fhaolain 34, 59, 74
Inverliver 44, 70
Inveroran Inn 46

Kentallen 69
Killichonan Burn 172
Kingshouse Hotel 91, 97, 100
Kinlochleven 95, 99, 100
Kinloch Rannoch 153, 168

Lagangarbh Hut 74, 91
Laggan Dam 179
Lairig Eilde 87, 88
Lairig Gartain 81, 88
Lairig Leacach 135, 140
Lancet Edge 163
Larig Noe 25
Larig Torran 26

Leanachan Forest 140, 142, 146
Leum Uilleim 99, 101
Loch Achtriochtan 65, 82, 93
Loch Ba 51, 98
Loch a'Bhealaich Bheithe 154
Loch a'Bhealaich Leamhain 165
Loch Dochard 19, 40, 43
Lochan na h-Earba 161, 165
Loch Eilde Mor 103
Loch Ericht 152
Loch Etive 19, 69
Loch Ghuilbinn 159
Loch Killin 193
Loch Laggan 160
Loch Laidon 98
Loch Leven 95
Lochan Loin nan Donnlaich 153
Lochan Meall an t-Suidhe 118, 121
Lochan Sron Smeur 153
Loch Ness 193
Loch Ossian 1, 91, 148, 155
Loch Pattack 152, 156
Loch Rannoch 153
Lochan Sgoir 163
Lochan na Stainge 51
Loch Treig 100, 156, 160, 181
Loch Tulla 19, 33, 47, 55
Lochan na h-Uraich 63
Long Leachas, Ben Alder 152
Lost Valley 82, 90
Lubvan 162, 166
Lynwilg 191

Mam Carraigh 33
Mam Coire Easain 52
Mam na Gualainn 111
Mamore Lodge 103
Manse Barn, Onich 103
Marchioness of Breadalbane 55
Meall an Araich 43, 55
Meall na h-Aisre 192
Meall a'Bhealaich 151
Meall a'Bhuiridh 51
Meall Coire Choille-rais 177
Meall Copagach 31, 32
Meall Cruaidh 36
Meall Cuanail 21
Meall Dearg 92
Meall nan Eun 42
Meall Garbh (Loch Treig) 159, 166
Meall an Laoigh, Glen Strae 33
Meall na Leitreach 171
Meall Lighiche 66
Meall nan Ruadhag 97

Meall an t-Suidhe 121
Meall Tarsuinn 39
Meall nan Tri Tighearan 36, 40
Meanach 91, 135
Meeting of the Three Waters 74
Melgarve 185
Montrose, Marquis of 9
Moy 179
Mullach nan Coirean 110
Mullach Coire an Iubhair (Geal Charn) 165
Mullach Coire nan Nead 161

Naismith, Wm.W. 119, 161, 176
Na Gruagaichean 104
Nevis, Falls of 113
Nevis, River 113
Newtonmore 185, 186

Onich Hut 103
Ossian's Cave 86

Pap of Glencoe 94
Parallel Roads, Glen Roy 181, 182
Pass of Brander 1, 19, 22
Pattack, River 163
Polldubh Crags 133
Puist Coire Ardair 177

Rannoch Moor 47, 92, 98
Rannoch Station 1, 50, 100, 148, 149, 153, 168
Red Burn, Ben Nevis 121
River Calder 188
River E 192
Roughburn 179, 180
Roybridge 135
Roy Corrie Crags 183

Salachail 66
Sgairneach Mhor 171, 174
Sgorr Bhan 67
Sgurr a'Bhuic 138
Sgorr a'Chaolais 69
Sgor Choinnich 151
Sgurr Choinnich Beag 139
Sgurr Choinnich Mor 140
Sgorr na Ciche 93, 94
Sgorr a'Choise 71
Sgorr Dhearg 67
Sgorr Dhonuill 67
Sgorr Eilde Mor 103
Sgorr nam Fiannaidh 92
    Clachaig Gully 93, 101
Sgor Gaibhre 149, 157
Sgurr Innse 144

Sgor an Iubhair 108
Sgor Iutharn 157, 161
Sgurr a'Mhaim 108, 115
Sgor na h-Ulaidh 64, 72
Short Leachas, Ben Alder 152
Snechdach Slinnean 188
Sow of Atholl 171
Spean Bridge 135, 140, 144
Spean, River 140
Spey, River 189
Sron Coire na h-Iolaire 154
Sron na Creise 52, 56
Sron Garbh 94, 101
Sron a'Choire 177
Sron nan Giubhas 49
Sron na h-Iolaire 37
Sron an Isean 25
Sron na Lairig 87
Sronlairig Lodge 193
Staoineag 91, 135
Steall 106, 108, 113, 115
Steall Hut 103, 113
Stob an Aonaich Mhoir 172
Stob Ban (Glen Nevis) 109, 115
Stob Ban (Grey Corries) 140, 143
Stob a'Bhruaich Leith 50
Stob na Broige 80
Stob nan Cabar 81
Stob Coire Altruim 80
     Centre Gully 80
Stob Coir'an Albannaich 37
Stob Coire nam Beith 83
     The Pyramid 83
Stob Coire Bhealaich 138, 146
Stob Coire a'Chairn 106
Stob Coire na Ceannain 141
Stob Choire Claurigh 140
Stob Coire Dheirg 36, 45
Stob Coire Easain (Grey Corries) 143
Stob Coire Easain (Loch Treig) 147
Stob Coire an Fhir Dhuibh 138
Stob Coire Gaibhre 141
Stob Coire Leith (Glen Coe) 93
Stob Coire nan Lochan 82, 84, 90
Stob a'Coire Mhail 108

Stob a'Choire Mheadhoin 147
Stob a'Choire Odhair 50
Stob Coire Sgreamhach 81, 86
Stob Coire Sgriodain 159, 166
Stob na Cruaiche 97
Stob an Cul Choire 137
Stob Dearg (Ben Cruachan) 21, 22
     North Ridge 28
Stob Dearg (Buachaille Etive Mor) 80, 88
Stob Diamh 25
Stob na Doire 80
Stob Dubh 81
Stob an Duine Ruaidh 41
Stob an Fhuarain 65
Stob Gaibhre 61
Stob Garbh 25, 28
Stob Ghabhar 47
     Upper Couloir 56
Stob Mhic Mhartuin 94, 101
Stob a'Ghlais Choire 51, 52
Stob Maol 31, 32
Stob Poite Coire Ardair 177
Strath Ossian 149, 156, 161
Stronmilchan 21, 25

Taynuilt 1, 20, 44
Tigh na Cruaiche 100
Tom na Sroine 137
Tulloch Station 135, 159, 166
Turret Bridge 182

Uinneag a'Choire Lochain 190
Uinneag a'Ghlas Choire 162
Uisge Labhair 149, 151, 155
Unna, Percy 32, 75
Upper Couloir, Stob Ghabhar 56

Victoria Bridge 36, 37, 40, 44, 47, 50

Whitebridge 192, 193
White Corries Ltd 52
Window, The, Coire Ardair 177
Wragge, Clement 118

Zigzags of Gearr Aonach 85